The Arctic Schooner

Bowdoin

"Tonight I brushed my teeth at 11 P.M., in full daylight, in the middle of Davis Strait, aboard a schooner three times my age, in my underwear. It occurs to me that my occupation is not a natural one."

— Elliot Rappaport, first mate
aboard the *Bowdoin*, summer 1991

The Arctic Schooner
Bowdoin
A Biography

Virginia Thorndike

North Country Press
Unity, Maine

Published by North Country Press, Unity, Maine.

Cover photograph by Tom Stewart, Penobscot, Maine.
Map by S. F. Manning, Camden, Maine.
Design by Janet Robbins, Camden, Maine.
Composition by Typeworks, Belfast, Maine.
Printed at The J.S. McCarthy Company, Augusta, Maine, on recycled papers using soy-based inks.

Grateful acknowledgment is made to the following for permission to reprint previously published material:
    Larry Kaplan, *Song for the Bowdoin*, 1976, Hannah Lane Music, BMI, and *The Wreck of the Bay Rupert*, 1977, Hannah Lane Music, BMI.
    The Colby Alumnus, November 1934, article by George Crosby.

ISBN 0-945980-52-3
Library of Congress Catalog Card No. 95-069845

From the Author

*I*n the course of writing *Windjammer Watching*, a guide to the large sailing vessels seen on the coast of Maine, I was excited by each of the historic schooners on Penobscot Bay. But the *Bowdoin* stood out.

The *Bowdoin*'s history is unique. She has made real contributions to the scientific knowledge of our planet and to the lives of the hundreds of people who have loved her.

My interest in the *Bowdoin* only increased as I spoke with people who knew her, sailed on her and worked on her. Every person had a different tale to tell, yet each one's life was affected by his or her connection with the vessel. And certainly the schooner's own life was affected by these people; she owes her life today to the dedication of her sailors and enthusiasts, moneyed and hammer-wielding folk alike.

I want to thank each and every one of the people who shared their experiences with me. The story I have tried to write is really theirs, and could not have been put together without them. In particular, I appreciate the many hours that Andy Chase, Braley Gray, Deborah Harrison, Stuart Hotchkiss, Ed Morse and John and Sue Nugent spent with me; just as important is each of dozens of others with whom I spent less time. Sadly, one other special member of the *Bowdoin* family, Helga Morse, has passed on. In her memory, a small endowment account has been set up for the *Bowdoin* at Maine Maritime Academy. With a lot of help from friends this fund will grow to significantly aid in the upkeep of the *Bowdoin* and keep the schooner sailing north.

I also want to thank Bowdoin College for allowing me to quote from Donald B. MacMillan's logs, journals and manuscripts, and from William R. Esson's journal, which are all in the Special Collections at the College. The Special Collections at Dartmouth College provided access to Robert Goddard's photographs and papers, including a journal of the 1921–22 trip entitled, "Many Are Cold but Few Are Frozen," from which I have quoted a few short pieces. The librarians at both colleges were very helpful in my research, for which I am most grateful.

Contemporary journals, letters and photographs contributed tremendously to my project, and I must particularly thank the writers and photographers: Andy Chase, Bill Esson (posthumously), Braley Gray, Deborah Harrison, Stu Hotchkiss, Elliot Rappaport and Tom Stewart. Captain Jim Sharp was also more than generous, allowing me access to his photo collection and other papers as well as sharing some wonderful stories. I am also very grateful to Sam Manning for his cartography. Nancy Hauswald, my editor, was very patient and made a major difference in the end result.

Gratitude should also be given publicly to Phil Roberts, my husband, who was with me throughout.

Note: Arctic place names and their spellings vary a great deal through time, and from person to person. For the most part, I have tried to be consistent, if somewhat arbitrary, but in some cases I have changed names with the times about which I am writing. Thus, Baffinland becomes Baffin Island and Godthaab becomes Nuuk. In formal place names, although not in the generic, I adopted the Canadian convention of spelling "harbor" with a "u."

I have tried to use verb tenses to indicate when any quote was made. "Stu writes" or "Deborah says" shows recent communication directly with me. "Andy wrote" indicates words set down at a time closer to the events described, in a journal, letter or later manuscript.

Contents

Prologue: Deborah

*H*ello, gorgeous," I say.

She said nothing back. Not at first. I had to climb below, down to this little galley, and be quiet so she could make up her mind about me. I'm sitting here now, the golden May sunshine filtering through the hatch, reflecting warm and tawny off the mast and this old wooden table where I sit. She's so dirty and dusty now.

"Why are you like this, *Bowdoin*? Have you been abandoned all winter? I'll clean you up. I'll take care of you—promise. Look how beautiful you are under this dust. I think I'm going to end up loving you. I think I'm starting to already."

Then—"Hush!" she said. "Listen," she said.

So I put down my pen, and I listened. The sunlight faded and it grew dim down here, and still I listened.

It was then I knew we were not alone, *Bowdoin* and me. She rocked me, gently, gently, with the tide washing in against the dock. And she whispered some secrets, but I didn't understand all the words. Something about memories. Something about promises.

"I'll belong to you for a little while," she said. "But you—you will always belong to me."

These spaces will fill up with people and work and laughter, days at sea, shipmates-turned-friends. Then the *Bowdoin* will sit quietly again, but not alone. She will have her memories, after all.

She breathes history. I can't explain that, but I can feel it, just as solid as I can feel this old wooden table I'm writing on. She remembers all the men—and women—who have lived aboard

her, worked on her, loved her. She remembers. And later, someday, she'll remember me, too. Captain Mac loved her, and Miriam.
And all those college boys that Mac brought north—do you
remember them all, *Bowdoin*? Do you remember the men who
sailed on you during World War II?

I think you do. I can feel some of them now, here with us in
the stillness. Is it that they haunt you, *Bowdoin*—or is it that you
haunt them? Do you haunt all of us, after we leave? Is it back
aboard you that we come after we've died, to move quietly and be
sure you're treated well? Are you the final port for all those rest-
less souls who, in life, rode with you to search the far north?

*—Journal entry by Deborah Harrison, age 21,
on her first night aboard the* Bowdoin, *spring 1991*

Introduction

On April 9, 1921, a schooner came down the ways at Hodgdon Brothers in East Boothbay, Maine, one schooner within a long line of schooners, but unlike any other before or since. For the *Bowdoin* was built with an unusual mission, and cat-like, she has lived several lives.

The schooner's design and construction were carefully considered and well-executed, although neither was radical for their day. The vessel is unique today because of her specialized purpose — she is heavy and carries less sail for her displacement than most schooners because, in addition to the obvious ice hazards, the Arctic is known for having either no wind at all or too much.

But there's more to it than that. Through seven decades, so many of the people who have sailed or worked on the *Bowdoin* hold her in a special place in their hearts. Their lives were affected by her; she brought something significant to them. "The *Bowdoin* is the best," say more than one of her people, or "the *Bowdoin* is special."

The *Bowdoin* first crossed the Arctic Circle on August 23, 1921. A place unknown to most of the world, the Arctic had had few visitors from the south. Only sixteen years before, the goal of many generations of Arctic explorers had been reached when a northwest passage was traversed — a route which was, practically speaking, unusable, and after the construction of the Panama Canal, no longer necessary. Peary's North Pole expedition was merely a dozen years past. The last few Hudson's Bay and Davis Strait whalers had made their final trip home two years before.

The *Bowdoin* sailed north with MacMillan two dozen times, carrying scientists, adventurers and students. On July 30, 1991,

xi

again with students aboard, she came full circle, crossing once more to the sea where the summer sun never sets.

The past informs the future; for many, the journey to the far north mirrors a journey into themselves. It has been a long time since the *Bowdoin* was on the leading edge of science, but her contributions to those fortunate souls who sail with her are as great as ever. In people's search beyond the horizons, they can profit from looking to the past. The *Bowdoin* was a part of the quest for understanding for decades and now, under the ownership of the Maine Maritime Academy, she has returned to her own milieu, the North.

PART ONE

MacMillan's Days

ONE

Donald MacMillan

Early Days

*I*T IS NATURAL," MacMillan wrote in 1927, "for man to wonder what lies beyond the mountain peaks, what strange and interesting things may be below the encircling horizon." The southern Europeans had stumbled into the western hemisphere in the fifteenth century, opening vast territories to investigate for centuries to come. By the beginning of the twentieth century, the western frontier of North America had disappeared. Despite occasional expeditions over the course of several hundred years, the north and south poles were the last unknown earthly territories.

In the spring of 1908, Robert Peary, the great Arctic explorer, invited Donald MacMillan to come see him in New York. Over breakfast, Peary asked the young teacher to come along on what he felt would be his final attack on the North Pole. Peary suggested that MacMillan take a couple of weeks to think about it and warned him of the dangers of the trip—Peary very nearly hadn't come home himself, three years earlier—but MacMillan asked for a contract on the spot. Peary drew an envelope out of his pocket, the only paper he had at hand, and in pencil wrote an agreement appointing MacMillan to command a supporting party, act as ornithologist of the expedition, make tidal and meteorological studies, and make a running survey of the unknown fjords of Grant Land. MacMillan was not to write or lecture about the trip; any pictures he took would belong to Peary. There would be no salary.

MacMillan didn't hesitate to sign. Two weeks later, he returned to New York to gather supplies for the expedition.

Born in 1874 in Provincetown, Massachusetts, Donald MacMillan was the son of fishing schoonerman Neil and Sarah Gardner MacMillan, a shipbuilder's daughter. When the youngster was just nine years old, his father's vessel disappeared with all hands, driven down, said some who knew of Captain MacMillan's tendency to over-canvas his vessel. The lad had already made one sea voyage with his father, however, and had loved his father's tales of Greenland, Iceland and all of the Arctic.

MacMillan's older brother happened to be with his grandparents in Cape Breton, Nova Scotia, when his father's schooner went down, and he stayed there. Sarah MacMillan took in washing, but couldn't support the remaining four children, and allowed her eldest girl to be adopted by a family in Freeport, Maine. Young MacMillan added to his mother's meager earnings by skinning cod, peddling cranberries and lemonade, and diving for tourists' pennies, but life was hard, and Sarah MacMillan's exhaustion caught up with her. She died in 1885, leaving her children orphaned.

After a couple of years with one or another neighbor in Provincetown, Donald MacMillan and one of his younger sisters moved to Freeport to be with his older sister, now married; his other sister was taken in by another family in Freeport.

From Freeport High School he went on to Bowdoin College, and then started a career as a schoolmaster, all the while following the Arctic explorations of his Casco Bay neighbor, Robert Peary. In 1905 Peary invited the young man to go north, but MacMillan was unwilling to break a teaching commitment; fortunately for him, Peary's attempt on the Pole that year failed. Three years later, in 1908, MacMillan finally got to the Arctic.

Unlike many earlier explorers, Peary had learned from the whalers and from his earlier trips that the only way to live in the Arctic was in the manner and with the assistance of the region's native people. In August of 1908, when Peary's *Roosevelt* steamed north from Etah, she carried not only all the provisions she had brought from the south, but also 49 Inuit men, 17 women, 10 children and all the possessions of that nomadic community, including 246 sledge dogs. (Sledging was the only feasible method of carrying the supplies needed to cross the frozen Polar Sea.)

Not knowing in what direction he might return from the Pole, Peary sent MacMillan to cache supplies at Cape Morris Jesup, the northernmost point of land in the world, whose sole previous visitors from warmer climates were Peary and Henson in 1899. Making tidal observations and soundings, MacMillan then continued on to Fort Conger, where for two years in the early 1880s, Lieutenant A.W. Greely and the men of the Lady Franklin Bay Expedition had made their headquarters. Now, thirty years later, MacMillan was awed, coming across not only Greely's house and expedition debris but finding useful supplies that had been left behind. Cans marked "potatoes" turned out to be filled with rhubarb, but were enjoyed nonetheless. They also found a book inscribed in a childish hand: "To my dear father. From his affectionate son, Harry Kislingbury. May God be with you and return you safely to us." As MacMillan knew, Kislingbury, the single parent of four small boys had, along with several others, died of starvation in 1884 while waiting for rescue from Cape Sabine. MacMillan took the book home with him, and searched out Harry Kislingbury to return it.

Perhaps it was this personal connection with Greely's people that made MacMillan care so much about that particular Arctic expedition; one of the objectives of an early *Bowdoin* trip would be to formally recognize the Greely party.

MacMillan became enamored of the Arctic and its people on his first trip. It is easy from today's perspective to fault him for what seems to be a paternal attitude toward his Inuit companions who had never left their own world, but that he respected and enjoyed the Inuit people is undeniable. The ice country obviously attached itself to his soul as well; MacMillan was hooked by this life of adventure and exploration.

Not everyone who travels to the Arctic is caught by the area's appeal, but those who are feel an intense, often life-long itch to return. Some of the early explorers felt it, MacMillan felt it, and in 1991, the schooner *Bowdoin*'s first mate, Elliot Rappaport, felt it:

> In its scale, its utterly indifferent majesty, the Arctic places an individual life against a backdrop so vast that the complexities and encumbrances of such a life fade into insignificance. It is as an astronaut must feel looking back at Earth ... small, but more than that, reduced to scale — to some elemental and humbling appreciation of life itself.
>
> "Maybe," said Rockwell Kent upon finding himself shipwrecked in Greenland during the thirties, "we have lived just to be here now."

MacMillan made several expeditions north on his own before building the *Bowdoin*; in fact, each of the next eight years saw him in the north. He joined an expedition into the interior of Labrador in 1910, made a solo canoe trip along the Labrador coast in 1911 and a motor boat trip in the same area with a friend the following year. In 1913, sponsored by the American Museum of Natural History, the American Geographical Society, and the University of Illinois, he led his own Crocker Land Expedition north. During this trip the party disproved the existence of land north of Ellesmere Island that Peary had claimed to have seen and given the name Crocker Land. MacMillan and his fellows were the first to follow the trail of previous explorers — Kane in 1855, Nares in 1875, Peary in 1906 — and retrieved their records. They made scientific observations, started a dictionary of Inuit language that MacMillan would work on for years to come, and took great numbers of photographs and moving pictures. The trip which was to have lasted two years extended to four due to the difficulty of getting ships north, the same problem that ultimately caused the death of all but six of the 25 men in Greely's party. MacMillan's party all survived. In 1917, MacMillan returned to the United States and enlisted in the Navy for the duration of the war, eventually receiving a commission.

One more trip, in 1920, during which MacMillan served as second mate on the *S.S. Thetis* as she traveled to Hudson Bay on an unsuccessful commercial endeavor, convinced MacMillan that he was ready to be self-sufficient. He certainly felt comfortable in the Arctic. His knowledge and accurate recall of the navigational hazards of the northern sailing ground was well known and admired. It was time to have his own vessel.

The Bowdoin

MacMillan knew exactly how his own exploration vessel should be constructed. He hired the well-respected naval architect William Hand to design a schooner to his specifications, and agreed to pay each of the three Hodgdon brothers of East Boothbay, Maine, ten dollars per day to build her. Sonny Hodgdon, whose father was one of the principals of the Hodgdon yard and who still builds fine boats in East Boothbay himself, says that William Hand drew the *Bowdoin*'s lines, sail plans and cabin and deck layouts, but "he hadn't the least idea about how to build such a strong vessel. It was my uncle Charles who did the construction plans."

(Already the *Bowdoin* had started her pattern of training young men who would become well known in their own right. They included Wallace Goudy, who later would have his own yard and would maintain the *Bowdoin*, and Harvey Gamage, who built big wooden sailing vessels when no one did that any more, starting with the *Mary Day* in 1962 and continuing with the *Clearwater* — who herself comes into this story many decades later — *Shenandoah*, and *Bill of Rights*.)

At just 88 feet long, the schooner *Bowdoin* was small when compared with many earlier Arctic vessels, and had a relatively shallow 10-foot draft so she could hug the shoreline and hide behind rocks and reefs from attacking ice. The *Bowdoin* was built ruggedly to withstand the strength of Arctic ice. She was constructed of wood, so that if she were nipped by ice her sides would recover their shape. (A steel hull might distort, popping rivets and opening seams permanently.) The Hodgdon brothers built her with the extra heavy oak framing and planking of a Grand Banks schooner, with an airspace between her planking and her Oregon pine ceiling to minimize condensation. Cast concrete filled her bilges, because outside ballast would be ripped off by ice. An additional inch-and-a-half of ironwood sheathing started a few inches above and reached five feet below the waterline. Steel protected her bow. The *Bowdoin* was the last treenailed vessel ever built at Hodgdon Brothers.

MacMillan himself had less than ten percent of the money necessary for such a project, but with the help of his good friend Jerry Look and many others, some of whom bought shares at $100 each, he raised the $35,000 needed. He named his schooner the *Bowdoin* for his alma mater.

In the 1920s, the *Bowdoin* was a research center on a par with any of today's most serious laboratories. The tidal observations MacMillan made proved invaluable decades later when submarines passed under the polar icecap; his magnetic and meteorological studies were essential for understanding the planet. In her first decades the *Bowdoin*'s adventures were so exciting and well-publicized that she was known to every schoolchild; she fits into the continuum of exploration vessels that includes Columbus' *Santa Maria*, *Nina* and *Pinta* and the space shuttles *Discovery*, *Explorer* and *Challenger*.

TWO

The Scientists in Foxe Basin

The Voyage Begins

*I*N JULY OF 1921, the schooner *Bowdoin* was ready for her first voyage, to the Foxe Basin, on the western side of Baffin Island, then called Baffin Land. MacMillan wanted to reach the Fury and Hecla Strait, named by the British Arctic explorer William Edward Parry nearly a hundred years earlier in honor of his two ships that had been forced to turn back from that stretch of water between Baffin Land and the Melville Peninsula.

Sponsored by the Carnegie Institution, one objective of Mac-Millan's trip was to study terrestrial magnetism and atmospheric electricity. It is hard today to realize how recent is our understanding of the earth's magnetic poles. Although seamen had been using magnetic compasses for navigation since perhaps the twelfth century, Columbus was the first to notice that the needle didn't always point north. In the seventeenth century, the regularity of variation was recognised, but it wasn't until 1903, when Amundsen stood on the site that had previously been identified as the North Magnetic Pole and it was no longer there, that the location of the Magnetic Pole was documented as actually moving. The Carnegie Institution was studying the variation over time, and they wanted MacMillan's party to ascertain the horizontal and vertical intensities of magnetic attraction in several locations.

MacMillan, always interested in ornithology, also hoped to find the nesting site of the blue goose. The trip was to take a year; he wanted to establish a winter camp in the Foxe Channel from which he might explore the surrounding area.

Among the most important preparations for the trip was crew selection. Because the *Bowdoin* was small, and her men so few in number, MacMillan took great care in choosing the people who sailed with him. In addition to looking for obvious attributes—health, strength and vigor—MacMillan sought the more important traits of loyalty to the leader and to the expedition, optimism and faith in the successful outcome of the trip, and an accepting, patient outlook.

His first mate was Jonathan "Jot" Cook Small, whom he had known since they were both boys in Provincetown, and who had accompanied him on two other trips north. Although as a general rule, married men were not taken on such expeditions, as their loss would leave dependents uncared for, MacMillan took two married men, Harold Whitehouse, engineer, from East Boothbay, and Thomas McCue, cook, a Newfoundlander who had a great deal of sailing experience on fishing vessels and full ships alike. His general assistant was Ralph Robinson, and two magnetic observers, Dawson Howell and Richard Goddard, completed the crew, making just seven men.

MacMillan chose Wiscasset, Maine, as the port of departure, in part because it was a quiet harbor with a good loading facility and not far from his home in Freeport, and in part to recognize townspeople's support of the expedition. Among other donations aboard the *Bowdoin* were a marine clock presented by the Wiscasset Masonic Lodge and a sextant from the citizens of Wiscasset. Although Wiscasset was—and still is—a small town, on departure day, July 16, 1921, the dock was packed with people wanting to wish the travelers well. Governor Percival Baxter, who also happened to be a former classmate of MacMillan's at Bowdoin College, addressed the crowd. Finally, they were off, to the cacophony of the town fire whistle and the narrow-gauge railroad locomotive's huffing and puffing and screeching steam-whistle, and accompanied by a flotilla of power boats blowing their air horns all the way down the Sheepscot River. MacMillan wondered if there was room through the narrows for his schooner and all her attendants, but they reached the *Bowdoin*'s birthplace, Hodgdon Brothers in East Boothbay, in three hours with no mishap. The schooner spent the night there, where they rearranged the deck load and picked up William Hodgdon, who would ride along as far as Battle Harbour, Labrador.

On deck, the schooner carried dories, a canoe, the magnetic observatory equipment, coal, lubricating oil in wooden crates, and kerosene and gasoline in drums. The *Bowdoin* was loaded deep, her hold also packed full with materials and supplies, even including dolls and toys donated by local youngsters for Inuit children. One little girl had come down to the boat just before departure with an extra suit for her doll "to exchange for her travel-stained suit when she got there."

At 6:30 the next morning, everyone aboard was ready to leave Maine behind and head off on their northern adventure. They cast the lines and were underway—but just 20 yards from the dock, the *Bowdoin* grounded.

The tide rose, and within three-quarters of an hour, the *Bowdoin* floated off. MacMillan wrote, "She began to realize for the first time that she was especially constructed for Arctic work, and off she went, her bow in the air and belching forth black smoke from under her quarter as if she were determined to accomplish her task before fall."

MacMillan's vessel was dually powered. Sail not only lessened the need for fuel, but also provided a backup should the propeller or drive shaft be damaged by ice, as had happened to Peary's *Roosevelt* in 1909 on MacMillan's first trip north. In order to keep the crew safely on deck when they were changing sail, the *Bowdoin* carried a compact, pole-masted rig. In any case, MacMillan said that in the northern regions there was either no wind at all or much too much, so topsails or the additional sail area a bowsprit would permit would not be needed, and the supportive bobstay would be vulnerable. Ice catching on the bobstay could bring the mast right down.

The *Bowdoin* raced along under sail and power. She stopped at Seven Hundred Acre Island in Penobscot Bay to visit the illustrator Charles Dana Gibson. Mrs. Gibson sent a launch over to Dark Harbor to bring all the grade school pupils there (a half dozen children) to see the *Bowdoin*; John Yeaton was eight years old, but he remembers the visit clearly. "I was fascinated," he says. "I was surprised she wasn't any bigger, to go way off like that. They told us if she was any bigger she wouldn't have been able to make it. They'd close off all the decks and just let the water roll right over her, they said. And I remember how she was loaded — you had to crawl on your hands and knees to get into the cabins, she was so heavily loaded. And they had a little monkey aboard, to see how it would take the cold, I guess." (There is no mention of a monkey in MacMillan's account of the voyage — presumably, the monkey didn't fare well.)

MacMillan was pleased with his schooner's behavior in a strong breeze; she made the 335-mile trip to Halifax in 35 hours. They laid over there a couple of days, waiting out a strong gale, and left on a foggy Friday morning. A line of gas buoys marked the Nova Scotia coast, and the *Bowdoin* had a good compass and log. Each mark came along where it was expected, though particularly thick fog off Cape Breton required taking bow and beam bearings by sound to get a rough distance from Scatari, the turning point into the Gulf of St. Lawrence.

North Sydney was the jumping-off place for the real north, where the last mail was sent home and final provisions were purchased. MacMillan tied the *Bowdoin* up at the dock and went ashore on these errands. When he returned, the dock was buzzing with activity — the passenger/mail steamer *Stella Maris* had run directly into the *Bowdoin*. All her crew had jumped ashore when they saw the steamship coming, except for Whitehouse in the engine room. At impact, he erupted up through the hatch, yelling. MacMillan was told what Whitehouse said but didn't feel he ought to record the words.

The *Stella Maris*'s steel prow had struck on the *Bowdoin*'s port quarter almost directly in line with the after bulkhead. The ironwood sheathing and the schooner's planking were slightly crushed, the treenails were started and putty oozed out from some seams. The impact was so severe that the *Bowdoin*'s new three-inch manila docklines broke, and everyone expected her to sink on the spot.

But the schooner wasn't taking on any significant water and, despite the admonition of the local salts, MacMillan didn't feel it was necessary to haul his vessel. He put to sea, and his faith in the *Bowdoin* was justified; she was fine. Far worse would happen to her in the years to come, and always she came through.

To Labrador

The trip along the Newfoundland shore put the *Bowdoin* to test against weather, throwing a good southeast blow her way, during which she flew along close hauled with her rail buried. Discretion suggested putting into a safe harbor until the worst of the wind had passed, and MacMillan turned into Bonne Bay Harbour, a drowned valley, deeper inside than out, with an average depth of 49 fathoms. (Even eight miles into the fjord, a depth of 750 feet can be found.) MacMillan had to take the schooner right in close to shore to get a sounding of eight fathoms, and there they dropped anchor.

Leaving Bonne Bay that evening, the *Bowdoin* saw her first northern lights of the trip. MacMillan wrote:

> *With the Northern Lights playing across the sky in the northwest and beckoning us on, we all felt that night that we were on the borderland of the Arctic and had left behind us for a year and possibly longer green fields, stretches of woodland, for sterile grey hills, and a coast abraded and polished by the pressure of immense ice fields, the replica of our own now beautiful country at the end of the glacial period. All were weary of the conventional life at home and longed for the simplicity of northern life with its many lessons so simply told of how God works in the building of the world. And nowhere can the lesson be better learned than in the far North, where the pages of the book are open and beautifully illustrated.*

Upon reaching the Labrador, the rigors of sailing that coast soon became clear: the magnetic deviations caused by iron deposits coincided with fog at the Strait of Belle Isle, and there the men spotted their first icebergs. Rather than asking his schooner to fight her way into a harbor protected by two large icebergs as well as reefs that appeared to jump up out of nowhere, MacMillan chose to heave-to off shore.

In the morning, he wasn't certain of their location and headed north, peering into the fog for familiar rocks or islands. "The Cap islands emerged and with a look-at-me-quick action disappeared in the dim outlines of St. Charles Gull Island in the background," he wrote. At least then he knew where he was— MacMillan never forgot the geography of any place he had been before. A couple of hard turns of the wheel led the responsive schooner into the quiet, protected waters of Battle Harbour. There the men spent a couple of days rearranging the deck load, photographing the sights and being entertained by the local fishermen and residents.

With very few exceptions, the next 540 miles along the Labrador (as the goose flies) were uncharted. One crewmember was happy when the *Bowdoin* stopped at the Indian Harbour Grenfell medical mission, where he had an aching tooth pulled. "Relief for one man is always a relief for all, considering our intimate relationship on such a small craft," wrote MacMillan.

On the run to Hopedale, halfway up the northeast coast of Labrador, MacMillan saw three new lighthouses, built since his last trip, and there the *Bowdoin* met her first Inuit people, who were fishing from sailing outriggers. Hopedale was the site of the first Moravian Missionary, one of eight missions established by the evangelical Moravians between 1763 and 1900 along the Labrador. The English had granted these missionaries 100,000 acres of land to protect the Inuit. The Moravians tried to provide education to the native population without interfering in their way of life, and intentionally discouraged the Eskimos from learning English, believing that not knowing the language of the visiting fishermen would act as a bulwark against the corrupting influence of those passers-through. In spite of their best efforts, the Inuit population steadily declined. Epidemics of smallpox, measles, influenza, whooping cough, typhoid and syphilis had regularly attacked the Inuit since 1774. These southern diseases— common in their home habitats—had taken their toll. By the 1920s, only five of the original eight Moravian missions were still operating.

The native population had dropped and dropped; originally estimated at 3,000, by the early twenties the Labrador Inuit population had decreased to 800. MacMillan believed that these were mostly half-bred and that the Inuit would meld into the white race before long. He credited the Moravians with the perpetuation of those who remained.

MacMillan had planned to pick up an Inuit interpreter to travel with him the rest of the way; in the absence of an English-speaking Eskimo, the Moravians told him of a local resident, Abram Bromfield, who might go with him. Bromfield, who agreed to join the party, was one of two sons of a "liveyere" family (a term used to describe fishermen who chose to call the Labrador home). He had been born in 1879 in Jack's Bay and had never been south of Battle Harbour.

Another couple of hundred miles up the Labrador coast was Hebron, the site of another thriving Moravian mission. The *Bowdoin* was met by a motorboat full of Inuit looking for the overdue annual steamer from the south, their source of news and supplies from the rest of the globe. But it was with great cheer that they visited with the strangers aboard the *Bowdoin*; they curiously inspected every inch of the schooner and left, reluctantly, only when MacMillan announced that he and his crew were going to bed.

Mid-August found the *Bowdoin* approaching the farthest northeastern tip of the North American continent, Cape Chidley, where four- and five-thousand foot mountains rise directly from the water, with colorful fjords and plenty of fog. Increasing southeasterlies and a rising sea precluded calling at Port Burwell to report to Customs. Instead, the *Bowdoin* swung offshore and headed across Hudson Strait to Baffin Land. A short cross sea broke over the weather rail, and now and then a solid mass of water over the starboard quarter tumbled coal, grape juice, ropes, and boxes of pemmican into the lee scuppers.

As they sailed through Hudson Strait and the islands along Baffin Land's southern coast, the *Bowdoin* was joined by an American whaleboat crammed full of Inuit and their possessions: men, women, children, skins, rotten meat and dogs. The boat was escorted by a pair of circling kayaks, and the smell reached the *Bowdoin* well before the party. But MacMillan welcomed the visitors aboard, fed them, and played his Victrola. He was impressed at the Inuit ability to appreciate music he considered so much more sophisticated than their own.

Baffin Land

MacMillan and his men needed to find the Hudson's Bay Company outpost at Cape Dorset, on the Foxe Peninsula, as that would be the last connection with their own civilization; should the *Bowdoin* be lost, they would have to return to Cape Dorset. They also would leave mail there to be sent home on the fall mail boat.

Scanning the skyline looking for marks that were customarily built upon high points of land and at turning points, they found first a beacon, then another mark, and abreast of that, a second beacon, then an anchoring buoy, and a boat, and a flag pole, and then there they were, at the HBC—Hudson's Bay Company. (HBC was said to stand for "Here Before Christ" because the company had been on northern shores so long—since 1670—although the Cape Dorset outpost wasn't established until 1913.) The factor in charge, John Livingstone, was suspicious of MacMillan's intent when he came alongside, but became friendly when assured that there was no plan to set up a competing trading company. Livingstone and the crew of the schooner enjoyed one another's company before the *Bowdoin* set off, north and west again along the western shore of Baffin Island, through Foxe Channel, around King Charles Cape and north into Foxe Basin.

MacMillan knew that his schooner would confront ice on every trip. And he knew that ice was a serious adversary. Because it floats with only 10 to 12 percent of its mass above water, an iceberg 250 feet by 200 feet, standing 200 feet above the water, weighs in at more than five billion pounds. Even a common icepan 50 feet by 30 feet and rising only three to five feet from the water, weighs considerably more than two million pounds. The northern ice pack sometimes allowed passage, but more often did not. In the past it had caught and dragged—or destroyed—many vessels.

"Starboard, starboard!" or "Hard a port!" MacMillan or the mate would call down to the helmsman from the crow's nest, where one or the other always stood, watching for shoaling reefs. Not only were there ice and ledges to threaten the schooner, but strong tidal currents sometimes ran as fast as six knots.

The schooner first met the ice pack as she crossed the Arctic Circle. It was just as described by Parry in his search for the northwest passage, a hundred years earlier: heavy, hummocked, and covered with sand and small stones. It was the same odd dirty ocher color George Back reported in 1836; MacMillan was puzzled by the color until he realized that the many shoals' bottoms consisted of sand and mud. He believed that the polar ice in the Foxe Basin didn't move from its locality; he wondered if it might even be the very same ice as those earlier explorers had seen.

The *Bowdoin* wriggled and wormed her way through twisting narrow leads in the ice pack, but she was restricted to travelling in those directions the leads happened to take her. Through sunset, Arctic twilight and sunrise again, her steel-plated bow glanced over the ice, crunching through until after six in the morning. Then the pack completely prevented her from going north or west, as MacMillan wanted. They tied onto an ice pan and filled their water tanks from the pool of fresh water always on the surface of floe ice, and then headed out to the southeast under power.

That the tension extended to the crew is shown in Goddard's journal. "Had a wonderful watch below turned in, hearing Cap'n Mac in the crow's nest ordering the helm. Tried hard to find the wheel but couldn't, and so groped about for four hours avoiding ice in my sleep."

Seven hours later, in open water again, a big, ancient, compacted chunk of ice suddenly came at them from nowhere. The helmsman's first response was wrong. In correcting his course to avoid the growler, the schooner hit it squarely. MacMillan, in the crow's nest at the top of the foremast, would have been thrown out if he hadn't been well down in the barrel. "The *Bowdoin* bounded like a rubber ball, and went serenely on her way," MacMillan reported.

Threatened by the Pack and the Ground

The *Bowdoin* recrossed the Circle once, trying to get around the pack. She squirmed her way north again through the leads before getting hemmed into a cul-de-sac in the moving ice. MacMillan was finally convinced that he'd better get out of the pack, but there was no opening toward shore. Steadily and cautiously they worked their way eastward. Twice, the propeller blades struck ledge and the *Bowdoin* shuddered and vibrated in protest. Held in the wind-blown pack, and drifting along with it, the men were "not exactly in rapport with their surroundings," MacMillan wrote. (Goddard reported that Bromfield said, "This place must be handy to where the devil lives.") Listening to his crew's remarks about this being an awful place to winter, MacMillan broke out the motion picture projector. "Old Torngak of the North must have peeped through our port hole and become disheartened over his vain attempt to bring us unhappiness, for when the theatre closed good weather greeted us."

The *Bowdoin* was off in a good northwest breeze, carrying one reef and a bone in her teeth. They regained the lost distance, coming into a group of reddish colored islands which reflected oddly on the water. Suddenly, the schooner touched bottom. She bounced forward leaving mucky water in her trail, struck again, and stopped. It was just after high water.

Among the specifications MacMillan had made of the *Bowdoin's* designer, William Hand, was that she should be able to float off a grounding before water reached her hatches, and that she be rugged enough to handle such groundings. MacMillan could only wonder, though, how she would handle a dropping tide. The bottom seemed to be safe enough—but it surely would be better to get her off and not put her to the test.

The first step was to get her turned about, and there was no time to spare. MacMillan told his men to lower the main and fore so the headsails would pull her around, and to turn the wheel hard-a-port and run the engine full speed. The schooner swung on her stern until she had her back to the wind, but even with all her sail raised again, she wouldn't budge. The two strongest men went out in a dory, tugging her bow back to windward, but still she clutched onto the mud. MacMillan trimmed the main and fore in hard until the schooner heeled over with her scuppers under, and the men in the dory pulled with all their might. At last a strong blast of wind hit, and the *Bowdoin* shook herself free and moved off.

The ice pack was swinging around and threatening any retreat the *Bowdoin* might attempt. It was a race between the pack and the schooner, and soundings showed the ground beneath her to be shoaling beyond comfort. The only escape was to leeward, over the shoals. The largest pieces of ice were aground already. First Mate Small on the hand lead was calling out fathoms: "Five, four, three, two and a half, two—it's getting shallower all the time!" But there was no choice but to keep going.

Crash! The *Bowdoin* struck heavily on rock, and someone on deck hollered to cut power. Down in the engine room, Whitehouse knew better, and opened the throttle. The *Bowdoin* bounded ahead, striking ledge again and again but never halting. Ever so slowly, the soundings increased to three fathoms, three-and-a-half, but never more than four. On went the schooner, MacMillan steering for a growler grounded a mile eastward. The berg showed two feet above the water, indicating enough water below for the *Bowdoin*. And there was free water beyond.

One hundred and seventeen miles north of the Arctic Circle, still making progress to the north, at 68°30' the *Bowdoin* was still 65 miles short of her objective, the Fury and Hecla Strait. It was August 29. Summer was gone. The west shore was blocked, the middle passage was shoal, the pack was aground to the east and north. Reluctantly, they turned back to follow the eastern edge of the pack southward until they could find an opening to the unknown western shores of the Foxe Channel.

"Port!" hollered the lookout in the crow's nest. But the man at the wheel wasn't quick enough, and the *Bowdoin* struck an ice tongue with what MacMillan described as a "fearful thump. She gained headway and wobbled on complaining of such harsh treatment by excessive vibration which indicated a bent shaft or badly twisted blades."

The schooner's engine was crippled, but she still had her sails. When the anchor watch reported that they were hemmed in on all sides, they spent a night jogging back and forth under sail, breaking newly forming ice. To be immobile in the ice for three or four days in September meant spending ten months there—and no one wanted to spend the winter frozen in a floating ice pack. Although the *Bowdoin* was not designed as an ice-breaker, MacMillan believed that she wouldn't hurt herself and in the morning he set the *Bowdoin* to bucking ice.

MacMillan's faith was well-placed. The *Bowdoin* had been designed with an easy entry, a sharp turn of the bilge to elude the grip of ice, and wide quarters to shunt ice away from her propeller. In addition, her stem had been extra-heavily reinforced inside and out. MacMillan slowed the schooner when direct impact was near, asked for full speed when prying two floes apart, and his vessel made progress faster than he expected. By the end of the day, they were again in open water, with no land in sight.

Celestial sightings determined that, according to the chart, their location was 15 miles inland.

The Search for a Winter Harbor

Maps and charts of 1921 showed Baffin Land clearly enough, but the island was not where it was shown. The *Bowdoin* worked her way back eastward, looking for land, but there was none to be seen. MacMillan and her crew knew that land was there, they'd seen it themselves, a week or two back. She hove to overnight—"with the helm hard down, jumbo flat, and foresail with started sheets, she lay like a duck, slowly jogging to windward," wrote MacMillan. They started eastward again at four in the morning and passed through a herd of walruses; although the mothers sheltered their young, none of the animals seemed alarmed by the schooner. Fortunately for the animals, there was no time for shooting.

Finally, at daylight, hills appeared to the east, ending sharply on their north end. The hills were at Cape Dorchester, on the north side of the Foxe Peninsula.

When the Cape's location had been mapped 290 years earlier, it had been located 31 miles too far west and 55 too far north. In 1921, on the charts available to the crew of the *Bowdoin*, Baffin Island remained mapped in this way.

It was time to search for a good anchorage for the winter. Sailing along to the east, they found nothing but shoals and ledges and exposed water, offering no protection at all. The schooner returned to Cape Dorchester, where the inner section of the bay looked good, until the crew saw the green cast to the water. Too shallow.

And then they heard four rifle shots! MacMillan wrote that he felt like Robinson Crusoe finding Friday's footprints. Ahead on the shore were three tents. Deep in the water was a whaleboat with a load of natives. MacMillan anchored in eight fathoms of water and welcomed aboard the boatload of strong-smelling Inuit: old women, mothers and babies, all laughing and cheerful.

The schooner once again became a motion picture theatre, as MacMillan showed the Inuit movies of Eskimos in Greenland and Hudson Bay, as well as their first view of life outside of the Arctic. Some of the guests were so absorbed in the moving pictures that they sat like stone images.

However, the outer bay was too exposed to stay for the winter, and through the interpreter, MacMillan confirmed his thoughts about the coast to the north—it was scarcely above water, unapproachable due to shoals, and without the seals, walrus, or bear necessary to survive the winter. The *Bowdoin* weighed anchor and headed southward again, amid tearful natives. "Our visit was like the flash of a meteor out of a dark sky and now we were gone," MacMillan wrote.

MacMillan headed west to make one final attempt to reach the Melville Peninsula and be closer to the Fury and Hecla Strait. The days were shorter as the equinox approached, and as there was not the slightest zephyr blowing, they flung a line over a pinnacle of a growler to hold them during the night's darkness. MacMillan left orders that if any breeze arose or if they moved, he was to be awakened. Within an hour, the man on anchor watch called the captain; he had taken a sounding and there was no bottom, yet he'd seen lights and heard a locomotive puffing, dogs barking, wolves howling and people crying, sighing and groaning.

MacMillan could explain all the strange phenomena. The lights were phosphorescence. When there is no wind and the air is heavy with cold, noises travel extraordinary distances, and some of the sounds were just what they sounded like. Narwhals blowing and whales humming accounted for the locomotive and some of the human utterings.

In 1921, the ice field hugged the shores of Southampton Island and blocked the strait completely. It was at this same time of year, 85 years earlier, and very nearly at this place, that Captain Back in the *HMS Terror* had been trapped by ice. For more than ten months, ice toyed with the rugged, 340-ton ship, once throwing it forty feet up a cliff, and nearly destroying it the following summer when the ice finally broke up. The leaking, waterlogged and lumbering vessel slogged back to the coast of Ireland, where her captain beached her just hours before she would have gone down for good. MacMillan recognised it was time to quit, and turned back.

The *Bowdoin* made her way back to King Charles Cape on the Foxe Peninsula, where she had been a little more than two weeks earlier. A perfect harbor awaited her crew there: good depth even at low tide, freedom from the pressure of ice and currents, and a good supply of game and water. They were below the Arctic Circle, at 64° 24′ North Latitude, and 78° West Longitude. They named their winter home "Bowdoin Harbour." (A dozen years later, though, MacMillan would name another harbor for his schooner and alma mater. Today, the harbor shows on charts as "Schooner Harbour," still honoring the schooner *Bowdoin*.)

The men spent the eighth of September and the next few days stripping the *Bowdoin* of her running rigging. They left the sails on the booms because stowing them below would take up precious space, and they'd be certain to mildew. They set out the heaviest anchor, ran a hawser to a large rock on land, and turned the *Bowdoin* to face what they guessed would be the prevailing winds. The deck load and all provisions and camping gear were stashed ashore above the high water mark in case the schooner should burn, as other Arctic vessels had before her. They erected a spar as a flag pole, from which they flew a pillowcase to let the Inuit they had met earlier know that they were there.

A few days later, two Inuit hunters, brothers, and their wives happened by with a polar bear carcass. The brothers helped set up the magnetic observatory ashore while the women made sheepskin garments for the crew. Using moranic stone with two layers of beaver board inside, they constructed a building 23′ by 18′, and six feet tall, setting cement pillars inside for the magnetic instruments. A trysail was stretched over the top for a ceiling, and a canvas pitched roof covered the whole works. A second observatory, just a tent, was also constructed.

Soon this Inuit family moved on, but the MacMillan camp was ready for winter.

Settling In

Snow fell on the camp on the 20th of September, but inside the schooner, the men felt secure. By the 24th, the building work was completed and the men were hunting at every opportunity. But in the Arctic, with no familiar points of reference, it was easy to be misled about the sizes or even the identification of objects.

During earlier expeditions, owls had been mistaken for caribou, a small dory for a 500-ton steamship, and distances estimated to take six hours to cross had taken 18. Bromfield and Whitehouse, perhaps the most serious hunters in the group, had a great war with a polar bear, shooting him a couple of times in the head, before they realized that their bear was a rock. The men found that tent life wasn't as comfortable as the "snug little *Bowdoin*," and stayed close by.

By October 27, the harbor ice was so thick that the men could walk from the schooner to shore. The *Bowdoin* was 50 yards off the beach, stern to, held in place with a second anchor and the strongest line aboard. MacMillan wanted to move her closer to the land in order to run electric cable to the observatory, so the crew chopped ice astern of her and hauled her in. Just when MacMillan thought his vessel was finally ready for the winter, a huge southerly wind arose on October 29. A six-inch manila line wore right through and the schooner leaped forward to her earlier home in the ice. Then, to everyone's surprise, the surrounding ice started moving toward the sea, taking the *Bowdoin* along. She dragged her anchor and 80 fathoms of heavy chain. Just short of threatening rocks, she finally held her ground, "and there she held humming and vibrating under the strain of her steel chain, bursting up through and cleaving the field as it swept down past us on its way to the harbor entrance," MacMillan wrote. By evening, all the ice was gone from the harbor, and the *Bowdoin* was left on a lee shore with just two feet of water beneath her at low tide.

It was two days before the weather settled enough so they could move the *Bowdoin* back to her original anchorage. Once there, the men ran their power lines ashore and hooked up their recording instruments, and within ten days the *Bowdoin* was frozen in for real, not to move for 274 days.

The day after freeze-up, November 10, was MacMillan's 47th birthday. He and his men feasted on tomato soup, roast eider duck with grape jelly, boiled new potatoes, plum pudding, nuts, figs, raisins, chocolates and coffee, and topped the banquet off with cigars.

New routines were established for the winter. The men maintained a fire hole in the ice near the *Bowdoin* to supplement the vessel's chemical fire extinguishers. A tidal gauge was set up beside the vessel and MacMillan established watches to record the rise and fall of tide. He also scheduled the men to fetch fresh water from shore. He didn't believe it was necessary to plan physical exercise for the men, as had some other Arctic explorers—these men were active on their own. Trapping was a popular endeavor; white fox pelts made fine presents for ladyfriends at home. MacMillan encouraged hunting, too, both for the men's enjoyment and for fresh meat, which was essential for their health.

It amused MacMillan how ignorant Europeans and Americans still were about preventing scurvy. It was even still a law that ships on long voyages had to provide crew members a specified amount of lime juice daily. MacMillan knew that fresh meat prevented scurvy. The traditional Inuit diet contained, at most, two pounds of vegetable matter in an average year; only if starving would an Eskimo eat seaweed. Even though the whalemen knew this, and long ago had learned that a cure for scurvy among their crew was to send the afflicted ashore to live and eat with the natives, doctors wouldn't believe it, and for an extraordinary length of time, notwithstanding disastrous results among their men, northern expeditions from Europe and the United States continued in the ways traditional to their own parts of the world.

MacMillan described the *Bowdoin* as "cozy" even in the worst weather. Her wooden interior was more comfortable than that of a steel vessel, on whose walls condensation collected and froze regularly, freezing bedclothes and books to them. The *Bowdoin* had a sturdy interior ceiling, which discouraged some condensation, and later during the winter the men built igloos on deck to allow air circulation and let moisture out.

The men enjoyed watching nature's spectacular light shows. MacMillan listed a dozen different effects they saw, from sun pillars to coronae and mirages. Holidays and birthdays were made much of, and Thanksgiving was celebrated by a rifle shoot, which was won easily by Bromfield, the interpreter from Labrador.

In early December, the brothers Kovavau and Nipatchee appeared, whom MacMillan had hired as assistants and dog drivers. (In Baffin Land, because there was a shortage of meat for dogs, it was common for two men to share ownership of a dog team.) Wherever an Innuk traveled, all his relatives came along; Kovavau and Nipatchee were happy that their wives, children and parents were welcomed into the *Bowdoin*'s camp. They chose to set up their own houses, though, rather than sleep on the *Bowdoin*. Within a couple of hours of their arrival, they had built two snow houses, 12 to 18 feet in diameter, using for each house about 50 snow blocks cut and lifted into place from within. Every block was beveled so that the whole structure was self-supporting. The men placed the blocks, and the women chinked with snow from outside. By bedtime, their houses were functional, complete with beds of snow raised off the floor, covered with skins. A porch connected the two dwellings, which shared a single entrance, and a four-inch hole in the roof provided ventilation.

The next day the brothers replaced some of the snow blocks with clear ice cut from a pond. Now, their houses had windows. Later, they built a wall around the igloos for further protection and insulation. "Lined with seal skins or an old tent, seal oil lamps lighted, pot boiling and Victrola going, it is a palace to an Eskimo, and a home to the white stranger from the south who has had a long march through rough ice against a cold biting wind," MacMillan wrote.

From his new Inuit friends, MacMillan was able to fill in some gaps in western history. Until then it had been a mystery what had happened to Captain Grant's 1911 expedition north. One Eskimo told MacMillan how Grant's ship had run aground, and the Inuit aboard were sent ashore onto a nearby island. When their women and children were safe, the Inuit men were to return for the white men. But the Inuit were unable to return, and during the night they heard gunshots aboard the ship, which they took to mean trouble. (MacMillan suspected that the gunshots were a distress signal.) When daylight came, there was no sign of the ship. The Inuit spent the winter on the island, and ultimately returned to Baffin Island not far from where the *Bowdoin* was spending this winter. The Eskimo told the story a number of times, until MacMillan felt he had memorized all the details.

Within the vast and sparsely settled Arctic world, MacMillan often observed a special closeness between people. He met an old woman who had lived on Captain Spicer's ship for several winters, 30 years earlier. Between the Inuit of Baffin Land and Labrador there were close connections; the dog-drivers' grandfather had migrated from Labrador. Many of the stories Mac-Millan heard in Baffin Land were repetitions of tales he had heard in Labrador and even Greenland. One old woman told him, "We cannot put down our thoughts in *strokes* as you do. What I have learned I have learned from my mother. What my mother knew she learned from her mother."

The sun showed just over the crest of the hills south of the harbor on the shortest day of the year, three days before Christmas. It was 25 degrees below zero. But the Christmas celebration was as festive as any. There were presents for all, a real Christmas tree from Bustins Island, Maine, and a huge dinner, much of it courtesy of the S. S. Pierce Company of Boston, who had sent a Christmas greeting along with their boxes of food. After the *Bowdoin* men finished their holiday dinner, MacMillan invited the Inuit aboard, and each was served a heaping plate of turkey and fixings. Cigars were passed around and Nipatchee's wife played an accordian she had bought at the Hudson's Bay Company for two white fox skins. Fireworks and a huge torch, set in the snow and illuminating the schooner, completed the celebrations.

The end of the year brought nature's own fireworks. MacMillan described them:

December 28th and 29th are to be remembered for their
wonderful display of northern lights. It will interest the reader to
know that such were generally to the south of us. On this occasion

the whole southern sky was a mass of bands and streamers, contracting and expanding, and ever changing in their appearance. On the 29th the display began with a low arch extending from west to southeast, simply a band of light. Within an hour there were three sinuous curtains reaching from low in the south-west to the Zenith, constantly changing position and shooting forth sharp needles of light. The lower edge of the curtains were colored a light red. The ends turned toward each other, met and formed a perfect ellipse.

Gradually the bands and streamers worked northward, passing the Zenith and Polaris and finally disappearing when about fifteen degrees above the northern horizon.

Most mysterious and most awe inspiring phenomenon of Nature! Just what it is and why no one knows. "Spirits of the dead at play," the Eskimo's assertion, one could readily believe, who stands on a clear cold night amid that great expanse of whiteness, and beholds a yellowish-white tint of the finest lace gradually taking form and color and then darting with almost lightning like rapidity toward the earth soon to be joined by the countless hosts which join hands and enter joyously and in utter abandon into the great whirling mass of ever-changing color.

Winter

On the first day of 1922, some of the *Bowdoin*'s men cut through three-and-a-half feet of ice and went trout fishing in one of the nearby lakes. (The harbor ice was only 2 feet 6½ inches thick.) They also started banking the vessel with snow and finished the igloos over the hatches. A few days later, Mr. Livingstone of the Cape Dorset HBC came by with some Inuit from the south and three dog teams; they built three more houses on the shore, making a veritable village near the schooner. MacMillan showed his movies and slides of the Crocker Land and Peary expeditions. Goddard appreciated a fine New Year's dinner, in part from S. S. Pierce cans: "The spinach was the finest I ever tasted."

In February, MacMillan's assistant, Robinson, accompanied

Livingstone on the first major trip away from the schooner by any of her crew. They intended to trek 700 miles to the northernmost HBC post, but they heard from Inuit they met along the way that the post was low on the supplies they were after, so they turned back. In mid-March, Robinson was again off, this time with Whitehouse, for a month. They investigated the inland lakes and sledged a great number of miles before returning. They visited with most of the other white people in Baffin Land, including the HBC and a reindeer company at Amadjuak Harbour. (The reindeer company hoped to show the Canadian government the superiority of reindeer over dogs as draft animals. Its owners believed that reindeer were less trouble, because they could feed themselves, and more versatile, because they could be eaten and their skins were useful. But a large number of the herd imported from Lapland had died in the winter, and the animals that remained seemed weak. It was Robinson's belief that dogs were more functional.)

At the reindeer company, the men were treated to a home-like dinner, eating from china on linen table cloths. They learned of a young Innuk hunter who had recently been washed to sea on an ice pan "three strides" square. He had gone three days and nights with nothing to eat, was swept off the pan, climbed back on again, considered jumping off to end his torment, but decided to see what God would do with him (he had been influenced by the Anglican missionaries), and finally floated back into shore. He dismissed his ordeal with the remark, "I've come."

Robinson and Whitehouse returned to the *Bowdoin* in mid-April, and Robinson commented that he had been able to carry out very few of the instructions he had been given. His conclusion was that observations and charting could far better be undertaken in summer.

Sometime during the winter, Whitehouse tripped over the *Bowdoin*'s seismograph, triggering the recording of the biggest earthquake of all time.

The end of April saw magnetic observer Howell off on a survey trip to Lake Harbour, where he was to board the HBC steamer *Nascopie* and, on his way home, continue his magnetic study. He ended up on the *Bay Chimo* instead, which took him to Ponds Inlet, the northernmost point of Baffin Land, and ultimately to St. Johns, Newfoundland. He reached Boston in October, an entire month after the *Bowdoin* was home in the United States.

Spring

A hint of spring showed on May first, and the sun was up well over half the day again. Following a week of warm weather, the men sleeping on the *Bowdoin* were awakened by a great crash. The big igloo over the after house had fallen in, burying everything beneath it. The same night, the Inuit on shore worried about their own houses. A falling snow block, turned to ice from the warming inside the igloo during the winter, could be lethal. In the morning, they abandoned their winter houses for tents provided by MacMillan.

With the advent of spring the numbers and species of wild life increased quickly. Seals and many different birds reappeared. (MacMillan was pleased to find the nest of a rough-legged hawk, the first recorded sighting north of Hudson Strait.) In late June, white and blue geese flew northward overhead. One day, while MacMillan watched, a dazed white goose fell suddenly from an overhead flock, a little duck hawk after him. MacMillan wondered how a little hawk could have struck a blow hard enough to stun a six-pound goose. The Inuit explained it to him — the smaller bird struck the goose with his breast bone.

The numbers of birds attracted the hunters as well as the ornithologically inclined. Nipatchee was out shooting ptarmigan one day when a shell he had loaded himself exploded, blowing his gun into pieces, cutting his face and slashing an arm. Robinson, acting surgeon on the trip, sewed him back up. A few hours later Nipatchee was back out hunting ptarmigan again, this time with his wife, who carried a gun on her shoulder. Nipatchee was only along as guide and game-bearer.

In early June, after the blossoming of the first flower, the

Purple Saprifrage, bees and flies and mosquitoes arrived. Mac-Millan charged his crew with collecting specimens of insects along with birds and other animals; some of the crew members became more involved in this project than did others, whose interest remained in hunting game. McCue, the cook, met Bromfield coming in from the hills one day; each carried his rifle over his shoulder. "What did you get?" asked McCue. Imagine his scorn when Bromfield answered, "Two spiders and three flies."

As the ice outside the harbor was beginning to break up in early July, two dories went off to Trinity Island in search of eggs. In the first dory were Kovavau, Nipatchee and Goddard; the second held Robinson, McCue and a third American. The Inuit compensated for the strength of the current and got to the island easily; the second dory was carried off into rapidly running ice which was piling up into pressure ridges. The men pulled on both sets of oars with all their might, and still made no progress. Then Robinson "caught a crab"—caught the water with his oar on the backstroke. That should have meant certain death for them all, but through a stroke of luck, the way the dory swung around saved their lives. Robinson was able to clamber out onto an ice pan and hold the dory's bow just long enough for the others to follow. They ran back over the moving ice, dragging the dory along, until finally they managed to reach a safe place. The men immediately fell into a deep, exhausted sleep. When they awoke, they found it was slack water and were able to row back to Trinity Island. Their companions had found not even a single egg, just one white fox and a lot of eggshells.

Summer

On July 2, the harbor entrance finally started breaking up, although it still would be awhile before the *Bowdoin* could leave her winter quarters. And although the ice was melting around the edges, the harbor ice was still four feet thick, so the men sprinkled forty bags of sand around the *Bowdoin* and 30 yards ahead of her to the big anchor to draw the sun's heat. It took three weeks to melt a channel. They powered up the schooner, pulled forward, weighed anchor, reversed and went back toward land. At high tide, the *Bowdoin* was able to creep along the shore between the remaining ice and the land to a small bight at the eastern side of the harbor entrance. At low water, taking advantage of the schooner's shallow draft, MacMillan beached the *Bowdoin* to work on the propeller which had been so severely damaged coming in through the ice the previous fall. As the tide ebbed, over she went. Whitehouse removed the propeller and, using a sledge hammer and a rock as an anvil, pounded it back into shape and replaced it on the shaft.

As the tide flowed in, the water crept up the side of the schooner and in through the scuppers and up on the deck. Slowly, the *Bowdoin* righted herself—exactly as she was designed to do—and on the high water quietly floated off. MacMillan anchored her a short distance out and the men prepared to leave in the morning. They visited the Inuit families ashore, taking dolls, needles, thimbles, ribbons, soap and clothing as gifts for the women and children. The Inuit said they would follow the schooner down the coast and meet them at Dorset, but the men thought they were saying their final good byes.

For 306 days the men had made observations from their land-based station. The lowest temperature they recorded was minus 50°F on February 10. There were 244 cloudy days, 62 clear. The prevailing wind was northwest and averaged 7.6 mph. It was now early August.

The channel out of the harbor, ice free the day before, was now nearly blocked by a huge ice pan that had drifted in on the flood tide. But the *Bowdoin* squeezed through between the pan and the rocks, and was at last free of her long-imprisoning harbor. There was heavy drift ice in the Foxe Channel, but by noon, there was nothing but blue water ahead. They sailed to the HBC post at Dorset, where they stayed a few days taking pictures and cataloguing botanical specimens. On the second day, in came their Inuit friends, their boat loaded to the rails with skins, dogs, and children. The goodbyes all had to be made again, but at last the schooner *Bowdoin* was headed for home.

On August 12, safely anchored under the big hills on the western side of Cape Chidley, the *Bowdoin* faced the worst gale of her entire trip. "Heavy pack ice, grinding and crunching against our anchor chains and greenheart sheathed sides, prevented sleep and naturally gave me no little concern over the safety of our little ship," wrote MacMillan. It was five days before the winds and the seas subsided enough so they could move on.

To save time, MacMillan wanted to pass through McLelan's Strait, a beautiful eight-mile long fjord that leads directly through Cape Chidley, but is tricky to pass unless the tide is right. Mac wrote:

> *The* Bowdoin *came through beautifully when she once found the door, and bowed gracefully to the heavy swell rolling into the mouth of the run from the outside ledges white with surf. Under sail we skimmed along the shore on the inside run close under the snow capped mountains of one of the most awe inspiring and striking bits of scenery in North America. One need not be of primitive mind to agree with the native that it is the home of the evil spirits. Almost straight up from the sea these rugged hills rise, terminating in serrated peaks at an altitude of 4,000 and even 5,000 feet. Not a single one has ever been climbed and but a few even named....*
>
> *Stretching southward outside of our course was the "Iron Strand," a long and almost continuous line of reefs marked by breakers, the formidable outer guard of the Northern Labrador, which denies entrance in heavy weather to a ship seeking a quiet harbor, and growls and shows its white teeth to one who would like to get out.*
>
> *With darkness coming on and shoal ground everywhere, I deemed it wise to enter a bight on the starboard hand and anchor for the night. Although a quiet looking place from the outside, it was very different in; for the wind dropped from the high hills with such force that wer were compelled to seek shelter well up under the lee with the nose of the* Bowdoin *almost against the mountain side, and could only hold on then with our largest anchor and 40 fathoms of chain.*

When they reached Hebron, no ship had been in yet that summer; natives swarmed the schooner looking for news of the outside world. They soon recognized MacMillan and realized that he and his people were as eager for news as they were.

The *Bowdoin* went to Port Manvers by way of the Mugford Tickle, "quiet and deserted now for the flu claimed all at Okah," MacMillan wrote. An influenza epidemic had ravaged the Labrador three years before, wiping out whole villages, including Okah. Missionaries had been horrified to arrive at dead towns, where starving dogs had dragged bodies out of houses and were chewing on the remains. A hut on an outer island had presented a sadder picture yet—huddled in a corner, starving, terrified and being protected by a pet dog, they had found a little girl. Her dead parents and siblings had all been eaten by dogs.

On September 9 as they sailed along the Nova Scotia coast, nearly at the final turn toward home, the sky was so clear they could see seven navigational lights at one time, some well beyond their theoretical range. But the next day, as it so often is, Cape Sable, on the southern tip of Nova Scotia, was fogged in. The strong tides there rendered the log reading uncertain. But MacMillan climbed aloft onto the spring stay, from where he could see out over the fog to both Seal Island and Cape Sable.

Next stop—Maine! At 4:45 A.M. the *Bowdoin* headed straight for Monhegan Island, where MacMillan had promised to meet friends and relations on the eleventh for a peaceful layover before the official homecoming. The schooner made Monhegan at midnight on the tenth, unbeknownst to his welcoming party, which had retired to the hotel for the night. By morning, the fog was so thick that the *Bowdoin* was invisible from the land. But an island fisherman spotted them, and soon they were deluged with visitors.

That afternoon, MacMillan sailed on to Boothbay, thinking they could rest quietly there prior to the official reception on the twelfth at Wiscasset. Word had gotten out, however, that the *Bowdoin* was coming, and there was a tremendous crowd awaiting them at Boothbay.

"When the knockabout bow of the *Bowdoin* shot around the northern end of Westport Island, everything that could make a noise did its best," wrote MacMillan. "Whistles that had called 'Goodbye' and 'Safe passage' more than 14 months ago, now shrieked 'Welcome home. We're glad to see you!'" Boats of all shapes and sizes accompanied the returning heroes all the way up the river to Wiscasset. A band played, colors flew everywhere, the governor greeted them, and their families swarmed around. The *Bowdoin* was home.

THREE

1923–1924—To Northern Greenland

Off Again

SEVENTEEN MONTHS AFTER the *Bowdoin*'s return from her first trip to the Arctic, three of the six men who had sailed with MacMillan to the Foxe Basin were back aboard the schooner ready to leave for a year's trip to northern Greenland. McCue left his position as cook to become mate, and Robinson and Goddard signed on again as Chief Assistant and representative of the Carnegie Institution, which again was sponsoring studies of the vagaries of the earth's magnetic fields and atmospheric electricity. Three new men joined the vessel, again making a complement of seven. For the first time, the *Bowdoin* carried a radio.

The second sponsor of the trip was the National Geographic Society, which wanted a tablet mounted at Cape Sabine to honor the men of A. W. Greely's 1881–1884 Lady Franklin Bay expedition, so many of whom had perished. It was their base camp at Fort Conger which MacMillan had visited in 1909.

Among the dignitaries to see the *Bowdoin* off from Wiscasset on June 23, 1923, was General Greely himself, along with Governor Baxter. The sendoff was mostly for show; the *Bowdoin* put in briefly at Boothbay for some final preparations, and actually left Monhegan on the 26th.

They set up one magnetic station along the Labrador coast, where MacMillan counted but a dozen Newfoundland fishing vessels where only fifteen years before there had been a thousand; in 1867, 3,000 had been counted through Domino Run.

At Jack Lane's Bay, Labrador, Abram Bromfield again joined the *Bowdoin* as interpreter. When he agreed to go along, he didn't know if they were staying in the area or going north but it didn't matter to him; overnight he arranged for a year's absence from his home.

The following day, as they left Jack Lane's Bay, the *Bowdoin* was waved down by two men in a small boat. When the schooner pulled up alongside, the men in the boat handed a pair of sunglasses across to MacMillan, who had left them at Battle Harbour's wireless station. The wireless operator had given them to another vessel, which had in turn passed them along to a third, and it was the mate and fireman from that vessel who had rowed out to await the *Bowdoin*. People looked out for each other along the long and difficult and sparsely populated Labrador coast.

Greenland

Because ice still blocked the eastern shore of Davis Strait, the *Bowdoin* headed across to Greenland and sailed up the coast. Along the way, MacMillan and his men established magnetic stations, attracting attention wherever they went because a vessel from the outside world was a rarity. The Danes had long had a policy of keeping Greenland closed to all, permitting no contact or trade with natives, but the Carnegie Institution had obtained special privileges for the schooner, and throughout his trip, MacMillan and his group were welcomed by the Danes in Greenland. He wrote that he felt insignificant in comparison with his predecessors along Greenland's rugged shores: the Norse settlers of almost a thousand years earlier, John Davis' sixteenth-century expeditions, other settlers and voyagers, and finally the whalers.

One unplanned stop had to be made for repairs. In order to increase the length of the radio antenna, MacMillan had had a short, flat bowsprit installed on the *Bowdoin*; well off Simiutak, in a heavy head sea, the *Bowdoin* buried her nose and the bowsprit snapped. MacMillan turned the schooner toward shore, and as they approached the black hills and jumbled mass of rocks on the shoreline, they came across a small fishing boat with two Inuit aboard. These men were happy to climb aboard and pilot the schooner into Simiutak, a halibut station, where boned halibut were packed in salt and shipped to Copenhagen.

MacMillan was fascinated by the variety of racial identities in this small village, where white, black, brown and blond skins were all visible. He had never before seen red-haired Eskimos. Again, he was concerned about the scarcity of full-blooded Inuit, particularly in South Greenland.

A more substantial bowsprit was fashioned for the schooner, and the following morning they were again away. MacMillan was glad to have seen the entrance to this harbor in stormy weather: "In navigating unknown waters a rough sea is always preferable ... it never fails to reveal its own dangers. Where white water cannot be seen, it is safe for the *Bowdoin* of ten-foot draft to hold her course."

The Arctic

On August 2, the *Bowdoin* crossed the Arctic Circle, a first for three of the men aboard. As much noise as could be mustered — foghorn, whistle, bell and rifle shots — brought the off watch up on deck "in much abbreviated costume" wondering what was going on. A toast was drunk to celebrate crossing the line, which they would not see again again for more than a year.

Two days later they saw the midnight sun as they approached Melville Bay, site of many disasters to whalers in decades past; in 1830 alone, 22 ships were crushed by ice there. In 1850 the Franklin search party took five weeks to fight their way through. Seven years later, the *Fox*, under McClintock, began the crossing on the eighth of August (just three days later in the year than the *Bowdoin*), was beset on the seventeenth and held for more than eight months, drifting 1,385 miles to the southward. But 1923 was a fortunate year; although the *Bowdoin* passed many icebergs, there was no pack ice to threaten her. She crossed Melville Bay in a single day.

At Cape York, three long blasts of the horn brought four kayaks out to the schooner. There had been no ship in during the previous two years, due to ice, and there was much news to share. Two of the Inuit MacMillan had known on Peary's North Pole expedition were dead. The dog driver MacMillan had employed for the four years of his Crocker Land Expedition had died during the worldwide flu epidemic in 1919. Other friends, too, were gone, either dead or having migrated south for better hunting.

As the schooner followed the shore north, MacMillan looked for encampment sites he'd known from his earlier travels in the area. There was no sign of anyone for miles and miles in any of the usual places; he realized that during the influenza outbreak a beneficent superstition had driven the Inuit from their traditional settlements. Finally, around a point came E-took'a-shoo, MacMillan's dog driver, whom he described as "the best Eskimo I ever employed." E-took'a-shoo soon was off to get his new wife and dogs and hunting equipment. With his brother Kah-ko-tchee'a, he signed on for the winter, knowing that white man's assistants were always certain to have food during the long night of winter. Inuit cache tons of food during the summer, but their tradition of sharing anything they had with visitors and their dogs meant that even a seemingly large food supply may not be adequate.

The *Bowdoin*, with her deckload of kayaks, tupiks, harpoons, skins, and 21 dogs, headed for Etah where a couple of tons of aged walrus meat for dogfood was added to the collection. Mac-Millan said by comparison with Peary's *Roosevelt* in 1908, with her 30 tons of rotten whale meat and 250 dogs aboard, "the *Bowdoin* seemed like a gilded ballroom!"

Coming into Smith Sound, MacMillan was reminded of those few explorers who preceded him—Hayes, Peary, Kane, Hall, Greely. This was his own familiar territory; the *Bowdoin* passed the point where MacMillan's Crocker Land Expedition had made its base from 1913 to 1917. It was an eerie sight for MacMillan to see the flat, debris-covered site where his 35-foot square building with its comfortable living room, shop, generator room, darkroom and four bedrooms had stood.

When the *Bowdoin* arrived at Etah, MacMillan's Inuit companions visited with their father, Panipak, who had worked for Peary on all his expeditions. Interviewed after Peary's last trip, Panipak was asked what he thought when the group was starving on the Polar Sea in 1906. "We didn't worry, we let Peary do that." His philosophy pleased MacMillan, who questioned the old man about the purpose of human life. "I have often thought about it, and wondered why—I can think of one reason only—be kind to each other and help each other."

Connections with the Past

In 1881 and 1882, as the United States' contribution to the internationally proclaimed Polar Year, Lieutenant Greely and his party of 23 officers and enlisted men lived on Ellesmere Island at Fort Conger, Lady Franklin Bay, 220 miles northeast of Cape Sabine. They were attempting scientific work, and reached the farthest point north that white explorers had attained to date. But the ship that was to come for them in 1882 didn't make it. In 1883 the party made the difficult trek south to Cape Sabine, where they found a message in a rock cairn which said the *Proteus*, their rescue ship, had been crushed in ice and sunk within sight of that spot, and her crew had headed away in their open boats. Still, Greely was confident that the American government would do everything it could to retrieve them, and the men built themselves a make-shift shelter and settled in. No one came that year. The following winter brought not only cold and darkness but starvation; when the *Bear* and the *Thetis* finally arrived for Greely and his men on June 22, 1884, there were only seven skeletal men left. One of those died on the trip home.

MacMillan had been to Cape Sabine in the winter of 1917

and hoped to take the *Bowdoin* there in 1923 to erect the commemorative tablet commissioned by the National Geographic Society. After a night at Etah, MacMillan set sail, only to come face-to-face with a solid jam of ice that stretched along Ellesmere Island. The schooner could get no closer to Cape Sabine than ten miles. The memorial would have to wait. MacMillan still hoped to make camp on Ellesmere Island, but in any case he knew he could reach the site by dog team once the sound had frozen over. He turned the *Bowdoin* back across Smith Sound to Greenland.

The schooner had just returned to Etah when they spotted the Canadian steamer *Arctic*, which soon joined them in their anchorage. From her radio, the men on the *Bowdoin* learned of the death of President Warren Harding. They immediately lowered their flag to half-mast, where it stayed for three days. Theirs was the most northern American flag honoring the late President.

The *Arctic* was on her way to Cape Sabine, where the Canadian government intended to establish a police station to protect musk oxen from Greenlandic Inuit. (MacMillan said that the policing forces would eat more musk oxen than would be shot by the entire Smith Sound Eskimo tribe, but that hadn't occurred to the Canadian officials.) MacMillan helped them find two Eskimos to assist at their station, although he thought it unlikely they would reach Cape Sabine in their steamer. Indeed, within a couple of days a member of the *Bowdoin*'s own party, back from reconnoitering wintering sites, reported seeing the *Arctic* fast in the ice, ten miles northwest of their objective.

After a few days at Etah, while Goddard recorded his magnetic data, MacMillan took the *Bowdoin* to Pandora Harbor, site of earlier expeditions' encampments. It was this harbor to which the men of the wrecked *Proteus* had retreated in their open boats and met up with another vessel. Ashore, forty years later, the men of the *Bowdoin* found the remains of their camp, and brought back to the schooner relics including fish hooks, knives, forks, and two broken cups marked with royal insignia and the words "Marine Service."

Another attempt to cross the sound to find winter refuge also failed. Part of the way across, with no warning, an ice

40

squeeze threatened, and the *Bowdoin* had to hurry away. Then came fog and squalls and MacMillan, aloft in the ice barrel, suddenly saw the color of the water change from black to yellow with boulders visible. "Hard a-starboard," he hollered, but his cries were too late. The *Bowdoin* was aground, on a falling tide, no less. But MacMillan's crew trimmed the sails in, ran the engine full speed, turned the wheel over hard, and the tough little schooner turned on her heel and scooted off. (The men did shoot five walrus during the day for dog meat, so the trip was not wasted.)

An overnight stop between Littleton Island and Little Duck took them out of the worst of the storm, although they kept watch all night. The Inuit gathered a bucket of eiderduck eggs from a cache and MacMillan visited the cairns built by earlier explorers on Littleton Island, starting with Inglefield in 1852. MacMillan could name every vessel from the outer world that had ever passed the island, a total of perhaps twenty, each with her own tale of hardship.

Winter

MacMillan decided to make his winter quarters 11 miles north of Etah, 689 miles from the North Pole, at Refuge Harbor, where the Kane Expedition of 1853–55 had headquartered. There were good hunting grounds, fresh water, ballast stone for the return trip, and from there MacMillan could easily reach Cape Sabine by dog team. Also, with the protective shores reaching around them, there was no danger of being crushed by ice. They settled the schooner in on August 18.

After unloading nearly all their winter provisions onto the beach, the men started work on the magnetic observatory, pouring cement piers. They began their meteorological observations which continued, uninterrupted, for 286 days.

During the coming months, the men got great pleasure from the radio. Friends broadcast to them from Chicago every Wednesday night throughout the long winter, and they listened to English and German news in the evenings. They heard concerts and church services from all over the United States and they received many personal messages on Christmas and New

Year's, including one from Greely. On Thanksgiving, President Coolidge wished them health, safety and success. But most significant was the first outgoing short-wave radio contact from the far north, messages sent and received, which came from the schooner *Bowdoin* on this trip, through Prince Rupert, British Columbia.

The sun set for the last time on October 25, and was not seen above the horizon again until February 18, but the *Bowdoin* was not in continuous darkness, as is often imagined. Throughout the months before the sun rose again, the middle of every day was twilight. (Total darkness isn't found beyond 6° of the Pole; the only white men who had experienced that were the sailors aboard the beset and drifting *Fram* in 1892–1893.) The moon stayed above the horizon for ten days each month, circling the sky over their heads. In addition, the *Bowdoin* had electric lights aboard.

The winter routine was rigid in order to maintain the observations on a regular basis. Breakfast was at 9, dinner at 3, and supper at 8. During the days, the men walked, hunted, skied or snowshoed, tended the snow walls about the vessel, and fed the dogs. Every day one of the men carried 20 gallons of water down to the schooner from a lake a half mile north; the duty rotated. Aboard the schooner, checkers, chess, fan-tan, and mah jongg kept everyone amused when their own studies, books and writing did not. They showed movies on Saturday nights. Again the schooner made a perfect shelter, insulated as she was with snow; her double sheathing provided air spaces, reducing condensation. A snowhouse built over the foc's'le skylight, which could be left cracked open, permitted good ventilation.

MacMillan, the Inuit, and others made a number of sledging trips, starting in October. The dogs, having been tied for four months, were glad to be moving again. MacMillan said the life of a sledge dog in summer is miserable, as they are not cared for and rarely fed. During the winter, however, they worked hard and were better cared for, as their handlers' lives depended upon them. Even in January, when the sun was down, E-took'a-shoo went seal hunting; the Inuit were out of oil for their igloos. He found a breathing hole the size of a fifty cent piece, sat beside it for 24 hours, and shot a seal. MacMillan and others made various trips out of camp during the winter, hunting bear because they all needed warm pants, or trapping fox, or hunting seal for oil, or collecting meat from caches, or just visiting. A number of old friends visited the *Bowdoin*, including Oo'tah, who had been with Peary and MacMillan on Peary's Pole expedition, and others who had been with MacMillan during his four years at Etah. The winter is important to Inuit, who enjoy visiting with one another; in the summer, they are separated by open water.

It pleased MacMillan to adopt native methods of transportation. He believed that dog sledges were infinitely more appropriate for carrying supplies than the man-power white explorers had persisted in using for so long. One trip that MacMillan took across Smith Sound took seven hours; earlier explorers, without dog sledges, had taken as long as 31 days. MacMillan believed that had Greely had dog teams, he could simply have sledged across to North Greenland with his men and lived with the Inuit there until the rescue vessel came.

MacMillan spent many hours learning about the customs and traditions of the Inuit people. They told him that the earth had been dropped from above, piece by piece—no one knew where the people came from. At first, it was dark all the time, and no one died. Later, when they were given light part of the time, they lost their immortality. That was better. Someday the people will all be together, living as they do now, but warmer, with more light and food. Stars are the spirits of the dead.

Before the sun reappeared, while the temperature outside was 45° below zero, an Inuit baby was born in the camp. A few weeks later, a young missionary came to the *Bowdoin* to baptise the baby. Word of the birth had travelled up and down the barren coastline, and the *Bowdoin*'s foc's'le filled with Inuit men, women and children who came to witness the baptism.

The Memorial

In March, E-took'a-shoo, Kah-ko-tchee'a, Bromfield and Mac-Millan made a reconnaissance trip to Cape Sabine to prepare for sledging the memorial tablet out and establishing a magnetic station there for future use of the Carnegie Institution. They built a snow house at Cemetery Ridge, where Greely's relief party had landed and the dead expeditioners were buried. The snow on the ridge was all blown clear, exposing the ring of rocks marking the tent site, the walls of the hut, and ten graves. The men awoke amid roaring wind and drifting snow and contrasted their own good fortune, with a comfortable shelter, warm fur clothing, food, fuel, dogs and sledges, with that of the remaining seven, starving men in Greely's group who, when they were rescued, were reduced to eating jelly made from boiling strips of their own sealskin clothing.

MacMillan and his men were met on their return to the schooner by an Eskimo boy looking for medical assistance. Ninety miles away, a young man was dying. From the description, Mac-Millan concluded the young man probably had tuberculosis, a disease recently brought to the Arctic by social changes which came with the influx of southern civilization—doors, for instance, which trapped foul air within crowded houses. MacMillan regretted he had to tell the youth that he had no doctor aboard, but he sent a box of delicacies in hopes of brightening the boy's last days. Despite the Eskimo's driving his dogs nonstop, his friend was dead when he got to him.

On Admiral Peary's birthday, April 6, the crew of the *Bowdoin* raised the flag in his honor. "It snapped at our truck as if signaling to the phantom *Roosevelt* steaming by on her way northward," wrote MacMillan. Later in the month, MacMillan and some of his men made another sledging trip away from the schooner, to the nearest village, Nerky, 30 miles away, to take movies of life in an Eskimo village. During the trip, MacMillan got a little careless and his dogs ran away with him, flipping the sledge several times. The sledge was wrecked, but MacMillan's Inuit companions mended it in short order. Instead of taking hours to bore lashing holes through the wood with a knife, as he might have done himself, the Inuit shot holes in the oak frames and quickly lashed the frame back together.

They were joined on their trip by several Inuit. The wind picked up, the snow drifted, and most of the company thought it unwise to continue on. E-took'a-shoo's sister, her husband and their child went ahead, while everyone else stopped. MacMillan pitched his tent, and the Inuit spent one night in igloos and then took shelter in a cave, fearing that the snowhouses would fall in. Some of the Inuit men made forays out for hare, so there was plenty to eat. Finally, they moved on into Nerky, where it remained so windy and miserable that MacMillan moved from his own tent, saying he was glad to sleep with the Eskimos despite the likelihood of getting body lice. The following day, more sledges arrived, making the communal bed even more crowded. Outside, 120 dogs and twenty pups howled.

But E-took'a-shoo's sister and her family had still not arrived, and MacMillan was worried. E-took'a-shoo laughed at him, saying they were fine, and indeed, the next morning, they arrived looking rested and happy. They had gotten tired, so they had simply lain down on their sledge and slept, with a caribou skin pulled over them. The snow covered them, but they just slept on "like tired children."

The stormy weather made MacMillan a week overdue getting back to the *Bowdoin*. His men were very worried, not only fearful that he might not be coming back, but because the schooner seemed to be leaking badly. But MacMillan wasn't concerned. He knew from past experience that in the springtime what appeared to be leaking was merely condensation melting next to the outside skin of the vessel.

In early May of 1924, MacMillan and eight others—five Inuit and three Americans—took six sledges across to Cape Sabine, carrying the memorial tablet which they installed on a huge boulder. It was inscribed:

> *To the Memory of the Dead who Under Lieutenant A. W. Greely Here Gave their Lives to insure the Final and Complete Success of the First Scientific Cooperation of the United States with other Nations, 1881–1884. Erected by the National Geographic Society, 1923.*

After another trip to Ellesmere Land, to photograph the musk oxen, they returned to the *Bowdoin* on the first of June.

There was no darkness by this time; the protective snow wall around the schooner had fallen, and the snow houses on deck had melted away. The ducks, dovekies, guillemots, and glaucous gulls had returned and were laying eggs. The Inuit were netting birds (one woman could net as many as one a minute) and caching eggs. By mid-June, there were flowers everywhere, frantic to go to seed before the cold returned. It was summer.

Leaving for Home

The men ballasted the *Bowdoin* for the voyage home using seven tons of small stones to replace the weight of the supplies used during their winter layover. The job took two-and-a-half hours, using two dog teams; had they waited for open water, it would have been a two-day job.

Most Arctic harbors lose their ice in June. Not Refuge, not in 1924. It was still there well into July. The schooner had been frozen in for ten months; MacMillan became concerned. Didn't it break out each year? "Some years it does, some years it doesn't," one of the Inuit told him. At the end of July, when a lead opened up along the shore, the *Bowdoin*'s men scattered ashes from the galley stove on the ice between the bow and the land ahead, and attacked the softened ice with an axe to draw the schooner into the lead.

But after travelling only a hundred yards, the schooner bumped onto a ledge. MacMillan ordered his vessel full steam ahead to see if she could bounce over the shoal. She hit hard, and wouldn't budge. He worried whether she'd fall off her perch and fill with water when the tide dropped—or whether her keel was caught between two rocks, and she'd twist it off. He ran masthead tackles ashore and out to the harbor ice, hoping to keep her upright. As the tide went out, her bow rose, her stern fell and the underwater rock became frighteningly visible. Crack! The schooner fell on her side, burying her lee rail. Buckets and boxes and oars and clothing flew everywhere. Men scooted around her decks "like flying squirrels," MacMillan wrote. Two went overboard. She broke one plank on her port side.

The men took everything off the vessel that they could, hoping that lightening the *Bowdoin* would let her float free on the
tide. First, they removed everything they would need to survive
in open boats should she not come off; then they emptied the
water tanks and stripped the anchor and chain. They caulked the
hatches, sealing her as best they could. The water rose along her
side and up the deck — and suddenly she righted herself, as Mac-
Millan described it, "until she looked us again square in the face,
as much as to say, 'Here I am ready for business, regardless of the
hole in my stomach!'"

But this tide was 18 inches lower than the last, and even in
her lightened condition, she didn't float off. "Well," said Mac-
Millan, "that was a rehearsal. Now we'll do the thing all over
again, only better." This time they keeled her toward shore, rest-
ing her bilge on the bed of rocks which they had seen at low tide.
She sat at a more comfortable angle — and then she slipped and
fell several feet, breaking two more planks.

"On the next high water," MacMillan wrote, "she gently floated
off herself, as if saying 'Let's go home.'" The cement in her bilges
kept her shape and her hull remained strong and safe. The crew
loaded her back up again, with all her own men and equipment
and 15 Eskimos and 75 dogs.

As they approached the end of the seaward channel, a huge
berg floated in, one finger blocking the way. After sawing nearly
through the finger, MacMillan pointed his vessel right at it and
charged, the *Bowdoin* playing icebreaker. She stopped short, but
the ice cracked, and there was no damage to her steel-shod oak
stem. Again MacMillan set her to full speed and attacked the ice.
This time she broke through. The *Bowdoin* was on her way home.

After 320 days frozen in place, the *Bowdoin* was again on the
seas. The next few days, as they disembarked at one village or
another, the Inuit said goodbye to MacMillan and his men.
E-took'a-shoo was the last to go; he had tears in his eyes as he said
farewell.

The schooner again had good fortune transversing Melville
Bay; the men saw no ice whatever and made the crossing in only
27 hours. The *Bowdoin* came into Godhavn, on Disko Island,

while a wireless station was being erected that would connect the town to Godthaab, which was already connected to Julianehaab, in turn to Iceland and finally Copenhagen. No longer would North Greenland be so isolated.

At Holstenborg, the *Bowdoin* was welcomed by the Danish authorities, and the whole town took part in the festivities arranged in their honor: kayak demonstrations, racing, a rifle shoot, and bag races for the men and children. An elderly woman wanted to enter the bag race, and was permitted, if only to humor her. But she had the last laugh; she beat the men handily.

They left Holstenborg in daylight at 2:30 A.M. on August 25, and recrossed the Arctic Circle more than a year after they had crossed northward. At Godthaab the town was abuzz because its whaling steamer was returning with a humpback lashed alongside. There, the *Bowdoin* took on ten barrels of fuel oil.

Four hundred and fifty miles across Davis Strait lay Labrador. The first day out, motor-sailing with a good wind the *Bowdoin* made 220 miles. The next day they paid the price, as they faced fog, an unfavorable wind, heavy seas and rain. But from the crow's nest, MacMillan could see over the fog and make out the coast. Studying each rock, reef and mountain peak, he identified their landfall as Saglek Bay, 20 miles north of Hebron. On down the coast they sailed, staying outside to avoid the dangers of the foggy inside runs.

On her way into Hopedale, the *Bowdoin* passed the *Wren*, the North Labrador mail boat. Before nightfall, the *Wren* was a total wreck, so they learned a few days later at Battle Harbour.

In Sydney, Nova Scotia, they took on a thousand gallons of oil and 300 of water, and the men had haircuts, bought new clothes, fruit and ice cream. Crossing the Bay of Fundy, a gale offered yet another test of the *Bowdoin's* seagoing abilities.

"You needn't be afraid of this one, sir," said the cook to MacMillan, "she'll always take you home!" And she always did.

On September 20, 1924, the *Bowdoin* was welcomed back to Wiscasset by 6,000 people from all over New England. She was home again, if only for a few months.

FOUR

1925–1930

1925—Greenland with Byrd

*U*NDER THE AUSPICES of the U.S. Navy and the National Geographic Society, in company with the steamship *Peary*, MacMillan again took the *Bowdoin* to Greenland in 1925. There were four objectives of the joint venture. The first was the Navy's interest in the Polar Sea, still a great mystery. More than once, earlier explorers had reported seeing land that later couldn't be found. MacMillan himself had spent four years looking for the Crocker Land which Peary thought he saw. The Polar area was inaccessible by ship and difficult to travel by dogsled; perhaps from the air, particularly from amphibian planes, explorers could more easily investigate this strange land.

The Navy was also interested in the potential of radio communications in the north. John Reinhartz was the electronics genius of his day. As a high school student, he was building short wave radios; he believed in short wave radio when no one thought it would ever amount to anything. He allowed himself to be convinced he ought to go to college, but by the time he was a junior, he had so many job offers that he left. He made his own innovations obsolete before descriptions of them could appear in the press. Reinhartz joined the expedition, and kept in steady radio contact with distant parts of the world.

The National Geographic also had two objectives. In the 1920s, scientists were only just beginning to understand barometric pressure variations around the earth and the movement of high and low pressure areas. By sponsoring this trip, the Society was underwriting the further collection of temperature, pressure and wind data from the Arctic, as well as the first color photography of Arctic flora and flauna.

The *Bowdoin* and the coal-burning steamship *Peary* went north together, the *Peary* carrying three amphibious airplanes for Lt. Commander Richard Byrd.

The *Peary*'s greater heft and pushing strength proved her far superior to the little schooner as an icebreaker, but the *Bowdoin* could work the narrow twisting leads through loose ice far better. Each had opportunity to extricate the other from unfortunate situations—the *Peary* pulled the *Bowdoin* free of a tight wedge, and the *Bowdoin* helped the *Peary* off the rocks in Labrador.

During the course of the trip, MacMillan got to fly over Smith Sound and across Ellesmere Island, seeing from 3,000 feet the sites of his previous expedition quarters, including the Greely camp where he had erected the memorial the year before. He must have marvelled at how easily he traveled over hills that had been major obstacles to his dog teams.

But the pilots could not accomplish everything they desired. They weren't able to fly as far as they'd hoped, and although they were able to drop supply caches at places where MacMillan believed summer air landings could be made in the future, two of their planes became disabled. Late in the season, with the favorable weather rapidly disappearing, Byrd proposed a final, heroic solo flight to Ellesmere. If he happened to get lost, he said, MacMillan and the Eskimos could come rescue him. "You can go off and get lost if you want, but I'm not coming to get you," MacMillan told him. They went home.

On the way down the coast, the *Bowdoin* hit hard on a ledge, and once again was stranded high and dry. As in her previous groundings, after the men unloaded the extra weight from 39 barrels of fuel and awaited the tide, she floated off safe and sound, and continued on her way. She broke her main gaff along the Labrador coast, but MacMillan ordered a new one over the radio; it was awaiting him when he arrived at Battle Harbour. The world was getting smaller.

1929—MacMillan's School

In 1929, MacMillan took materials north to build a school at Nain, site of a Moravian mission about two thirds of the way north on the Labrador coast. The *Bowdoin* carried lumber, books, desks, blackboards, food and clothing. The schooner then proceeded up the coast, where she had one of her more dramatic adventures.

Off the south end of Loks Land, where in 1578 Martin Frobisher had lost a ship, crushed by ice, the *Bowdoin* lay with an ice anchor out. Suddenly, the forty-foot tide grabbed the pan the *Bowdoin* was anchored to, and sent them all rushing northward. The schooner was being squeezed by ice, creaking and groaning, when Mac, in the ice barrel, suddenly saw an iceberg the size of a city block attacking her quarter. He commanded everyone to prepare to abandon ship, but the cook said he was too old to die in the cold; he sat below, his feet against the stove, and rolled a cigarette. With the engine full ahead, Mac ordered the helmsman to swing the schooner back and forth to maintain maneuvering room. At the last moment before the berg smashed into the schooner, he threw her bow hard to port, and the berg scraped the starboard rail as it roared by. There was no damage.

1930—Iceland

The *Bowdoin* made her only trip to Iceland in 1930. MacMillan planned to follow Erik the Red's track from Iceland to Greenland and Labrador, and as usual, he carried provisions for the missions on the Labrador coast. For the first time he took students with him; that the students had no sailing experience didn't matter. Within a few days they all had "welded into a competent and a prideful unit," in the words of Dr. Clifford Grulee, who had just finished his freshman year at college when he sailed to Iceland aboard the *Bowdoin*.

Grulee reports stopping at the French island St. Pierre, which then, during Prohibition, was home to the serious business of rum running. There the boys saw sailing vessels equipped with powerful engines, said to be able to outrun any Coast Guard vessel. They toured one vessel which had a shallow tank hidden beneath its deck that could be filled with liquor and then pumped out at its destination. Some of these vessels sailed all the way to the west coast of the United States, their cargoes were so valuable.

The doctor-to-be learned something about wound care from the *Bowdoin*'s old Portuguese cook. When Grulee developed an infection on his finger, the cook brewed a combination of water, vinegar and chewing tobacco; the young student, however, couldn't bring himself to immerse his finger in the unattractive concoction. But a few weeks later, the cook himself had a nasty cut, used his own medicine, and watched his injury heal rapidly. Years later, Dr. Grulee could understand the efficacy of the remedy; the tobacco would have reduced edema and contracted blood vessels, and the vinegar would have acted as an antiseptic. Grulee learned that sea remedies, although unorthodox, were not without their value.

The *Bowdoin* remained in Iceland for two weeks. The young men were impressed by the country's beauty, especially its volcanic mountains dropping their glacial ice nearly to the sea. The perpetual twilight made early morning watch idyllic for a young man with a cod jig, who knew his catch would be served for breakfast.

The first mate on the Iceland trip, Jack Crowell, was a lifelong sailor in both the Arctic and the Antarctic and had sailed with MacMillan on a number of trips. He later skippered various vessels for MacMillan, including the *Bowdoin* when she served as a support vessel in the early 1930s when MacMillan was surveying the Labrador coast from the air. Many decades later, Jim Sharp would be sailing the *Bowdoin*; in the 1980s, he taped Crowell's recollections of sailing with MacMillan:

After a period of time, the salt from saltwater ice, especially
when it has been broken and pushed up into peaks, jagged edges
and so forth, works down from the top, so the tops of these pieces
of ice are fresh. You can melt that ice.

 In the Bowdoin sometimes, we'd run short of fresh water.
I remember once, we ran from Iceland, going to the west, over
towards a place called Angmagsalik, and we got into the east
Greenland ice. It was open, but it was very heavy ice, what we
call floe bergs. At that time of the year, the ice was in all sorts of
fanciful shapes, and blue, on the last end of it. This ice was wave-
eroded on the edges so that it began to overhang over the rails of
the Bowdoin. So we started to get out of there. But before we did,
we wanted water. There were lakes on these big floes, ponds. Now,
if you're careful in the summertime after there has been a lot of ice
on the big floes, you can water your ship, but you want to be
careful that you don't dip down too low, because the wave-action
spray has gotten up in there and the salt water has settled
down there.

 Well, we had a fellow with us that trip, Franky Henderson,
from Provincetown, one of Mac's friends. I used to kid these boys
that they couldn't tell fresh water from salt, because they came
from nothing but a sandspit down there where they live in
Provincetown, and they had never had fresh water. Well, sure
enough, Franky was out there tending the hose, and we were
pumping it into the tanks. Jeez, the next day, we had salt water.
He got down a little too deep. So we kidded him all the rest of the
trip, he didn't know fresh water from salt. But you can get
beautiful water if you're careful.

 Franky Henderson nearly lost his life on one of those icefloe
water trips. The undercut edge of the floe broke loose under his
weight, dropping him into the sea which was narrowing quickly
as the floe moved toward the Bowdoin. Somehow he scrambled
back aboard before he was crushed or became completely numb
from the cold water.

 A few days later, a sudden lurch in a wave trough threw
young Grulee overboard, head first. Jack Crowell grabbed him,
hauling him back aboard. It all happened so fast that Grulee

hadn't time to be afraid, not until he started below for dry clothes. He found himself at the top of the fo'csle ladder, unable to move, shaking. Some weeks earlier, seasick, he had gone to the windward rail to vomit and his shipmates had ribbed him without mercy, but this time he was left alone to gather himself.

MacMillan had to abandon a planned stop at Baffin Island due to ice and because the trip was behind schedule and the vessel was provisioned only for four months. But they stopped along the Labrador in a number of harbors. At Indian Harbour, the approach was difficult, with an outgoing tide and a narrow channel; the *Bowdoin* took more than a half hour to negotiate the last 250 yards before the harbor opened up. Once inside, they found 27 Newfoundland fishing schooners at anchor. The vessels were mostly of the *Bowdoin*'s size, but scruffy and worn looking. The fishermen jigged for cod from dories and smaller boats until those were filled, then returned to their schooners, where the fish were cleaned and salted away in the hold. Because cod liver oil was the most profitable by-product of cod-fishing, the livers were saved in barrels on deck, unpreserved; Grulee reported the stench to be nearly unbearable. When a schooner could carry no more, she'd head for home, with perhaps as little as six inches of freeboard. It was a difficult trip, one which destroyed many a schooner.

In Nain, Bucky Pontagooniak, who had been a dog driver for MacMillan on the Peary expedition, taught young Grulee some Inuit phrases. It turned out that some of the phrases didn't mean what Grulee thought they did. The missionary at Nain and his wife tried hard to discover who had taught him this shocking vocabulary, but Grulee kept mum. Bucky expressed his gratitude by offering Grulee "freedom of his home" (and wife). As Mac-Millan had earlier explained this custom to the boys, Grulee was able to respond that he, like his Captain, always slept alone. No doubt Bucky thought this was odd, but the Inuit were used to MacMillan.

While the *Bowdoin* was taking on water and rock ballast to replace the weight of heavy electrical and other equipment Mac-Millan had delivered to Nain, Grulee saw a raggedly dressed man, one of the last remaining Nascopi Indians, who had been forced north by the Iroquois and then inland by the Inuit. Only 30 or 40 Nascopi remained in 1930 — there are none today. Mac-Millan brought the Indian aboard, fed him and gave him some food and supplies to take back to his family, which he took with no visible reaction.

By the end of the voyage, all the young men aboard were happy to be home, but at the same time, they were reluctant to end what they all knew was a once-in-a-lifetime experience.

FIVE

1934—The Boys

I N THE 1930s MACMILLAN found a reliable way to finance his future trips north. From 1934 onward, paying students always accompanied him. There was still scientific work being done aboard the *Bowdoin*, but perhaps it was no longer of as much significance as it once had been. For the "boys," as the students who sailed with MacMillan called themselves then and still do, sixty years later, the experience was momentous. These young men often said that between the physical challenges they faced and the personal character example of their captain, their future lives were shaped by the summers they spent aboard the *Bowdoin*. Braley Gray's trip in 1934 was probably a typical experience of many of those young men. "I thought it would be a great adventure," he says. "And it was. It was everything I thought it would be." Although Gray returned to Maine after his trip and never again went to sea, to this day he cherishes his experiences on the *Bowdoin*. It is with great respect that he refers to Mac-Millan as "the Admiral," recognizing the rank with which Mac-Millan retired from the Navy after World War II.

In years to come, the *Bowdoin* herself would depend upon the largesse of the "boys," now doctors and lawyers and businessmen; when she needed their support, they came to her aid.

The Voyage Begins

On June 16, 1934, promptly at three o'clock, as scheduled, the schooner *Bowdoin* steamed out of Portland Harbor. She was escorted by a large number of boats, big and little, power and sail, many fully dressed with their signal flags flying gaily, and all led by the United States Revenue Cutter *Ossipee*. About halfway out of the harbor, the Portland fire boat scooted ahead and started up all of her pumps, sending four big streams of water skyward. The members of the flotilla blew their horns and whistles in salute to the departing vessel, and the *Bowdoin* returned the honor with her own airhorn, convincing the students aboard that the horn could indeed carry thirteen miles, as advertised. The *Bowdoin* was on her way to Labrador.

Aboard the schooner were Captain Mac, as the boys called him, and his three professional crewmembers: first mate Captain Jack Crowell, engineer Leon MacDonald and cook Oscar Auclaire. The rest of the crew inclued ornithologist Dr. Alfred Gross from Bowdoin College, botanist Dr. David Potter from Clark University, and nine students: seven from Bowdoin, one from Clark, and one from Colby. MacMillan had visited Bowdoin College that winter specifically searching for students to join this voyage, because no other graduate of his alma mater had yet sailed on any of the *Bowdoin*'s trips north.

Prior to this trip, Gray had never been at sea, nor even aboard a large boat, although he was certainly familiar with smaller lake boats, coming as he did from the Old Town Canoe family. In preparation for the expedition, Gray had to take courses in astronomy and ornithology. "Birdology got me up awful early in the morning, and astronomy kept me up late at night, so I didn't get much sleep that spring." Perhaps the lack of sleep was as good training for his summer aboard the schooner *Bowdoin* as the academics.

Most of the expeditioners came along at least in part because they were interested in the specific research planned. Many of the Bowdoin boys were students of Dr. Gross. But Gray was an economics major. "The Admiral usually took scientifically-minded people with him. Well, I wasn't, so I signed on as an assistant engineer. My job was to help the engineer, and to do any job no one else wanted to do."

Every man had his share of jobs aboard, at least some of

which no one wanted. Right from the beginning, the crew was divided into two watches, the starboard watch under MacMillan, which was on duty from 6 A.M. to noon, and again from 6 P.M. until midnight. The port watch took the opposite times, under Jack Crowell. Each watchmember had only two hours of specific duty, one on bow watch and the second on the wheel. For two hours he was supposed to be available, "and the last two, if nothing was going on, you could sleep, though you were supposed to stay on deck," says Gray. "We spent a lot of time sleeping in coils of rope." All hands were called whenever sails were raised or lowered, which they tried to do at watch-change time, but the weather didn't always cooperate. The position of galley-hand rotated among the young men and was a job no one enjoyed, because any tendency to seasickness was aggravated by having to work below. As assistant engineer, Gray was always on call for troubleshooting engine emergencies.

Each boy signed a contract acknowledging "the complete authority and control of MacMillan ashore and afloat until the expedition shall have ended" and agreeing to "devote all his time to the work of the expedition, to execute all orders promptly and faithfully, and to the best of his ability to perform all duties which may be assigned to him." In addition, each paid $550 and provided all his own clothing and equipment. "'Course that was Depression time; it was hard to find that kind of money," says Gray. (For comparison, the previous fall Gray had spent $300 for a 1930 Ford Model A Roadster, and the following school year, he would pay $250 in tuition to Bowdoin College.)

The first leg of the trip was only 14 miles to Mackerel Cove on Bailey's Island, after first passing by Eagle Island to blow three long blasts in salute to Robert Peary's widow. During the evening the boys stowed their possessions and found their way about the schooner. Also that evening they played the first of many games aboard, in this case poker with matchstick stakes worth a penny apiece. By the fourth night, a continuing cribbage tournament was begun; the losers would all chip in nightly, with the pot going to the overall winner at the end of the trip.

To Sea

At sea the next day, the *Bowdoin* passed Monhegan Island at 10:55 A.M. and took a course of 120° (south of east) for Cape Sable, Nova Scotia. Cadillac Mountain and Isle au Haut were the boys' final sights of Maine and the United States for two-and-a-half months, but they were more excited at the time about the whales and porpoises swimming along with them. Some of the porpoises played under the *Bowdoin*'s bow, leaving luminous phosphorescent trails during the night.

Just as young Gray was coming off morning watch on the third day, the engine acted up, a forewarning of the long hours of work he might face along the way. He and Leon MacDonald spent most of the afternoon repairing an oil collector ring, finishing only in time for Gray's evening watch. His stints on the bow and at the wheel ("a cold and wearisome job") came the last two hours before midnight, eighteen hours from the start of his day.

The young men soon learned to sleep during any spare time, to sleep soundly through whatever came along, and to wake up quickly and ready to work. They ate well coming on watch and again as they went off—"We called ourselves the 'Peanut Butter Boys' of the Labrador," Gray says. "We ate an awful lot of that hardtack with peanut butter and marmalade on it. I don't remember too much of what we ate, but it was good food." It must have been; he gained 20 pounds that summer. "We had hams," he remembers. "We kept them in the bilge, where it was cool. They were encased in some kind of black tar or pitch, some impervious material, and when it was time for another ham, the cook would just hack that stuff off it, and that ham was real good."

Bill Esson, another Bowdoin student aboard, wrote in his journal on the third day: "So far we've had wonderful weather. No rain, no fog, no high winds, calm," adding the skeptical addendum "so Captain Mac and Jack say." In the next sentence he reported that the *Bowdoin* "can do a good job pitching" when she faces the ocean swells. "Where I am it feels like an elevator every time we go over one and we do that quite frequently, several times to a minute."

"Not much sea-sickness yet," Gray wrote home. "Gross kind of had a leaning for the rail yesterday afternoon and Luke has been a trifle indisposed a couple of mornings — oh yes, and Wait passed out completely on us at dinner yesterday — all on account of a few big groundswells." But soon the ocean flattened out, and the trip across the Bay of Fundy was the smoothest Captain Mac and Jack had ever made.

The evenings were chilly, although sometimes it was warmer just ten feet up the mast than on deck. That temperature change caused the mirages the boys saw from time to time during the voyage, starting the first night after leaving Monhegan Island, when the Cape Sable light appeared periodically, visible more than 30 miles before it was supposed to be seen.

By midnight the third day out, the fog rolled in when they were passing through the dangerous Canso gut separating Cape Breton Island from the rest of Nova Scotia. It was almost impossible to see any navigation lights so they had to steer by compass, the anchor at the ready to throw over if the buoys didn't show up as expected. But the fog lifted and they went on through the night to Port Hawkesbury and anchored. After breakfast, some of the boys rowed ashore to find the post office. "We had a swell time but the ground kept swaying," reported Esson. Crosby, the Clark student, claimed he hadn't felt motion sickness at all at sea, but on land once again, "everything began to rock and pitch much as the boat had. Whether the worthy villagers thought I was happily inebriated I don't know, but the sensation was not pleasant."

MacMillan brought the schooner alongside for water, oil and supplies. Gray wrote home that he spent the day with Mac-Donald "making order of the chaos in the engine room — don't believe anything had been done in the engine room but keep the engine running for the 13 years the boat's been in operation."

Told that the water was better in Port Mulgrave, they crossed to that village to find that, because a main had broken, water wouldn't be available until night. But by that time a southeasterly gale had blown in, and Captain Mac said he was glad they'd not gone out earlier as it would have been a very rough trip. The added stay in port allowed them to buy lobster for supper (at eight cents a pound).

That evening provided the boys with the first of many sessions spent listening to Captain Mac's stories of the north and of his schooner's early adventures. Bill Esson loved the stories; Gray said they were fun, but told his mother they were "pretty numerous and lengthy—sometimes a bit of undue prevarication or gross exaggeration pervades...." Perhaps some of the *Bowdoin*'s true escapades seemed like exaggeration to the young Gray. In any case, that the boys were already gaining respect for their captain was clear. And before the trip was over, they had added their own set of stories to the schooner *Bowdoin*'s repertoire.

Ornithology

In the Magdalen Islands, the boys first saw geography vastly different from that they were used to; the islands are sandstone, with white beaches, high red cliffs, and grass growing all over their tops. A few scraggly cattle and sheep grazed there, but the primary industry was smoked herring for the West Indies trade.

To this day, Gray clearly remembers his own adventure in the Magdalens. He and Crosby had taken MacDonald ashore to have a tooth pulled. The wind was blowing 45 miles an hour, they were told, but they started back for the *Bowdoin* in their dory, "figuring we could catch her as we blew by." And catch her they did, except the wind took Crosby's end of the dory away from the *Bowdoin* as he bridged the space between dory and schooner, leaving him "hanging with his feet in the water and holding the rail by his fingernails until they dragged him aboard." Gray, now alone in the dory, was blown far away from the schooner, headed toward nowhere, until he was noticed and rescued by a fishing boat which towed him back to the *Bowdoin*.

A second near disaster in the Magdalens was, luckily, averted.

Entering Grindstone, two buoys appeared to mark the good passage—the red buoy was to starboard and the black to port. In reality, though, the buoys marked the two ends of a reef. Fortunately, people ashore hollered when they saw the *Bowdoin* nearing the reef, and Captain Mac reversed the schooner in time to avoid going aground.

The Magdalens marked the beginning of the ornithological collection which was one of the purposes of the trip. Gray wrote to his mother:

> *The scientists hunted the elusive flora and fauna too long at Amherst, though, and the wind had risen pretty badly by the time they were ready to come back. Hubbard and the mate went after the first load in the dory and then I spelled Hubbard for the second load. We shipped a lot of water and it was a long hard pull—Mac swearing all the time at the way a damn professor will get wrapt up in work and pay no attention to the elements.*

Dr. Gross made one of the first finds for the ornithological study—a savannah sparrow nest, including the eggs. On Grindstone, the boys shot kittiwakes and terns and brought them back to the vessel. Despite laws against it, they took a grown gannet, an immature one and some eggs from the Bird Rock reserve.

The scientists continued collecting both birds and plants at every landfall along the way, ultimately gathering 20,000 plants and 200 birds of a score or more species. Four hundred birds were banded. The boys enjoyed the challenge of capturing live birds, and they brought a number back to the schooner, although those were soon killed. The crew ate the meat and preserved or stuffed the skins.

According to Gray, the puffins were easy to catch. "They were fearless. We had this heavy mitt. Puffins live in holes in the ground, and of course they have those big heavy bills. You'd put on that mitt, and stick your hand in the hole, and the puffin would grab right on and you'd pull him out."

The traditional sportsmen's endeavors of hunting and fishing were a part of life on the schooner *Bowdoin*. At many landings, hunting parties went off after seal or other game for the table, as well as birds for the collection. The boys reported that seal meat made a tasty meal. They often caught fresh fish, too, usually on jigs (Gray once caught three cod on a single jig with three hooks on it) although sometimes they set up nets.

Routine Jobs

There were always routine jobs to be done, large and small. Replenishing the water supply was one of the recurring tasks which, six decades later, remains strongly in the memory of the voyagers. The *Bowdoin* carried 400 gallons of water in tanks below, and another hundred on deck in milk cans. The boys took the cans ashore in dories, filled them in streams, either from waterfalls or pail by pail, and lugged them back out to the schooner, where they were hoisted aboard and dumped. It took about five dory trips to fill everything, and it was hard work. Water trips were made about every five days all summer.

Often when they weighed anchor, stowing the chain fell upon Bill Esson, who found himself being awakened for the chore; he performed it many times dressed in just his shorts and socks or even in his pajamas. When the anchorage was muddy, so was the chain; the water was always cold. Not a pleasant job.

Throughout the trip, a variety of projects filled spare time: helping to organize charts for the next part of the voyage, tightening a bumper on one of the dories, relashing the barrels on deck, reeving a new line through the blocks in a halyard. The schooner was always in need of cleaning; in honor of any expected meeting, the boys scrubbed paint and polished brass and coiled lines especially neatly. And they all wanted to learn the lore of a seaman: nomenclature, navigation, and small skills such as whipping rope, splicing, and rolling cigarettes. (Esson decided to continue buying his already formed.)

Weather

Heavy seas, rain, high winds and fog—above all, fog—dominated life on the *Bowdoin* in the summer of 1934, starting early in the voyage and continuing nearly to the end. The dangers of the trip were real, and the fog and rough sea in the Gulf of St. Lawrence were only the beginning. The visibility was so poor nearing the Canadian Labrador shore that they couldn't see land at all. They strained their eyes looking for breakers. Finally, they shut off the engine to listen for a fog horn ashore, to locate the point to change course. The waves came at them broadside, rolling the rails right under; the inclinometer showed that the *Bowdoin* rolled 40 degrees from the vertical.

Their first anchorage on the Labrador was Little Mekattina, a small harbor about seven miles beyond Harrington, their intended landfall. It provided fresh water and protection, however, and a few Inuit came aboard selling sealskin mittens and muskrat skins.

Their second day on the Canadian Labrador, the first with any visibility, the boys were impressed with the bleakness of the coast—there were still big snow and ice patches everywhere, few signs of human life, and the wind was bitterly cold. But it was sunny and a great sailing day. The mirage effect allowed them to see the coast of Newfoundland, and the schooner tore along at nearly nine knots. After supper they entered the Straits of Belle Isle. Fog banks awaited them, though, and Captain Mac turned the *Bowdoin* back to anchor at Anse Eclair. There, the boys saw evidence of the dangers along the coast—the wreck of a steamer still rested on a reef outside the harbor. She had gone aground and broken up five years earlier.

In the morning the schooner was under way at 4:35. The temperature was 36 degrees, it was overcast, and it looked like rain, but there was no fog. Soon after she passed the Point Armour lighthouse, the voyagers saw their first iceberg. It was only a small one, but at that, it looked bigger than the *Bowdoin*. They passed the wrecked remains of the British warship *Raleigh*, which had been lost during the *Bowdoin*'s first trip north; Esson reported "all that is left is several rusty pieces of scrap iron." Ice became more commonplace. They were out of the straits by midafternoon, and soon they dropped sail and proceeded under power alone through some tricky passages among islands and into Battle Harbour, whose approach was difficult; they were within 15 feet of shore in one place.

Battle Harbour welcomed the *Bowdoin* with rain and blustery winds, which before long felt like the norm. Crowell warned the boys to stay clear of the many dogs when they went ashore to check out the capital city of Labrador, a busy little town engaged in all aspects of the fishing industry. Salmon fishing, Battle Harbor's main enterprise, was part of everyone's way of life there. The boys watched two small motor boats tow into the harbor a little iceberg, which would be used to pack salmon in before being shipped to England and Canada.

They mailed letters home, paying $2.30 each for airmail stamps—the price of 39 pounds of lobster at Port Hawkesbury. Bill Esson made note of several species of birds they saw, and Dr. Gross's field expanded to dentistry as he applied a poultice on the bad tooth of a local resident.

Wherever he was, Gray always wanted to climb to the highest point of nearby land. Battle Harbour was no exception; he climbed up Battle Island, where he found that the surf on the windward side shot 50 feet or more into the air. "Frequently we'd be standing on a rock, high and dry," Gray wrote to his mother, "and then all of a sudden we'd be drenched with spray—or find ourselves surrounded by swirling white water. One wave caught Holbrook when he was down too far and knocked him over, scaring the life out of both of us."

The *Bowdoin* stayed in Battle Harbour for a day and a half while the sea ran heavy outside. When they left it was not because the weather had improved, but the contrary—the winds had increased. After the *Bowdoin* had dragged her anchor a second time, and after moving her once, and setting both anchors, Captain Mac decided to take her out to another anchorage. "Gee," wrote Bill Esson, "he sure knows just what the *Bowdoin* will do!"

Assizes Harbour was MacMillan's destination, and that of a large number of Newfoundland fishing schooners as well. Behind some adjoining islands, with both anchors out, for three days the *Bowdoin* faced the worst summer storm her captain had ever seen on the Labrador. The "old northeaster roared across our bows," said Gray in a letter to his sister:

> *Never saw such wind and the rain stung like pellets from a shot-gun if we stuck our heads above decks. . . . The wind and waves raised havoc along the coast here—ruining fish nets and sending lots of the fishermen's boats ashore. About 27 Newfoundland fishing schooners were in the harbor with us. They were all pretty much worried about their ships—because they never have heavy enough anchors and chains—one or two did drag onto a ledge a bit. Some wanted to tie up to us as we had very heavy chains and 2 anchors out, but Captain Mac wouldn't take any chances and had to refuse them.*

The *Bowdoin* seemed to weather the storm better than her occupants. "The scientists were nearly frantic at being cooped up in the ship so long," wrote Gray. Crosby wrote (with understandable overstatement of the time), "For five days we hove to with both anchors out and spent the long days reading, playing cards, and arguing. The latter sport was in vogue all along the trip and the less we knew about a subject the more we liked to talk about it." Even the entry from Esson's ever-cheerful journal ends with a plaintive sentence: "A rainy day on board the ship is rather trying as we are so crowded down below."

The weather finally settled down, the field trips ashore for birds and plants and water were completed, and the skipper was ready to leave. But the engine wouldn't start. The compressed air tanks had leaked and didn't have adequate pressure. The *Bowdoin*'s departure was held up another couple of hours. "Leon [MacDonald] and I will be sticking pretty close to the engine room till that little episode blows over," wrote Gray.

Moving North. Ice

It was twilight all night long, Esson wrote about the evening of July 3, "about what we usually have three quarters of an hour after sunset." The moon was out, and they saw a shooting star and northern lights, too.

George Crosby claimed that there was only one time on the whole trip he wanted to be home instead of on the *Bowdoin*:

> The Fourth of July came in foggy and cold, with a chill head wind. The holiday was celebrated by blowing the ship's horn several times, a performance which should please the most vigorous advocate of a safe and sane Fourth. With the thermometer around 30° F we felt that the above sufficed. I find in my journal the following entry: "To keep warm today, I had on two pairs of woolen socks, hunting boots, a woolen shirt, long underwear, chamois jacket, pea jacket, two pairs of mittens and a knitted cap. When it rained I just changed the hunting boots for regular ones and put oilskins over the whole outfit."
>
> As if this weren't enough for the Fourth, the fog came down even more thickly and we definitely lost our way. Shortly after our watch came on deck for the evening we saw several bergs dead ahead, having to alter our course by fifty or a hundred feet to pass them. In dense fog the bergs loom up as a dark, grey mass and suddenly come out in a chalky white when you near them. We managed to miss these only to find that what was at first thought to be a berg was a rocky cliff. Everyone was thoroughly miserable — it was becoming dark; it was cold and wet; and we were lost. I was put into the starboard chains with the lead line and presently found we had but two fathoms under us, and our draft is supposed to be just that! My hands were stiff from hauling in the line from the ice-cold water and any minute I expected to hear that heart-sickening crunch that would mean we had hit bottom.
>
> The Captain, however, betrayed no fear; turned the boat

sharply about, having to pass within two feet of a small berg to do so, and regained deep water. Within an hour he had identified the coast and we were at anchor in a comparatively safe harbor. It is at such a time that the seemingly uninteresting pastime of reading and listening to the radio before the fireplace becomes an ambition worthy of the greatest effort.

Each day of the trip north along the Labrador brought its own adventure, hardship and beauty. Dr. Gross was often sick, the crew sighted 152 icebergs by the fourth of July (and the ice had just begun), and the first of at least four groundings took place, although the schooner just touched, barely jarring her passengers. The residents of each little village they passed—Aillik, Hopedale, Nain, Port Manvers—visited gleefully with the people of the *Bowdoin*, the first boat to reach the northern settlements that year.

All the Inuit of Nain gathered at the dock to sing a welcome to the schooner and her sailors, and later, 55 came aboard to visit. Everywhere the *Bowdoin* came to anchor, natives brought trading stock aboard and the white missionaries and Hudson's Bay Company representatives brought tales of life in the north. The HBC stores were an attraction for the boys, and they ordered sealskin boots, slippers, and dickies (parkas), among other items.

Although the students' contract prohibited them from acquiring any articles from the Eskimos without the captain's express approval, trading was a part of every contact. Native clothing and folk crafts such as miniature kayaks had great appeal for the boys, and the Inuit were happy to take money, clothing or tobacco in trade. In many villages, the *Bowdoin* was welcomed by people who knew her and her skipper from earlier voyages, and the boys were made to feel comfortable everywhere they went. They stopped at the missions along the coast where the boys were given cake and cookies. The senior members of the party— the captain and the professors—sometimes went ashore for dinner with the missionaries. Although Inuit visited aboard the schooner, rarely—perhaps only once—did the boys visit an Eskimo home. That one visit was to deliver an alarm clock to a native who was going to join the schooner in the morning as a guide for one of the scientific expeditions ashore.

As is true with any voyage north, this trip was sometimes surprising and sometimes familiar, but it was never humdrum. The *Bowdoin* kept running into things; the second grounding occurred while approaching Port Manvers, where the water was very deep right up to the shore. One sounding showed 10 fathoms, the next, two, and the schooner was aground. MacMillan sent everyone forward onto the bow, to raise the stern up enough to allow the schooner to back off, and she went on her way to her evening's anchorage. Boys took naps at all hours in all places, fog came and went, high winds blew in and blew out. They got lost and unlost. Bill Esson packed and repacked his locker (he wrote that he never could find anything).

On July 10, after running all night, they reached Cape Mugford, the first scientific camp site. Dr. Potter, George Crosby and Bill Brierly were left there with three dory-loads of supplies. The *Bowdoin* was to return in a week to ten days after leaving another group of scientists on the Button Islands off Cape Chidley.

On his way back to the schooner from landing equipment, Crosby insisted on rowing through an arch in a big iceberg. Both MacMillan and Crowell were enfuriated.

A half hour later, the forty-foot thick arch, with a great roar and splash, collapsed into the ocean.

The *Bowdoin* headed north again. She traveled through a spectacular "tickle," as the passages between islands were known, perhaps because they were so ticklish to navigate. Sheer cliffs rose 800 feet on both sides and waterfalls fell directly into the sea. The schooner made her way into open ocean again and her crew saw a particularly striking light blue iceberg, gracefully shaped. Soon afterward they passed through a field of broken ice which kept snapping, making noises like hail falling. Captain Mac explained that an iceberg had just broken up, and the cold ice from the middle shattered as it came into contact with the warmer ocean water. A series of hard squalls came upon them, but luckily they hadn't full sail up. They continued on their way, hoping to reach Cape Chidley the following evening.

They ran all night; it was so light that few stars were visible, and when the sun came up the air was so clear they could see 70 miles up and down the coast. In all MacMillan's years of sailing the Labrador, he had never seen such a sight; he had always had fog. In the midafternoon they entered an ice field, and Crowell climbed to the ice barrel to give steering instructions. The ice bumping against her hull reverberated loudly within the schooner, but it barely jarred the *Bowdoin*. "Many times we just had to push ice aside," Braley Gray remembers. "Boy, that old mast would chatter. 'Course the schooner was built to ride up the ice, and either break it or push it aside. You had to watch, though, going through ice floes, that you didn't push one aside and then it would come back in onto the propeller. The captain, he'd pull the stern away from ice like that, but you went pretty slow, to give the ice you'd ridden up on and broken time to go a little distance."

None of the charts of this area were accurate. Although they showed a pair of tickles cutting through to Port Burwell, there was but one — Grenfell Tickle or McLelan's Strait, which the *Bowdoin* had passed through from the other side on her way home from Foxe Strait in 1922. In 1934, MacMillan attempted to run through it on his way north, because it would shorten the trip by 15 miles. But they just missed a favorable tide, and faced a six knot adverse current through the tickle. Progress was very slow — and then, suddenly, ice floes poured at them. They bucked the ice for a half hour, but finally, afraid of being caught in a jam, the captain ordered the vessel about. They tore back down through the tickle.

The next day's attempt to get around Cape Chidley to Fort Burwell was no more successful. Tremendous tidal currents pushed ice from Hudson Bay out around the cape. The way was impassable, and the *Bowdoin* ducked into a little harbor that didn't show on any of the charts. It was very well protected, and soon the crew had named their snug anchorage "Bowdoin Harbour." Some of the fellows went ashore and, on the highest point, built a cairn six feet tall, leaving a message in a bottle: "Fog and icebound in this place July 12, 1934, four members of the *Bowdoin*

MacMillan Arctic expedition climbed this hill and built this cairn." They celebrated the construction with a snowball fight. It seemed like a huge monument when they built it, but from the water it was barely visible.

The following day they steamed out of Bowdoin Harbour and headed north, and then west. The passage was open directly across to the Button Islands, where they were to leave Dr. Gross and four boys, but they were first required to go into Port Burwell to pick up a representative of the Canadian government who was to oversee their landing. Past Cape Chidley, behind a couple of islands, strong, whirlpooling currents swung the schooner this way and that. There was some ice, but they had no trouble avoiding it until they cleared the islands.

Outside was solid ice. Bill Esson wrote:

We saw a small opening and headed for it, but it closed up before we got through. The ice was old floe ice and very hard; some pieces were 10 to 15 feet thick. We hit them awfully hard and the bow rose way up but we didn't make much headway. We finally set the engine full speed ahead and we pushed several very large floes out of the way and got through to open water. I took movies of that and the jar was so great up in the masts that I couldn't hold the camera steady. We soon met another solid band of ice and had to break through that. This time was more exciting. We headed for a solid piece full speed and hit it a tremendous blow. We finally got in the ice with our bow stuck on one piece and a large piece at our stern so we couldn't move. The ice was in constant motion due to the heavy currents created by the tides. While locked in, a large piece bore down on us about 3 or 4 miles an hour and hit us broadside by the foreshrouds. I was up in the mast and I felt sure it would stove in a side. It gave the boat a tremendous jar but did no damage. In fact it knocked our bow off of the cake in which it had been locked. We then had open water for awhile. . . .

It became apparent to MacMillan that they weren't going to get through the icefield, and the best bet was to head ashore for protection. A narrow opening on the starboard side appeared to lead to a well sheltered harbor, and there the captain headed, dead slow, taking soundings all the way. At three fathoms, with kelp on both sides, he was tempted to turn back, but kept on. When they arrived at deep water inside what appeared to be an inner harbor, he was surprised to see ice driving to the westward. They weren't in a harbor at all, but rather in the midst of a number of small islands. They anchored in a protected cove to wait for the ice to pass by.

A shore party found a cairn and cross erected by a Newfoundland captain, Sam Blandford, master of the *SS Neptune*, who had called the place Port Harvey. There were also remnants of an Inuit village, and a number of Eskimo graves, which the boys inspected.

Almost as an afterthought in his journal, Esson wrote: "Apparently the ice we met this morning was rather dangerous. If we got stuck in it, the motion of the ice caused by the currents might crush us. Several boats have been lost here because of the ice, and Capt. Mac has nearly lost a vessel here because of ice."

The next day the ice had blown offshore, and despite bumping the bottom on the way out of Port Harvey, they had no difficulty getting to Port Burwell, and indeed, took the time to collect a few fulmars.

Waiting

At Port Burwell, a young Royal Canadian Mounted Policeman told the boys that the village was a dead place. The crew of the *Bowdoin* was about to have the opportunity to determine that for themselves. They had to wait for the Canadian government representative they were required to take along for their landing on the Button Islands; he was coming on the steamer *Nascopie*, which was due any time, as was a Hudson's Bay Company supply schooner. Arriving on July 14, the *Bowdoin* was the first vessel to come into Port Burwell in 1934.

The first day at anchor at Port Burwell was a Sunday, and the boys went to church, did laundry (Esson dyed all his clothes pink, washing them with red-topped socks), went hunting, read, had haircuts, traded with the Inuit, and visited with the white people living in the area, of whom there were five: two Mounties and three Hudson's Bay Company men. These men were young and interesting to talk with, and they spent the next three evenings aboard the *Bowdoin*. All wanted to leave their northern positions, and enjoyed the radio when it finally came in on the third night. Everyone listened to music and the news (trouble in Vienna, strikes in the United States).

The next day marked one month out of Portland. The weather was clear and relatively warm, so the *Bowdoin*'s sails were hoisted to dry, and the boys cleaned her from stem to stern. After lunch, they started on the sides, but were interrupted by the attack of a huge ice pan which floated in alongside, threatening to rip up the anchor and push them against the cliff, or at the very least, crush the dory. The boys jumped onto the ice as it lay next to the schooner; someone dared Gray to strip and get in the water pooled on the top of it, "so of course I took the dare. I didn't swim very long—boy, that was cold!" Pinochle and jigsaw puzzles kept the company amused in the evening.

The third day there was still no sight of either expected ship. The boys fetched water and hunted seals from the dory. Tired from rowing after seals, they sat on an ice pan and waited for seals to come to them. Neither approach was successful. Inuit brought bird specimens for Dr. Gross. MacMillan worked on his Eskimo dictionary all day.

The fourth day the boys polished brass and spiffed the *Bowdoin* up to look her best for the *Nascopie* while Capt. Mac rowed over to the site of a Moravian mission he had visited in 1911. It was empty now, in bad repair; in a few years it would all be gone.

By the fifth day, they thought they might go on to the Buttons in the afternoon, Canadian representative or no, but fog rested outside, and they stayed put. Still no sign of either *Nascopie* or the schooner.

The sixth day produced more hunting expeditions, maintenance projects, reading and trading. Esson traded a pipe and a couple of plugs of tobacco for a pair of mittens and a tiny skin of some kind "which was really too much, but you sort of pity the Eskimo so that you don't like to drive a hard bargain."

On the seventh day the fog had moved inside, with rain and a high wind to boot. Esson spent the morning reading a mystery magazine and the afternoon playing pinochle and checkers, both regular and "give away," whose object is to lose all your men first. After supper a group went hunting birds, with great success, providing plenty of skinning chores for the next day. They saw a flock of 300 Red Phalaropes, which was noteworthy as no more than 15 had ever been reported in the area before.

The eighth day, Sunday again, saw a lot of birds skinned. And finally, at midday, the schooner came in, followed that evening by the *Nascopie*. They both had been fog-bound and lost for ten days. The *Nascopie* in that time had somehow drifted through Hudson Straits and found herself 80 miles west of Fort Burwell.

Finally, Back to Work

July 23—Off for the Buttons! These islands had never been explored by white men, although they were familiar enough to the Inuit, and the bird studiers were excited to learn what birds lived and nested there. The *Bowdoin* left ashore Dr. Gross, four boys, and a one-eyed Eskimo guide named Bobbie, who was along, MacMillan wrote, to supervise the party in case the *Bowdoin* didn't return.

From the journal of one of the boys, the most significant aspect of the Buttons expedition appears to have been sleeping late every morning. But they did look for birds, and though they found fewer than Dr. Gross had hoped, they identified purple sandpipers, snow buntings, ptarmigan and sea pigeons. They hunted game and ate a great deal of seal meat (provided by Bobbie). They saw bear tracks, and sighted a fox. The only adventure, other than difficult rowing in the windy passages between islands, was the kitchen tent catching fire in the middle of the night on the second night. (Happily for the boys, no food was lost.)

The *Bowdoin*, after leaving her group on the Buttons Islands, high-tailed it for Cape Mugford. Sgt. Anderton, the RCMP officer from the *Nascopie* came along, but he didn't enjoy the rough seas, the worst the *Bowdoin* had met that year. He wasn't alone; even Jack, up in the ice barrel, was nearly sick.

They ran all night; the sunset was beautiful, and the moon rose, way to the south, and set again in two hours. Northern lights played over the schooner.

In the morning fog set in, but they kept moving along, knowing they were going to be late picking up Dr. Potter and the boys. Toward noon the fog lifted and they could see all the way to Cape Mugford. Right after supper they reached the camp site; a signal of the whistle brought its residents running!

Cape Mugford

The first week at Cape Mugford had passed quickly for the three campers. They had quickly dubbed their campsite "Camp Clark-Colby" and labeled it with white rocks. The scientists photographed and collected plants, surprised by the variety and adaptations of plant life growing in the harsh locale. Willow and birch trees grew five or six inches tall; a variety of flowers and other plants were also found. The men's food was good, a fresh water source was handy, the weather was pleasant and there were many plants to photograph and collect. Their gasoline lantern stopped functioning, but they made lard candles in peanut butter jars, which worked well, even if they made the sleeping tent look like an Arabic household instead of an Arctic camp.

The 20th of July was their tenth day in camp, and with no sign of the *Bowdoin*, they were getting anxious. They had thought they would be picked up in a week, or perhaps ten days—

certainly no longer. Their food was getting low, and they cut their meals to two a day. From George Crosby's account:

> *Sunday, July 22, was the worst day we experienced on the entire trip, but we were too concerned with our immediate situation even to think of home, which was about 2,000 miles away by boat. During the night a heavy gale and rain storm had been working up, and at six in the morning our sleeping tent fell down with a groaning swish. We had dressed previously, expecting something like this, so we dashed outside to see what had become of the work tent which stood in the shelter of the larger sleeping tent. It was of course flat, but that was the least of our troubles. Our dory was about ten feet off the shore and headed seaward and cooking utensils, cotton, stuffed birds, and plant presses were taking the same course. The wind was strong enough to blow Dr. Potter down twice, but in spite of it all the dory was brought back, but Bill had to wade up to his waist to do it. Then, everything that we could catch we weighted down with rocks. There being no natural shelter on the island to which we could go, we threw a few of the rocks from the center of the large tent, dumped some water from depressions in the canvas and climbed into our sleeping bags, cold and wet. We tried to smoke but the wet cloth flapped up and down in our faces to make it almost impossible. For ten hours we lay shivering beneath the tent while the storm blew itself out. About five in the afternoon we ventured forth to a scene that would have broken anyone's heart, for strewn all along the beach were remnants of our once excellent equipment.*

The next day, an Innuk in a small power boat came by, and the campers negotiated with him to return for them in three days and take them to Nain. On the 24th, they had decided that the *Bowdoin* must have been wrecked. "Most of our food was now gone and nearly all day long we just lay around wondering what we would do. We went to bed early—around 7:30—and had not been there long when we heard three long blasts that sounded very familiar to us—the boat!"

Back to the Buttons

The *Bowdoin* ran back up to Cape Chidley as fast as she could, using both engine and sails, although the sails didn't help much of the time. After breakfast on July 26, they struck the sails. It was very foggy, but the distance run, and willow leaves, bird feathers and twigs in the water all suggested they were near the Cape. MacMillan turned the vessel toward the land, and in twenty minutes a breaking ledge appeared right under the bow. The *Bowdoin* avoided that only to find a huge black cliff looming before her. They ran along to the southwest, just outside the breakers, trying to keep the land in sight and looking for a familiar landmark. A few times they had to steer hard-a-port to avoid rocks. Finally, they tucked into a quiet harbor which Mac-Millan believed to be the one they'd called "Bowdoin" two weeks earlier, though they couldn't see the cairn and weren't certain until a party went ashore.

The fog stayed thick all that day, and was thicker yet the next few. The crew amused themselves as they waited for the fog to lift with the usual chores, games, and hunting expeditions; more haircuts were given, some better than others. They built a second cairn, lower down, where an approaching vessel could see it, and Jack, with the help of a couple of the boys, mapped the harbor and made lines of soundings through and across it. It is more than a mile long, with a nearly uniform depth of six, seven and eight fathoms and a mud bottom, making it an excellent anchorage.

Finally, five days later, the fog lifted and the *Bowdoin* was able to head for Cape Chidley. They had beautiful traveling weather, and no ice, but half way across to the Button Islands, the wind freshened. The current was running hard, making rough tide-rips followed by large whirlpools. They dropped anchor a little beyond Dr. Gross's camp but the schooner dragged. They moved nearer the shore and settled in an eddy where they rode, oddly, stern to the wind for awhile. After the bird-watchers rejoined the schooner, the *Bowdoin* crossed back to Port Burwell. However, the foul current was so strong that even running full speed, the *Bowdoin* was pushed backwards sometimes. The normal two hour trip took seven.

The Great Grounding, and the Turn Toward Home

Leaving Port Burwell again was even more eventful. At 4:30 on the morning of August 1, some of the fellows who had been ashore celebrating came on board with the RCMP and Hudson's Bay men, making a great noise and waking the rest of the crew. The weather could not have been better, so after goodbyes were said, shortly after 5 A.M. the anchor was hove up and MacMillan ordered the engine started and idled. But the *Bowdoin* went forward. MacMillan rang for full astern, but still the *Bowdoin* went forward. He ran for the engine room hatch yelling, "She's going ahead!" and hollering to Crowell to lower his anchor. The anchor went down, slid for a second, then caught, and the *Bowdoin* swung to port, up onto a pile of rocks right next to the cliff. The engine was killed. With the falling tide there was no chance of getting her off, and the *Bowdoin* "settled down comfortably into a mass of rocks and waited patiently for the tide to return," as Mac-Millan wrote in his journal.

While everyone took pictures of the *Bowdoin* high and dry in her rocky cradle, MacDonald and Gray worked on the propeller's reversing mechanism. About 9:30 A.M. the *Bowdoin* floated off, but nearly hit the cliff on her way out of the harbor.

Everyone was excited to be headed for Baffin Land. But once away, they saw that Hudson's Strait was full of ice as far as they could see in all directions. Captain Mac turned the *Bowdoin* back; they had gone as far north as they would go, and were now heading toward home.

He offered as consolation a second attempt on Grenfell tickle (McLelan Strait), this time from west to east. The tide was with them and roiling along; the *Bowdoin* shot through the eight mile passage only to find the Atlantic side enveloped in fog. They crept through reefs and shoals in the fog and found a small protected harbor. MacMillan wrote the next day that something, or somebody, was protecting them on this trip. He had been tempted to pass farther up into this harbor before anchoring, but something told him not to, and in the morning, on the low tide, they saw two nasty black rocks just where he would have dropped anchor.

They spent a day or two in this harbor, and then went a few miles to another, which had fresh water, and which they named Clark Harbour. Some of the boys were upset that they hadn't been able to go to Baffin Land, and they approached MacMillan with their concern, but he convinced them that it was better not to try. Even if they were able to push through the ice, it might take so long that they would lose their opportunity to stop along the Labrador going south again. "Capt. Mac sure is a good leader," wrote Esson.

On a warm, calm day they at last headed out for Eclipse Harbour, and Dr. Potter climbed to the ice barrel for the first and, so he announced, the last time. The peaks surrounding Eclipse Harbour stood 5,000 to 6,000 feet, and naturally, Gray and some others had to attack. They got to 2,250 feet, where Jack caught a ptarmigan by hand. Gray caught some feathers. The mosquitos were terrible. As long as the boys kept moving, they were all right, but the second they stopped, the mosquitos chewed them up.

Sailing along under jumbo and foresail with the engine running, they picked their way through the rocks along the shore. Just as they passed through the lee of a high cliff, with reefs on the other side, the engine quit. When the wind came in from dead ahead, they dropped anchor to keep the *Bowdoin* off the rocks while MacDonald blew out the fuel line. In an hour they were on their way again, and soon they were past the shoals and could proceed under sail alone. It was a difficult sail, though— sometimes the schooner was sailing scuppers-under and other times she barely carried steerage way.

They ran all night. It was the darkest night they'd seen, and they turned on the running lights for the first time in many weeks. The port watch complained that the starboard watch was too noisy to allow them to sleep; Esson tried to sleep on deck, but was too cold. But the port watch showed their mettle when they lowered the sails alone, the first time it was done without calling all hands. Four of them dropped and furled the mainsail alone, and felt pretty smug about it. They anchored in the morning at Cape Mugford behind Brave Mountain in water so clear they could see bottom at seven fathoms. Gray and some others went ashore to climb the mountain, but they only got three quarters of the way up, to 2,800 feet. They put on one dory load of water, and headed off again, taking bearings all the way, as MacMillan was making a sketch of the run to Nain. They passed fishermen for the first time in weeks, and in their anchorage that evening two more schooners were anchored; one was a Newfoundlander and the other a big trawler from Lunenburg, Nova Scotia, whose crew was cleaning the day's catch, still at it after dark, working by flares. The captains visited the *Bowdoin,* and one of them asked MacMillan to telegraph a message home for him. The mosquitos were vicious; the men covered the *Bowdoin*'s hatches with cheesecloth in an attempt to keep them out, but that made it very hot below.

They sailed for Port Manvers at three in the morning, and then for Nain, arriving there midafternoon, again accompanied by mosquitos. Mail awaited them in Nain, the first they'd received since they left Portland. A two-week-old *New York Sunday Times* was a great hit.

At Nain they picked up a young man, Higgins, who had been hired to mine Labradorite, a colored feldspar, on one of the islands nearby. He and another young fellow had been encamped on the island for a month cutting and dynamiting as much of the mineral as they could, which was to be picked up by a ship some weeks back, but the ship had broken down. Higgins was hitching a ride back to the island, where he and the other man would wait another ten days, and if the ship hadn't come by then, they would get home the best way they could.

That night shone the most spectacular northern lights of the trip, bright enough to cast shadows. The colors were bright green, pink and purple, and the boys had never seen anything like them.

Once Higgins was dropped off on his island, the *Bowdoin* became a beast of burden, carrying material to and from Mac's camp, where the captain alarmed his crew by taking the schooner within two boat-lengths of the shore, in such shallow water that when they dropped anchor, only five feet of chain payed out. The boys landed and delivered provisions for MacMillan's Eskimo school, made some last purchases from the trader and the Hudson's Bay store, and took on water. The professors both had good luck collecting; everything has grown and bloomed since the schooner was last in Nain. The mosquitos feasted well.

The *Bowdoin* traversed a narrow, twisty passage called the Rattle on her way into Davis Inlet; the last time she went through, she had struck bottom, lost part of her shoe, and been aground for six hours. Happily, she had a safe trip this time.

The schooner dropped some of the boys off to cross overland to the next anchorage. They were going to collect birds along the way, but the collecting wasn't very successful — except for mosquito bites. Gray remembers that trek to this day. "Luckily we all had hooded rain capes; I've never run into mosquitos like that in my life."

Civilization

And so the trip down the coast continued: more and more fishermen (MacMillan had never seen so many Newfoundlanders on the Labrador), mosquitos, stops to band birds, gather plant specimens and get water. Steamships. They kept moving along by day, anchoring most nights. They spent one day at Indian Harbour, banding and gathering puffins from a nearby island, and during the next few days there were puffins everywhere on board — stuffed puffins, a pet puffin, puffin breasts for dinner. They didn't stop at the whale factory at Gready Island, but saw a whale boat coming in, towing a whale. They picked up mail in Battle

Harbour, then found big seas in the Gulf of St. Lawrence. In Red
Bay, some of the boys went aboard the *George B. Cluett*, Grenfell's
140-foot schooner. "Her fo'cas'le put ours to shame as far as size
was concerned," wrote Esson, "but we're fixed up much better."
Red Bay was the northernmost telephone connection—"It seemed
strange to see telephone poles," wrote Esson. They sailed into
more big seas and water came in through the forward hatches
when the *Bowdoin* put her bow under one big wave after another.
Nearly everyone was sick; Gray remembers he "was lucky as the
dickens. Coming back along the west coast of Newfoundland, we
got into a hell of a storm, with the wind blowing from the west.
It had the whole sweep of the Gulf of St. Lawrence to blow
across. The Admiral and Captain Crowell and the engineer and
the cook were okay, but there were only a couple of us boys on
deck. Everyone else was sick below."

On August 25, in Sidney, Nova Scotia, they came to real
civilization. They picked up mail (Esson got a letter his mother
had mailed on June 17), went to a barber shop, an ice cream shop
and a hotel, where they took hot baths and held a farewell party
for the sergeant.

The *Bowdoin* passed through the Bras d'Or Lakes, a beautiful,
protected, pastoral route completely unlike anything else the
boys had seen that summer. A canal and lock lead out of the lake
on the southern end, and it was there that the *Bowdoin* had her
last breakdown—she destroyed her propeller as they were leaving the lock. Ultimately, MacMillan arranged for the *Bowdoin* to
be towed to Port Hawkesbury, where she was hauled and her
spare propeller was installed.

Underway again the next day, the *Bowdoin* passed swordfish-
ing schooners off Halifax, with a couple of dories deployed,
showing they'd harpooned at least that many swordfish. The
moon was out for their last night at sea and the sailing conditions were ideal; Esson spent most of the night on deck. By
11 A.M. they were in Rockland, Maine, and everyone sent telegrams home and bought ice cream. "It seemed good to be back
in the U.S.A., but it sure was warm," wrote Esson.

Saturday, September 1, 1934, at 3 P.M. as scheduled, Captain

MacMillan brought the *Bowdoin* into Portland harbor, saluting Mrs. Peary. They were met by an Eastern Steamship line boat, a couple of small motor boats and a tug. The boys' families met them pierside and came aboard to help them unload. They all said their goodbyes, and went their separate ways.

The next day, with a party of his friends aboard, MacMillan sailed for Boothbay, stripping the *Bowdoin*'s sails after they passed Southport in order to get them stowed before wet weather set in. Another trip done.

Braley Gray remembers the trip for many reasons, not the least of which, he laughs, was "because of the trip I got to know my wife, Corinne. She'd spent the summer as a riding instructor at a camp in Vermont, and hadn't seen any boys, and I'd been on the schooner *Bowdoin* all summer, where there weren't any girls, and I guess we looked pretty good to each other." They were married on June 25, 1937; Corinne died on June 24, 1988, one day shy of their 51st anniversary. "That trip got us together."

Fitting out at East Boothbay, Maine, 1921. Note that the ice-barrel is not yet in place. (E.L. Boutilier
Collection)

An early embarkation.
(Maine Maritime Museum)

Donald B. MacMillan at the wheel of the *Bowdoin*, 1921. (The Peary-MacMillan Arctic Museum, Bowdoin College)

A group of Inuit visitors to the *Bowdoin*, Baffin Land, 1921-1922. (The Peary-MacMillan Arctic Museum, Bowdoin College)

The *Bowdoin* on the rocks, leaving Refuge Harbour, 1924. (Courtesy of Maine Maritime Academy)

The *Bowdoin* frozen in at Refuge Harbour, North Greenland, 1923-1924. (Dartmouth College Library)

Newfoundland fishing schooners, Assizes Harbour, Labrador, after the storm, 1934. (Braley Gray)

"The Boys," upon embarkation, 1934. Left to right: George Crosby, Robert Wait, a visitor, Henry Hubbard, Braley Gray. (Courtesy of Braley Gray)

"The Boys" at the cairn in Bowdoin Harbour, Labrador, 1934. Clockwise from lower left: Bill Esson, Henry Hubbard, Luther Holbrook, Oscar (the cook). (Braley Gray)

Port Burwell, Labrador, 1934. (Braley Gray)

The *Bowdoin* in dry-dock upon joining the U.S. Navy, Portsmouth Navy Yard, 1941.
(Courtesy of Jim Sharp)

Lt. Stuart Hotchkiss in command of the *Bowdoin*, 1942. (Courtesy of Maine Maritime Academy)

Ed Morse holding on to fellow crew members aboard the *Bowdoin*, 1947. (Photo by Rutherford Platt, courtesy of Jim Sharp)

Jim Sharp and his son Topher with Mac, 1968. (Courtesy of Jim Sharp)

Mac and Miriam at the wheel of the *Bowdoin*, 1950s. (Courtesy of Jim Sharp)

Miriam, Helga Morse, and longtime friend Moravian missionary Katie Hettasch, late 1970s. (Courtesy of Ed Morse)

Mac in the *Bowdoin's* ice barrel in Umanak Fjord, approaching Rink Glacier. (Courtesy of Maine Maritime Academy)

John Nugent driving a spike through a deck beam into the shelf, 1982. (Courtesy of Anne Bray)

Miriam, Clayton Hodgdon, and Clayton's dog, Timber, at the launching of the *Bowdoin* after her rebuild, October 1984. (Boutilier Photos)

The *Bowdoin* being towed to Boston, November 1984, in the bitter cold. A single person can be seen on the deck of the *Bowdoin*. (Neal Parent)

The Statue of Liberty's 100th birthday, 1986, at which the *Bowdoin* led the Tall Ships Parade. (The Boston Globe)

SIX

Miriam

Childhood

IRIAM LOOK WAS THE daughter of MacMillan's closest friend, Jerry Look, a civil engineer who summered with his family in Casco Bay. Look had been very important in raising money to build the *Bowdoin*. Miriam's hero-worship of Mac started soon after his return from the 1908–1909 North Pole Expedition with Robert Peary. She was a tree-climbing, kitten-loving child, and a make-believe Arctic-adventurer (who had to play the role of Donald MacMillan or none). Whenever MacMillan made a journey north, he brought a present home for Miriam—carved ivory, a fur, a beaded ornament, and once, an Eskimo puppy.

Miriam started writing letters to her idol before she had mastered the nuances of English grammar. A note Mac received at Etah as he left on the Crocker Land Expedition in 1913 (she was then seven and he 38) said, "I wish you was my brother." He saved this letter, along with a number of others he'd taken along on that trip, and Miriam found them thirty-five years later. (On one, unopened and sender unknown, was written, "To be opened when everything has gone dead wrong." MacMillan said things had never gotten that bad. It is now in the care of the Peary-MacMillan Arctic Museum at Bowdoin College, encased in plastic.

Miriam wanted it that way. If Mac hadn't wanted it opened, she wouldn't permit it either.)

The teenaged Miriam had a small power boat, the twenty-five-foot *Sea Pup*, in which she learned the beginnings of seamanship as well as the moodiness of motors. The *Sea Pup*'s temperamental two-cylinder engine was a far cry from today's outboards with push-button starters. Even after many repeated attempts to start the thing, it often remained balky and silent, while Miriam grew limp with fatigue. She was not speechless, however. (Miriam believed that her amateur's command of blue language was ultimately inspirational to the recalcitrant motor.)

But *Sea Pup*, once started, rarely let Miriam down. The little boat took her among the ledges and around the evergreen-covered islands of Casco Bay. To be sure, Miriam sometimes found herself grounded upon a ledge and had to wait until the tide lifted her off, but in the *Sea Pup*, she learned to love the sea. And although he let his daughter feel her own way around, her father kept a watchful eye on her.

In September of 1922, when Miriam was sixteen, the Looks went out to Monhegan Island to welcome Mac home after the *Bowdoin*'s first year in Greenland. A few days later, they spied the schooner dropping anchor at Bustins Island in Casco Bay. Miriam and *Sea Pup* were off. The engine started right up. The little boat crossed to the schooner; its skipper eased her boat alongside the *Bowdoin*, landing as gracefully as a pro and, surprising herself, invited Mac aboard for a ride. She was further surprised when he agreed, asking her to take him to South Freeport for a dinner engagement. They breezed into the bay, and he complimented her on how well she handled the boat.

But then the motor sputtered, banged, burped, and died. There they sat. Miriam investigated spark plugs, carburetor, priming cups and anything else she could think of, even though she knew nothing about engines (nor did he). Mac suggested perhaps there wasn't any gas in the tank. Nonsense, thought Miriam, only a real greenhorn would go off with a nearly empty tank. But he was right. No gas.

The ever-watchful Jerry Look appeared in his own power

boat. Quietly, sheepishly, Miriam handed him a line and accepted a tow home. Mac was a half hour late for his dinner engagement.

True Companion

In 1931, the *Bowdoin* left Wiscasset on a voyage to the Far North amid the usual speeches and wishes for safe return. Bands played, whistles blew, and the now-grown Miriam was on the dock, thinking only of the *Bowdoin*'s captain. And as the schooner swung her bow toward the open ocean, Mac hollered across to her, "I'll be looking for you when I get back." She nearly jumped aboard. She desperately wanted to visit the land of the Eskimos, see the icebergs and the walrus, but even more, she wanted to be with Mac. She found herself wondering if he would ever settle down to marriage. When he did return three months later, it was with talk of returning to Baffin Land.

MacMillan made another trip or two before finally, in 1935, he and Miriam were married. She was 29, he 60. His home in Provincetown, full as it was with Arctic memorabilia, became her home. Together they sorted through Mac's artifacts. They donated some to museums where they could better be preserved, they catalogued others and filed his photographs and negatives. They documented the 150,000 feet of movie film, until Miriam felt she knew intimately all the Eskimos her husband knew so well. Outrageous though it was, Miriam wanted to go north herself; at the same time she knew that was impossible. Women couldn't go on expeditions like her husband's. So that first summer, Mac and Miriam traveled to Europe. It was obvious to Miriam, however, that Mac's heart wasn't in the uneventful trip on an ocean liner. He missed the dangers, the suspense, the storms, the ice and the cold of the Arctic.

The next year, 1937, Mac planned another expedition north, this time on the famous racing fishing schooner, the *Gertrude L. Thebaud*, which was larger than the *Bowdoin* and could take more people. Miriam talked her way onto one day's sail of the voyage—

if she could get herself halfway up the Labrador coast in time to meet her husband at Hopedale she could sail with the *Thebaud* to Nain and spend the summer there with Mac's missionary friends, the Hettasches. If she couldn't get to Hopedale in time, he couldn't wait.

Miriam's connections—two trains and a steamer—went smoothly until she arrived at St John's, Newfoundland. There, she boarded a mail boat scheduled to make ninety stops on the way up the coast. Miriam was sure her luck had run its course. At each stop, though, interesting sights awaited young Mrs. Mac. From her husband's movies, she even recognised the first Eskimo she saw, coming out of the fog in a fishing boat filled with natives. But although there was no word yet of the *Thebaud*, she wanted to take no chances, and was anxious to be on her way.

Coming into Hopedale, the mail boat was, as always, the center of attention, but this time, everyone was screaming something about MacMillan. Miriam was worried that they were all saying he'd come and gone, but no, she herself seemed to be the attraction. Everyone on the Labrador always knew everything that happened up and down the coast; word had gotten around that MacMillan had married and that his wife was aboard the mail boat. Her husband's friends just wanted to welcome her. And the mail boat had beaten the *Thebaud* into port.

Miriam and Fan, her friend who had accompanied her to Hopedale, soon got into the spirit of local custom, and dressed themselves in Eskimo fashion, with cloth and trim purchased at the Hudson's Bay Company store and sewn into dickeys and other articles by Inuit women. Sealskin boots completed the costumes. They learned variations on Eskimo greetings, and practiced them on all they passed.

A couple of days went by with no word from the *Thebaud*, and Miriam feared the schooner had been damaged in the ice pack, or grounded in fog, or perhaps, even, that due to adverse conditions Mac had decided to bypass Hopedale altogether. But as the sun set on the third evening, the *Thebaud* was sighted, and a yell went up, awakening the village. Everyone, Miriam and her friend included, ran for the dock, and jumped aboard any available vessel — skiffs, motorboats, anything afloat. These small boats all circled the ship, everyone calling out Eskimo words of welcome. And their greetings were returned graciously by Mac-Millan at the rail of the *Thebaud*. But he gave no special recognition to his wife until, anchor dropped, he took the time to peer carefully at the boat she was in and finally recognized her in her Eskimo clothing.

The next day, the *Thebaud* sailed with two women aboard, Miriam and her friend. Mac pointed out where the wreckage of the *Bay Rupert* had come ashore, the Hudson's Bay steamer that had come to grief on an underwater rock a decade earlier. Mac had seen her before she went down, broken amidships. The stores aboard had not been lost; they were scavaged by the natives, who set up their own sales counters, selling butter, flour and sugar. Calico from the ship decorated the village, but of the steamer herself there was nothing left.

In 1937 very little of the Labrador had been charted, but Mac knew his way through the rocky passages, bays and inlets. He said he had learned the hard way, by bumping rocks and ledges. One of the few charts available was of the entrance to Nain, which had been mapped using aerial photographs MacMillan himself had taken a few years back.

At Nain they were met by the usual reception committee — the entire village population in small boats, in this case led by a boat with a brass band playing "Now Thank We All Our God." Missionaries Dr. and Mrs. Hettasch and their daughter Katie and another teacher at Mac's Eskimo school welcomed them as well; Miriam felt she had known these people forever (and indeed, she was close to them for the rest of her life). They were all pleased that Miriam and her friend would be spending several weeks with them. Mac, too, was happy to be back at last, and enthusiastically showed his bride through his northern home. Miriam saw that she had a job here too, determining what the school needed. It was hard for her to watch the *Thebaud* leave, but Mac didn't look back. He was probably humming, Miriam wrote; in times of sadness or stress, he had often told her to sing, as the Eskimos did.

Sometime, she intended to really sail with him.

The summer of 1937, however, Miriam spent learning about the changing—modernizing—life of the Eskimo, of the traditions and the needs of the native population and the Newfoundland fishermen who came after cod each summer. She learned of the history of the Moravian missionaries in Labrador, of the efficient way they won the Eskimos' trust without interfering with their native customs, how they helped protect the Inuit from foreign diseases, and helped to settle the fighting between visiting fishermen and the Inuit. And she learned of dog fights, and the threat they provided to small children, and of mosquitos.

When the time came for Miriam to start her trip back to Gloucester, Massachusetts, in hopes of meeting the *Thebaud* when she came in, there was no way anyone could know, but Mac and the schooner were far from returning. They were grounded in Frobisher Bay, Baffin Land, where a forty-foot tide rises and falls each day. The *Thebaud*, with three crushed planks, didn't float off the punishing rocks. Instead, she lay on her beam ends, flat in the water. They readied to abandon her, removing food, sails, and all important supplies. But a final check showed the schooner to be at last trying to right herself on the rising tide. They manned the pumps and, using everything that would hold water, all hands formed a bucket brigade. Thirty-five people pumped and bailed, and took tons and more tons of water from her foc's'le, hold and after cabin. Gradually, they emptied the water the vessel had taken on, the sprung seams closed up again, and finally, the *Thebaud* floated comfortably into deep water. The engine still had to be taken down and cleaned, but the *Thebaud* was back in business.

Mac headed onward to the Arctic Circle as if nothing had happened. They photographed the wildlife they'd come to study, and when they did head south again, they took their time along the coast, collecting rocks and birds and flowers. When the *Thebaud* came back into Gloucester, everything aboard was still soaked, and much was ruined, but Mac had finished his mission and was already planning the next one, which would again be on the faithful *Bowdoin*. And this time, Miriam intended to be along.

If Mac were not to come home from one of his voyages, wherever he was and whatever happened, she wanted to be with him.

In 1938, MacMillan had any number of arguments why his wife shouldn't sail with him—he had never sailed with a woman; it would be too rough and cold and difficult for a woman; she'd be seasick; the schooner might be crushed by ice and they would have to trek over the ice pack to Greenland, dragging dories; they might have to stay in the Arctic all winter; the crew would get sick of her and throw her overboard. Although none of these reasons seemed significant to Miriam, MacMillan had answers for her every objection. So she embarked upon a campaign of silence. She worked on all aspects of readying for the voyage without mentioning her hope of going with her husband. She ran errands, fetching paint, tools, and netting; she sent telegrams, mailed packages, and wrote letters. She prepared all the stores for the Eskimo school at Nain, purchased presents for all their friends on the Labrador, and helped outfit the vessel, all without saying a word about going north herself. And ultimately, shortly before sailing time, Mac admitted he hated to leave her behind. He blamed the crew; they wouldn't like having a woman aboard. Suddenly, he agreed to take her as far as Nain. She turned aside so he wouldn't see she was overcome, both with happiness and with mental and physical fatigue.

With captain, first and second mates, engineer, cook, doctor and seven college students interested in a variety of subjects and with a variety of plans, the *Bowdoin* left Boothbay Harbor. Also aboard was Miriam, the first woman ever to make a voyage on the *Bowdoin*.

As usual, the new sailors spent the first few days learning the ways of being at sea. Miriam had plenty to learn, too—the names of the parts of all the equipment the schooner carried, how the daily shipboard routine worked, and how to get dressed in a cross sea that made the schooner roll violently. Miriam's berth was opposite Mac's in the after cabin, which doubled as navigation station; she had a hard time sleeping the first night because she was so curious about everything going on. Someone would come below to check the chart and she'd wonder where they were. She'd hear booted feet pacing overhead and orders being given to listen for fog signals and wonder how bad the fog really was. At 4 A.M., she couldn't stand being out of the action any longer, and joined the oilskin-covered men on deck.

She loved being on the sea and feeling the schooner plunge into the waves and throw salt spray in her face. Within a week they were in Battle Harbour, where they were greeted by the postmaster who, perhaps under the influence of a little more rum than he was accustomed to, dubbed Miriam "Lady MacMillan." The name stuck, usually shortened to "Lady Mac."

The *Bowdoin* continued up the coast, in fog and among the uncharted rocks and reefs of the various runs and tickles, and too soon for Miriam, they were approaching Nain. At the first sitting for supper, her last day on board, one of the crew members handed Miriam a folded piece of paper. She thanked him, and put it into her pocket, wanting to read any farewells in private after the schooner had left Nain. But the crew insisted Miriam open it and read it to them.

> *MacMillan Greenland Expedition.*
> *Be it enacted by the members of the MacMillan Greenland Expedition. . . .*
> *Whereas, Thirteen is an unlucky number for the crew of any vessel.*
> *And, Whereas, 'Lady Mac' is a good scout,*
> *Therefore, be it resolved: that we the undersigned unanimously vote that Mrs. MacMillan be elected an honorary member of the expedition, and request that she continue on the voyage to points north, to be classified aboard ship as Official Hostess and Cribbage Partner of the* Bowdoin.

Every member of the crew had signed the document. And Mac, as surprised as Miriam, asked to sign also. Then and there Lady Mac became a permanent member of MacMillan's crew. Mac took the *Bowdoin* north nine more times; Lady Mac sailed with him on every trip.

Miriam wrote of her life with MacMillan in her 1948 book,

Green Seas and White Ice, which is known affectionately by some of the *Bowdoin*'s followers as *Green Seas and White Wash*. This interesting but definitely rosy tale makes the trips north sound adventurous but always happy. ("She even makes the mosquitos sound fun," says Andy Chase, who would later sail the *Bowdoin* north again, "and I'm here to tell you, they aren't.") But Miriam's enthusiasm and love for her husband, the Arctic, and the schooner *Bowdoin* permeated the lives of all of the *Bowdoin*'s people for decades to come.

SEVEN

World War II

The Bowdoin Joins the Navy

ORLD WAR II CHANGED life for the schooner *Bowdoin*. Although she started the war under the command of her own skipper, she soon passed into other hands, and ultimately almost lost her life.

With the outbreak of the war, the military wanted the *Bowdoin*. The Army offered to charter her for $1,000 a month, but MacMillan, a Reserve lieutenant commander in the Navy, wasn't sure that was best. He traveled to Washington to discuss it with a Navy admiral, who told him he might do better to sell the vessel to the Navy. This didn't appeal to MacMillan either; the *Bowdoin* was part of his life. But it was agreed, finally, that he would sell the schooner. Although both MacMillan and the naval surveyors agreed it would cost $50,000 to replace the *Bowdoin*, and the Navy was willing to pay that, MacMillan wanted just the $35,000 she'd cost him, so he could return that money to his investors. (He never did understand the concepts of inflation or making money on money invested. He never had enough himself to worry about it.) Mac would skipper the vessel for the Navy himself.

On his desk, the admiral had orders to take the *Bowdoin*, whether or not they had come to an agreement; luckily, they had.

In 1941, Mac and a Navy crew sailed north to help establish

two airfields on the west coast of Greenland, one at Sondres-trom, on the Arctic Circle, and the other at Narsarssuak. The *Bowdoin* was available for other work at Sondrestrom, but she had no clear mission, and by fall, Mac thought he should be doing something more significant for the war effort. He announced to the other Naval officers in the area that he was going home. Without orders? To please them, Mac radiogrammed the Secretary of the Navy, informing him that if he didn't hear to the contrary in three days, he was taking the schooner home. There being no word in three days, the *Bowdoin* steamed down the fjord. It was midnight when she reached the open ocean; snow fell heavily, and a ship offshore was calling for assistance. By radio, Mac talked the huge steamer in to the coast, up the fjord and into harbor, and then he headed out again. Early the next day, he received orders to do what he was already doing, going home.

Along the Labrador coast he was warned again and again about German submarines, but Mac said he would just shine a spotlight onto his mainsail after dark, and no one would think the *Bowdoin* anything other than a fisherman. They did see what looked like an island off Cape Sable one night, an island they knew wasn't there; a week later, the President of the United States announced the presence of German submarines off the northeast coast.

Once back in Boston, Mac was ordered to prepare the *Bow-doin* for another trip to Greenland in the spring. The schooner was taken to Lawley's yard in Neponset, Massachusetts, where she would spend the winter.

Lt. Stuart Hotchkiss Takes Command

While MacMillan spent the next three years with the Hydrographic Office in Washington, editing charts of Greenland and working on his Eskimo Dictionary, the *Bowdoin* continued her naval career without him. A young lieutenant, Stuart Hotchkiss, was given her command in April of 1942.

Lt. Hotchkiss was well prepared to take over the *Bowdoin*. After his sophomore year at Yale in 1933, he had spent a year as an apprentice on the *Parma*, a four-masted bark flying the Finnish flag, one of the last grain ships. "An apprentice," he says, "was the lowest form of life." He cleaned pig sties and furled the royals and did anything no one else wanted to do. He was introduced to the realities of sea life: during a hurricane he huddled on deck and watched thirteen sails unfurl and shred themselves. And, when an improperly secured staysail-sheet preventer tore apart the fife rail to which it was made fast, young Hotchkiss watched helplessly as a man was swept overboard and lost.

In 1935 he refit a 49-foot Nova Scotia-built, former fishing schooner, the *Vagabond*, and raced her from Newport to Bergen, Norway. (This crossing, too, was tragic. In heavy weather, a father and two sons were lost overboard from another vessel.) While the *Vagabond* was laid up in Norway, Hotchkiss navigated *Stormy Weather* in the Fastnet race (which she won) and sailed home aboard her.

In 1939, following two more transatlantic passages, Hotchkiss raced across the Pacific in the San Francisco-Honolulu race, and again won. By the time he took over the *Bowdoin*, his deepwater credentials were impressive; the schooner would be in capable hands.

His first assignment in the Navy also served him well in preparation for the *Bowdoin*. He joined the Navy full time in April 1941, and was sent to the minesweeper *Barbet*, being built at Ipswich, Massachusetts. He was with her through inspection, commissioning, shake-down cruise, and finally, in November of 1941, he went with her to New London, where he learned about icing conditions at sea. The sweep gear froze up coming aboard in the winter's northwest gales. It was so cold that salt sea ice formed, and everyone on deck was thoroughly uncomfortable.

It was during this tour that Hotchkiss, now a lieutenant, was given command of the *Bowdoin*. He presented himself at Lawley's prepared for a transfer of command ceremony such as he had just held on the *Barbet*. But that wasn't how things were on the *Bowdoin*. He found the schooner on the marine railway and her exec and radioman were surprised to see him. MacMillan hadn't been seen in a number of weeks, and no one knew if or when he would return. (He had been called to Washington to make charts, consult on all Arctic expeditions, and compile an Eskimo dictionary. Hotchkiss never did meet him.)

Lt. Hotchkiss gave his new charge a thorough inspection. He found some rot under the eyes of the rigging, which was easy to repair, and more in a large section of the inner three of the five aprons strengthening her stem, which would require serious rebuilding. On deck sat a massive air compressor, waiting to be installed; it had a primitive one-lung engine, cooled by pouring water into a reservoir on the top. The machine was to provide compressed air for starting the Fairbanks-Morse diesel when it lost starting air, as it had done a number of times during the last trip. But Hotchkiss wanted an electric air compressor and a 7 ½ kilowatt generator driven by a small diesel engine, instead of the archaic monster on deck. A second generator was also installed as a backup, as were a Sperry Gyro Compass and an oil-fired space-heating boiler.

When all this equipment was in place, the *Bowdoin* was heavy at the bow; Hotchkiss calculated that 1,000 pounds of lead ballast aft would trim her up. A duo of commanders from the First Naval District came down to see why so much lead was required; they declared that the problem could be solved by moving the two, 500-pound anchors aft to the wheelbox. Hotchkiss respectfully suggested that with this arrangement there might be difficulties in anchoring and getting under way. Apparently the commanders accepted his argument, for the next day the lead appeared.

The folks in charge at Boston wanted the *Bowdoin* to start for Greenland in mid-April, but fortunately, as it turned out, the schooner wasn't able to leave until the fourth of May. (As it was, they reached their first survey site only days after the ice went out.) In addition to Hotchkiss, there were nine enlisted men aboard, the executive officer, and two survey officers, Joe Gorman and John Stirton. (Stirton left the *Bowdoin* for the schooner *Effie M. Morrissey* in Frobisher Bay soon after they got north. The exec, David C. "Beanie" Nutt, had made a number of trips in previous years along the Labrador in the *Effie M. Morrissey* and, after the war he would continue to make regular trips north in his own schooner, making surveys and studying bird and animal life in the Arctic.)

The first day out from Boston there wasn't much wind, which was just as well since the crew hadn't sailed together before and several of the men aboard had never been to sea under sail at all. Hotchkiss set a policy that they would not run the engine unless the *Bowdoin* could not make four knots under sail alone. The second day provided a fair wind and good sailing as they reported to their superior, Commander Destroyers Atlantic Fleet in Casco Bay. From there they proceeded for Argentia, Newfoundland, where a torpedo net had been strung across the entrance to the harbor; the *Bowdoin* was greeted by the patrol vessel, the YP62, to which Hotchkiss himself had been assigned some thirteen months earlier in New York. Outside Argentia, the *Bowdoin* rounded up to wait for the lead into the harbor, and the YP62 waited, and the *Bowdoin* waited. "Perhaps they thought we would take in our sails," says Hotchkiss. But Lt. Hotchkiss didn't believe in using the engine when he didn't have to. He saw where the net gate was, and so finally filled away and headed for it. "We gathered headway quickly as the strong wind filled our sails. The YP62 abeam to port started in a leisurely fashion and as she began to drop astern, we could tell from the doughnuts of exhaust coming from her stack that she was laboring to catch us. She never did."

Given a signal to proceed alongside a tanker on a mooring, the *Bowdoin* "rounded-to, dropped all sail, and berthed gently alongside." Their show of seamanship was the talk of the officers ashore for some time to come.

A small amount of diesel oil topped off their tanks; the next day, they left for Greenland. The trip across the Labrador Sea had its share of great sailing—sometimes the *Bowdoin* flew along at ten knots—and days of shortened sail and discomfort as a result of gales and squalls of sleet, hail and snow.

"One night the seas were heavy and steep. They broke on-board like surf breaking on a beach. It was 35° Fahrenheit, and I was at the wheel when I saw a big one coming. I dropped to my hands and knees alongside of the wheel box. The sea broke over me and carried away the brass binnacle cover for the magnetic compass. It also filled my seaboots to the top. . . . It is interesting how quickly one's feet and legs warm up the cold salt water in a seaboot," wrote Hotchkiss.

On a broad reach, the entire rig would surge forward as the schooner slid down the back of a passing sea; Hotchkiss was worried about the strength of the rig, and indeed, three days out of Greenland, the main gaff snapped. But in yet stronger winds, the heavily loaded *Bowdoin* was happy under foresail, staysail and main trisail.

Lt. Hotchkiss used the engine infrequently on the way to Greenland, doing so only when the wind died south of Cape Farewell. In the calm approaching Greenland, they came close by a drifting mine. They circled it several times while some of the men shot at it with rifles. Finally, on his first shot, Hotchkiss punctured it. When they were certain it had sunk, they motored on. "Fools rush in," Hotchkiss says in retrospect.

They met floe ice about 60 miles from Greenland, first a few growlers and then within just a few minutes, they were sur-rounded by a field of ice. Beanie Nutt stood in the ice barrel to spot leads of open water headed in approximately the right direction. After slowing their progress a good long time, the ice disappeared as quickly as it had appeared.

Sondrestrom Fjord

The *Bowdoin* reported to the Coast Guard's Commander Green-land Patrol at Narsarssuak, Greenland, on May 21. Although a Navy vessel, during this duty the *Bowdoin* operated under the Coast Guard. Her assignment was to perform hydrographic surveys of the fjord at Sondrestrom, which straddles the Arctic Circle, as well as the fjord at Narsarssuak, further south. The work would be used to prepare charts to aid ship navigation in the waterways up to the airbases. Sondrestrom was first. After several days layover, while the gaff was repaired and Hotchkiss fashioned some running backstays to support the mainmast, off she went, following a kind of a road map north along the inland passage. There were almost no soundings marked and only a sketchy outline of the approximate locations of the many rocks and islands, with a route line marked through them. (Fifteen months later, under another skipper, the *Bowdoin* would return to survey and chart this area.)

During the summer, there was very little wind on the Greenland coast. The *Bowdoin* traveled a lot under power, including most of the trip to Sondrestrom, and they got there only a day or two after the ice cleared the fjord. The rest of the summer was spent working on the survey, building survey signals on shore and establishing a triangulating network for control. Joe Gorman describes one memorable workday:

> *I, with two assistants, set about one morning to establish a baseline over a terminal glacial moraine. We worked tirelessly at the task and, when finished, rowed the dory back to the ship. When we arrived and went below to get that hot supper, we were dismayed to find that it was past midnight and everyone, including the cook, had retired for the night! The long summer daylight at that high latitude had played a trick on us!*

The shoreline was delineated using overlapping air photos. Lastly, lines of soundings were run up and down the fjord. When the job was all done, the final measurement of the 85-mile-long fjord came out within millimeters. There was only one little problem, Hotchkiss says—the level of survey they were doing didn't call for a wire drag, so they didn't discover a pinnacle beneath the water just outside Fishmasters Harbor. Someone else did, unhappily, not too long afterwards.

With 24 hours of daylight, there was plenty of time for hunting, fishing, mountain climbing, and learning about the tundra and the icecap. "Frequently I would return from hunting at one or two A.M. only because one must sleep sometime," says Hotch-kiss. He remembers one anchorage: "There were boulders all along the shore, and betwixt them all, mallard ducks would get up and fly off. On the next occasion I went ashore—not more than a couple of days later, here were all these critters running and dodging among the rocks. I couldn't make out what they were, until I rowed in further, and saw that the mallard ducks had all molted, they had no feathers at all; it was the mallard ducks running around."

A point of interest for the crew of the *Bowdoin* was the *Halma*, a former Danish ship, put under Panamanian flag when Germany took Denmark. She had run aground part way up the fjord several months before. When Hotchkiss and his shipmates first saw her, she was on an even keel and looked as if she was ready to go to sea—but she was dead, deserted, motionless. Hotchkiss berthed the *Bowdoin* alongside for the night and they climbed aboard. Everything was in perfect condition. At first they were very quiet as they checked out the ship. "We had the feeling that the ship at any moment would suddenly spring to life and we would be caught trespassing like naughty boys." But they realized that there really was no one aboard. With great pleasure they discovered a supply of beer and other alchohol. The *Bowdoin*, like any Navy vessel, was dry; during their stay in Sondrestrom fjord, the men enjoyed visiting the *Halma* from time to time. In addition to the alcoholic attractions, they found parkas and mackinaws which had been soaked in oil, but they discovered that the aviation gasoline aboard served as drycleaning fluid.

Hotchkiss was surprised on one trip down to the *Halma* to find that Inuit had come aboard and taken all appealing items to the beach. "I felt mean indeed as I drafted a radio message to the Base to send a vessel down the fjord to retrieve the valuable loot." Later, he felt meaner yet when he learned that the Americans sent out in response to his request had made a fortune selling whiskey at the base. Before long, a salvage vessel took the rest of the *Halma*'s cargo off, pumped her out and patched her enough to tow to Boston for repair.

While the survey officers were at work, the *Bowdoin* stood by, giving the rest of her crew a good chance to get the schooner into topnotch condition. They greased the masts, varnished the rigging and all bright wood, shined the brass and painted the hull and decks. "If only we could dispose of the lumber pile on our starboard deck the ship would be very nearly the perfect yacht," Hotchkiss wrote home in July. In August, they aced a surprise inspection.

MacMillan had ordered a motor boat to assist in the survey work; it arrived soon after the *Bowdoin* got to Sondrestrom. The boat was about 18 feet long and had a little diesel engine. As it turned out, the boat caused no end of trouble. Hotchkiss says her "crowning misadventure" was at the end of August when, under tow, she sank. In an instant, she went under and hung vertically on her painter. Fortunately, the painter was new, and was able to hold the 2,000 pound boat until they could hook onto it with the halyards and haul her back up again.

Although the men had little occasion for socializing while they were at Sondrestrom, even up there, more than 2,000 miles from home, a couple of times Hotchkiss ran across men he'd known before. He had even sailed with one, Fred Sturgess, in the 1937 Fastnet. One evening, Hotchkiss and Sturgess were startled: "Something was quite wrong with the moon. Earlier it had been full and now it was only half." Hotchkiss wrote that perhaps the bottle of whiskey they had consumed the better part of might have slowed their comprehension of the eclipse they were observing. "As we watched, it went into total eclipse—a beautiful sight as the night was fine and clear. Through the binoculars the moon looked opaque."

In September, when the days grew shorter and the sun stayed lower in the sky, Hotchkiss headed the *Bowdoin* out of the fjord for the last time, "almost with a feeling of nostalgia." He was happy to be sailing again, taking the schooner 300 miles south to Narsarssuak. They had great sailing weather: "As daylight faded, the breeze freshened. This was what *Bowdoin* liked. The old girl picked up her skirts and reeled off the knots. The sea built up and crested with foam that gleamed white in the starlit night. The vessel would run down one sea and swing up as the next one lifted her transom before the cycle was repeated. The action was rhythmic as one sea followed the other."

The magnetic variation along the Greenland shore was in excess of 50 degrees, as was the declination. In a seaway, the compass card revolved in its bowl because the horizontal magnetic directive force was so weak. "It's a little distracting," says Hotchkiss in his understated New England way, "when the compass card starts rotating like a roulette wheel." They were thankful for the gyro compass.

The backstays worked well, steadying the rig, and the *Bowdoin*, lighter than on her trip north, remained dry. She was given a good test; with the winds increasing to gale force, the main had to come off and be replaced with the storm trysail. "As she came up amidst the roar of flapping canvas she took a heavy sea across the starboard rail and rolled deeply to leeward burying her lee deck. Mr. Nutt claimed that he was swept right outboard, but fortunately had a good hold on the lee main rigging. It was just as well as we were doing about eleven knots at the time. . . . That night I was again impressed by one of *Bowdoin*'s qualities. The wind and seas could roar on deck but down below in the after cabin she seemed steady and silent as a church."

Southern Greenland Village Life

The *Bowdoin* and her crew spent the winter surveying fjords and passages in the Narsarssuak area, which was very different from Sondrestrom. The fjords were broader and the mountains not as tall or steep. There were many islands, but not consistently good anchorages; often the water was too deep. Sometimes the *Bowdoin* was fortunate to have a 2:1 scope and a depth of 20 fathoms. Even then, their stern might be perilously close to the rocky shore, and they would run stern warps ashore. "Some nights," Hotchkiss reports, "with a gale blowing, snow pasting down, zero visibility, we would be lying there with a sounding lead over the side to detect any motion. I'd have a lad on deck reporting every ten minutes. We spent some very uncomfortable nights that way."

Narssak, where they centered their southern survey operations, provided more than just a good harbor; it was a village of 20 or 25 houses, complete with a white, wooden, steepled church and schoolhouse. The schoolteacher and the trader lived in wooden houses, and the natives lived in stone and sod huts. The men of the *Bowdoin* found themselves part of a community: "'Umiakshua,' the Eskimo name for 'big white boat,' became the community social center each time we dropped anchor in the harbor. Typically, as soon as we would enter the harbor the umiaks would come out and cluster alongside. Conversations would start, particularly with the young people, in a polyglot of English, Eskimo and sign language, always with giggles and laughs. Always they remained in their umiaks until specifically invited on board."

The indigenous culture was in a period of transition. The older people still dressed in traditional sealskin clothing and offered model kayaks and sealskin mittens and other items in trade for cigarettes, while the younger ones dressed western-style in clothes from the Danish Trading Monopoly, except for Sunday best, when many returned to the beautiful and intricately decorated Inuit garb.

Hotchkiss described Narssak life:

> *The life of the village was very simple and the entertainment was entirely self-made. It was surprising how many of the people could play musical instruments and had other personal accomplishments to contribute to the entertainment at a gathering. It frequently made us realize how few our own personal accomplishments were and how much we rely on outside sources rather than ourselves.*
>
> *Frequently we would visit in the people's houses. Sometimes a dance would "happen" to the music of an ancient wind-up gramophone with scratchy records. Often we would be offered "imiak," the native home-brew beer. Though we tried to be polite, this was an unpalatable and weak concoction, but occasionally our hosts would get quite tipsy on it.*
>
> *The houses provided an interesting contrast. The stone and*

sod houses were primitive in the extreme. The walls were built of stone very thick, as from time immemorial. Some of the more fortunately situated houses were built into the hillside facing south. The roofs were thickly covered with sod which presumably had some insulating value. A door and a window completed the structure. Most of the interior was devoted to a low platform which served as a communal bed space. Light was provided by a soapstone lamp which held a pool of seal oil and a wick. Faggots of wood were burned for cooking and warmth.

On the other extreme, however, the trader, who was the most important personage in the town, lived in a tidy, well-appointed wooden house.

The economy of the town centered around the Danish Trading Monopoly. To obtain the necessities such as cloth, salt, sugar, and other basic foods, powder and shot to load their shotgun shells and many other items, the people hunted, fished and raised sheep.

For transportation of goods and people beyond the capabilities of umiaks, the town had a motorboat. This could sometimes be seen loaded with brush and small wood collected for fuel at some remote crevice between the hills along the fjord. At other times it might be seen loaded with live sheep headed for Julianehaab.

It also might be used in the event of severe illness beyond the capabilities of the local nurse to take a patient to the hospital in Julianehaab.

The Greenlandic people were becoming westernized, in lifestyle and in blood. The Narssak trader was a Greenlander whose features indicated considerable Caucasian blood; at least one other member of the village was also of mixed ancestry. The people of the *Bowdoin* were accepted into the village just like anyone else. When they were operating in and out of Narssak, they took some of the local boys with them.

One calm, frosty morning, the fjord had frozen over with a one-quarter inch glaze which the *Bowdoin* easily pushed through. They were about at their furthest range from the base when Hotchkiss realized that they were in trouble. The *Bowdoin* was more heavily laden than when she had traveled north with Mac-Millan and amidships, her greenheart planking wasn't protecting her hull. "The thin ice was cutting through like a knife" into *Bowdoin*'s oak planking. They took the *Bowdoin* into a nearby sheltered harbor and radioed the base. A steel-hulled trawler was sent out with galvanized sheet iron, 2 X 10 planking and galvanized boat nails. While the rest of the crew sat perched "like chickens roosting" on the main boom swung out over the opposite side, heeling the schooner over, Lt. Hotchkiss and another man circled her in a dory, installing more protective sheathing. The boat nails were brittle in the cold, and the two men broke many before they developed a reliable technique.

Work stopped completely for a while in November. They were in the lower reaches of the fjord when the engine seized up and they had to return to the base for a major overhaul. Hotchkiss wrote:

> *That night it snowed hard, but early in the morning the storm passed leaving us with six inches of snow on deck, a clear sky and a fine fresh breeze blowing up the fjord. Never had I had a more glorious sail. With sheets eased on a broad reach* Bowdoin *swept through the icy waters while the snow covered hills looked down from either side of the fjord.*
>
> *The arm of the fjord upon which the base was located was filled with slush ice.* Bowdoin *made an eerie sound as she swished through the imperturbable layer of gumbo until at last we dropped all sail and let her slide gracefully into her snug berth on the inner side of the pier.*

The airbase was located directly across from the site of a settlement established by Erik the Red in the tenth century, traces of which could still be seen. The base itself was a self-sufficient entity, with no contact with the Greenland of which the *Bowdoin* and her men had become a part. It served as a refueling point and center for the Coast Guard cutters assigned to Greenland waters. The *Bowdoin*'s berth was beside an oil barge which was in the care of an unkempt-looking wheeler-dealer whose trading schemes allowed the *Bowdoin's* crew to profit remarkably from the Inuit souvenirs they had obtained for a few packages of cigarettes. The Danish authorities eventually heard of these activities, and Hotchkiss and his crew were officially restricted from contact with the natives. "It was ridiculous," Hotchkiss says. "Narssak was the only harbor in the area where we could lie over." And no one could see any harm coming from the contact. At any rate, the restriction was not enforced.

Back at work again, the *Bowdoin* faced no further lack of wind. Greenland experiences unique "Foehn" winds which develop from a particular combination of temperature and atmospheric conditions over the ice cap. These were both good and bad for the *Bowdoin*. Any wind discouraged ice formation, making the survey work possible, and the Foehn was accompanied by a rise in temperature. But the Foehn always built to hurricane strength, sometimes quickly. Hotchkiss wrote:

> *Our first experience was brief and unpleasant. One morning as we lay in the harbor at Simiutak at the entrance to Skov fjord the warning came. The air temperature, which had been at its normal level of about 10° F quickly rose to 20° and then to 30°, then 35°. When this occurs the wind is never far behind.*
>
> *The harbor is long and narrow, extending straight into the heart of the solid rock island. The axis of the narrow sleeve points toward the fjord and beyond that toward the treacherous ice cap. At anchor, we braced ourselves for what might come, prepared to get underway at a moment's notice should this seem necessary.*
>
> *The first gust of wind confirmed our worst expectations. It blew directly into the entrance of the harbor, converting the uninviting shoreline into a direct lee shore. Quickly we got under way in the desperate hope that we could find protection elsewhere.*
>
> *Our 120 HP diesel labored as we pushed toward the entrance of the harbor but with* Bowdoin's *bow directly to the wind we made sufficient progress. Once clear of the narrow waters, however, wind and sea conditions became rapidly worse.*
>
> *To starboard, the rocky shore dropped precipitously to meet the seas which were crashing high against the cliffs.*

*We gained a little offing before a breaking sea drove
Bowdoin's bow off to starboard laying her in the trough of the
sea. Tom McColgan in the engine room stood on the throttle to
extract the last ounce of power from the engine to bring the ship's
head to the fierce wind again. As the wind roared the top of the
wheel box beside me blew off and skated to leeward across the
water. But suddenly she made it. For a few minutes head to wind
we re-gained some distance from the murderous lee shore.*

*Then it happened again. Again we were in the trough
drifting rapidly toward certain disaster. Suddenly, Beanie Nutt
called from below — "Fire in the lazarette!" The iron handhole
plate in the otherwise lagged muffler was red hot and had started
some nearby gear to smoldering.*

*Miraculously we again got Bowdoin head to wind but this
time we headed back for the dubious protection we had left with
the roaring wind astern and the seas lifting us on. At a point
where I knew the bottom of the harbor rose we dropped both
anchors and rounded up to ride out the gale with the engine
turning over ahead to ease the strain on the ground tackle.
Meanwhile a little lighthouse which had been built on the island
above the head of the harbor blew away.*

That evening the wind departed as quickly as it had come.

*At about 2 A.M. as we lay in the quiet harbor the ice came in.
At first a few small pans appeared, then quickly and stealthily it
came in quantity. We hastily got under way and escaped before the
harbor became completely blocked.*

*During the storm we had watched the barometer descend
rapidly until the needle fetched up on the stop at the bottom of the
scale. The next day it was still there and I suspected that the
barometer was broken. When we hailed a Coast Guard trawler in
the fjord I asked for his barometer reading— 27.67 inches. Our
scale ended at 27.70! Eventually our barometer recovered none
the worse for its experience.*

During their second Foehn wind, the *Bowdoin* was berthed at
Julianehaab, alongside the *Tintagle*, a rusty old steamer resus-
citated from the scrap heap for wartime. The lines were all

doubled and extra steel cables were run ashore from the *Tintagle*. All available fenders were hung between the vessels. For five days the wind never dropped below 75 miles per hour, and the crew maintained round-the-clock sea watches, always ready to get under way. The *Bowdoin* rolled and rolled and rolled until treenails started backing out; from time to time her crew reached over and reset them with a mallet, surely a tricky chore.

The winds of yet another Foehn were clocked at 165 miles per hour before the anemometer blew away. Fortunately, the *Bowdoin* had a snug berth.

Survey work was slow and uncomfortable, due to the temperatures (mostly minus 10°F to 10°F) and to the short days—there were only six hours of sunlight daily by December. The signals they built were blown down by Foehn winds, and Joe Gorman's fingers and toes froze as he worked ashore. He writes:

> *Occupying the survey stations during the winter months was a tiring, and sometimes dangerous, chore. Garbed in heavy Arctic clothing, we had to carry the heavy theodolite case and tripod up steep, rocky slopes which were sometimes icy.*
>
> *On one occasion, my feet slipped on some ice, and I began a swift slide downhill toward the icy water. Fortunately, I was accompanied by the bos'n, a burly man of great strength, who planted his feet in a toehold and caught me as I came careening downhill. This happened twice on the same day. In my heavy clothing and snow boots, had I hit the water I would have sunk like a rock!*
>
> *Operating the theodolite in windy, freezing weather was a real challenge. The wind was occasionally so strong that I hung rocks from the theodolite's plumb line to hold the instrument down and somewhat steady. My cold, numb hands would require rotation of gloves; while I operated the theodolite, my assistants would warm a change of gloves under their armpits.*

Joe Gorman had to produce the work sheets for the next phase of the project, but all the others, except the cook, had no responsibilities beyond maintaining the schooner. Hotchkiss and Nutt, as senior officers, lived aft. The rest of the men lived in the *Bowdoin's* foc's'le, always cramped and even worse in bad weather, when the area was not only crowded but steamy as well. The galley was in the foc's'le compartment, too, and the cook was autocratic—sometimes abrasive—in his management of his domain.

The pressure of being the only surveyor became too much for Joe Gorman, and he finally exploded, raving at Hotchkiss about slavery. The storm blew itself out, and after a good talk, work continued.

In February, rumors of tragedy floated about the dock, and soon ships came in carrying a few survivors—and a larger number of bodies—from the *Dorchester*, a transport that had been torpedoed a hundred miles offshore. Some life rafts and boats had gotten off safely, but the people not picked up immediately died due to exposure. "The sea was literally covered with little bobbing lights on the life jackets of these frozen men," Hotchkiss wrote. Among those lost was the *Bowdoin's* previous cook, Lambert, who had been in the hospital in Boston when she left that port. Someone had forgotten to change his orders, and he was on the *Dorchester*, unnecessarily en route to rejoin the *Bowdoin*.

There was an effort made at security about convoys after this sinking, though there was an ironic contrast between headquarters, where conversation was furtive, and the docks, where everyone knew everything about the expected arrivals and departures of convoys with complete accuracy. During this time there was a report that a submarine had been sighted in the fjord at Narssak. There were no Allies' subs in the area. Hotchkiss was asked to investigate.

> Soon we were on our way down the fjord. We made our visit to Narssak seem as casual as ever and in due course we found our man.
>
> These easy-going, friendly people when asked a question will try to answer in the manner they think will please you most. We, therefore, were careful to avoid any leading questions. Had he seen anything in the fjord? Our friend answered, "Ap" (Yes).

Producing a pencil and paper, we asked him to draw a picture.
He drew a perfect submarine complete with all essential details.
It had disappeared quickly and he had not seen it again.

At the end of March, the winds stopped. Ice formed on the fjords and the *Bowdoin* was frozen in for a month. The men used the time to work on refurbishing her, scraping her topsides down to bare wood and recaulking, smoothing and repainting. Hotchkiss repaired some rot around a through-fastening by chiseling it out and filling it with cement, much like a dentist filling a tooth. Deckhouses, bulwarks and rails were refinished and the schooner again "glistened like a yacht," Hotchkiss wrote.

Hotchkiss learned during the spring spruce-up that he would be replaced aboard the *Bowdoin*. He prepared to leave Greenland, shipping his books, sealskin suits and other possessions home on the Coast Guard cutter *Escanaba*. "I was never to see those things again. The *Escanaba* was torpedoed and sunk on the voyage south."

Lt. Hotchkiss was transferred to Miami, Florida, to the Sub Chaser Training Center, where he joined the Navy's growing fleet of destroyer escorts. He was ultimately given command of a destroyer escort which saw fighting duty in the Pacific.

Meanwhile, the *Bowdoin* was taken over by Naval officer John Backland from Seattle, whose pre-war job sounded like heaven to Hotchkiss. During summers, Backland and his father had operated a four-masted trading schooner, the *C. S. Holmes*, trading along the coast of Alaska.

Under Backland, the *Bowdoin* surveyed the inland passage from Narsarssuak to Ivigtut, and in early October of 1943, she sailed uneventfully back across Davis Strait, down the Labrador, then west of Newfoundland, to Nova Scotia, traversing waters which had seen the end of numerous allied ships due to German U-boat activity. Joe Gorman sounds as if the trip home was a perfect pleasure cruise:

We made a restful stopover for a few days at Sydney, Nova
Scotia. Departing Sydney, we headed south through the fresh
water Lakes of Bras d'Or. What a delightful passage that was:

110

*no heavy seas, and just the soft purr of the diesel engine as we all
enjoyed a quiet night of rest. . . . The passage close in shore to the
Nova Scotia coast was an interesting one wherein we could see the
quaint and colorful fishing villages ashore. Finally, rounding
Cape Sable we met fair winds and a following sea and sailed
along wing and wing at ten knots toward New England. When
nearing the coast Bowdoin ran into heavy fog and our position
was not well established. Not daunted, Beanie Nutt spied a
fishing vessel dead ahead and heading westward, and said "Follow
that boat, the locals know where they are." Sure enough, the
fishermen led us straight to the breakwater entrance to Gloucester
harbor and there our voyage ended.*

From Gloucester, the *Bowdoin* was taken to Boston, where she
was decommissioned and sat until the end of the war.

EIGHT

Back to Mac

Hulk #51

ULK #51, AS THE Navy had classified the *Bowdoin*, was a derelict.

Her masts, grimy and black, stood loose in their rigging. What paint she had left was filthy and peeling. She had been stripped of her running gear, her water and fuel tanks, her machinery and all equipment, even the knobs and hinges from her lockers. In short, everything that could be taken from her was gone. Her interior partitions had been smashed with an axe. All that remained were the hull, the masts, and the propeller.

Looking at her, Miriam wept.

On January 19, 1945, after the Navy agreed that everything in the yard that belonged to the *Bowdoin* was included in the deal, MacMillan paid the asking price of $4,000 and once again owned his schooner. Rummaging around in the boat yard, he found booms, sails, anchors, chains, the windlass, some blocks and running rigging, and her binnacle and wheel, the latter hidden in the grass by someone who thought it would make a fancy chandelier. No engine, though.

MacMillan, then a retired rear admiral and more than 70 years old, spent the summer of 1945 putting his vessel back together, commuting daily into Boston from Provincetown, more than a hundred miles each way. He had the Cummins Diesel Company of Cambridge install a 100-horsepower diesel engine; when the time of reckoning came, the company's president made him a gift of the engine.

By the end of June 1946, the *Bowdoin* was ready to go to sea again.

Helga Knudsen

During the war, the MacMillans acted *in loco parentis* for Helga Knudsen, the daughter of an old friend of theirs, Aage Knudsen. Through the MacMillans, Helga met a young medical doctor, Ed Morse, and in 1946 they were engaged to be married. In years to come, the Morses would be a very important part of the *Bowdoin*'s life. But how Helga, in particular, came to join the *Bowdoin*'s family is a story in itself.

Helga Knudsen's father was the Regional Governor of Greenland when she was born in Godhavn, Disko Island, in 1923. She grew up there, driving dog teams and doing all the things young people did for amusement above the Arctic Circle, until she was old enough to go off to school in Denmark. In 1940, when the Germans invaded Denmark, Helga was seventeen years old. In order to rejoin her parents in Greenland, she embarked on the kind of journey movies are made about.

Brazenly, Helga approached the German authorities, knowing they didn't want people around who couldn't support themselves. They granted her permission to leave Denmark, but only if she first went to Berlin for three weeks' observation. Helga went to Berlin as directed, where every part of her was stripped and searched. The Nazis checked her clothes as well, but neglected her coat where, stitched in a sleeve cuff, she had hidden photographs of the "peaceful" German invasion, which showed the sky blackened with airplanes of the German Luftwaffe. Afraid that the inspectors would think of the coat later and take it apart, Helga drew the inspectors' attention to that as well, and they checked it perfunctorily, without finding the contra-band photographs.

After the required three weeks in Berlin, the young girl took a plane across France. When the plane made a stop in unoc-cupied France, she hadn't the required papers, so she hid in the plane's bathroom. Again she escaped capture and continued on to Barcelona, where she was to have taken a plane to Lisbon — but it crashed coming in.

It seemed that everyone in Europe was trying to get to some-place else; people were waiting months for transport out. For-tunately, Helga's father knew someone in Barcelona who helped her get train accomodations to Lisbon. The train was packed with all manner of people (and lice) and there was no way to know who was Gestapo and who wasn't. Every twenty minutes the train stopped and everyone had to disembark to be inspected.

Helga made it to Lisbon, but had no connections there. The porters at the railroad station wore hats with hotel names on them, so Helga selected her hotel by choosing the porter who looked the friendliest. By good fortune, she chose well. One day, after several weeks of unsuccessfully trying to get passage to the United States, the only way to reach Greenland, Helga was sitting in the lobby of the hotel when she noticed a man looking at her as he went by the window. He walked by again, still looking at her. Again, a third time, he passed. He came into the hotel and talked with the desk clerk, who glanced up at Helga and nodded. The stranger approached Helga. "You're Miss Knudsen, aren't you?" Reluctantly, she said, "Well, if you're so sure you know who I am, who are you?" Upon being told that he was Commander Fairbanks of the United States Coast Guard, Helga broke into tears of relief, embarrassing the commander mightily.

A few weeks earlier, Fairbanks had been in Greenland and Helga's father had shown him her picture. Now in Lisbon, Com-mander Fairbanks had specifically been looking for Helga. He took the pretty young girl to his ship where she was well enter-tained by the crew. They took her dancing and she had a great time. And through Fairbanks she met officials from one of the passenger lines, who arranged passage for her to New York that winter.

"I was met in New York by the Danish consul, who ensconced me in this thing on Fifth Avenue with mirrors on every wall and chairs trimmed with gold. It was huge apartment, and people would come from the Greenlandic delegation and take me out to lunch. In winter there was no way to get to Greenland, but before a month was out, I'd had it."

Miriam MacMillan, who had known Helga's parents for years from the *Bowdoin*'s trips to Greenland, had written to Helga in Denmark telling her if she was ever in the U.S. to come and visit. So Helga called Miriam in Provincetown, and accepted an invitation to visit the MacMillans for a week. She never left until spring, when she could finally reach her parents in Greenland.

It was while Helga was in Greenland that summer of 1942 that Dr. Edward Morse first wrote to her. Mac and Miriam had told Morse's father, their dentist, of Helga, thinking Ed might like to meet her. Today, Morse confesses he wasn't very enthusiastic about the idea. "She never answered, anyway," he says.

Helga returned to the United States in the fall; the MacMillans had arranged for her to attend Oberlin College. Morse says he had to have a look at this girl who hadn't answered his letter, so while Helga was in Boston before she started college, he asked her out. They went to dinner — at the Café Rouge at the Statler — and to the Ice Capades.

When Helga arrived at Oberlin, her talent for playing bridge in almost any language stood her well. The first weekend she was on campus, she joined a dorm bridge game and enjoyed the opportunity to become more fluent in English. On Monday, she met with the Dean of Women, a proper lady dressed in tweeds, with her hair carefully arranged, to plan Helga's courses. One of the classes Helga hoped to take conflicted with another.

"Oh shit," said Helga.

"I beg your pardon?" the Dean said in horror.

Helga obligingly repeated the remark. The Dean was silent a moment, and then asked, "Do you know what that means?"

"Oh yes," Helga assured her.

"Tell me what it means."

"It means 'too bad,' " said Helga.

"You go back to your dorm, and find out what it means, literally. You know what I mean, literally?"

"Well, it made me," she says today. "I was the only one who'd ever said that to the Dean."

Dr. Morse joined the Army and Helga continued her studies at Oberlin; they saw each other on vacations and during his leaves, and their relationship developed. Morse proposed to Helga by phone from Germany. "In those days, you had to plan a long distance call a week in advance. The phone company would arrange that the person you were calling would be there, and you'd make your call at that certain time." Morse smiles, thinking back. "Miriam always kidded Helga—Helga suspicioned what the call would be, so she got all dressed up for it."

In 1946, Helga, engaged to be married, was torn between going to Denmark, where her parents happened to be, and sailing with the MacMillans on their maiden, post-war trip. The *Bowdoin* won.

(So often, throughout her life, people have connected to the *Bowdoin* in random but recurring ways. In 1942, as part of his Coast Guard duty, Commander Fairbanks, Helga's rescuer in Portugal two years earlier, worked on the *Bowdoin* at Lawley's yard prior to her trip to Greenland under Stu Hotchkiss's command.)

The Vacationers

On June 29, 1946, the *Bowdoin* left Boothbay Harbor on a 35-day shakedown cruise north to Labrador. Instead of his usual student crew, MacMillan had a mixed group, with only two paid members: the engineer, whose services were donated by his employer, Cummins Diesel Company, and Clayton Hodgdon, the cook, who was just off a pair of Navy tours and wasn't sure he wanted to go to sea again. Among the other "idlers" – those members of the company who didn't pull watch duty – were "Sparky," whose duty was to man the radio, Miriam, Helga Knudsen, and Mac himself. The two mates' positions were held by former naval officers with sea experience. The medical man, Guy Abbate, had sailed on the *Bowdoin* as Chief Pharmacist's Mate for nearly three years during her time as a Navy vessel.

The rest of the crew were "vacationers," people taking breaks from their normal lives. They included the presidents of two companies, the vice presidents of Oberlin College and a bank, a museum director, and a representative of the Audubon Society. Two were more than seventy years old—as was MacMillan himself. Another was seventeen, ready to start college in the fall. (He got chain locker duty. Perhaps that's why he was taken along.) All of the vacationers contributed to the cost of the trip, and they enjoyed their voyage, filled as it was with good-natured harassment and teasing, although each needed reminding from time to time that he was on vacation, especially when he was awakened at 4:15 A.M. or took his turn as Scullion-of-the-Day.

Each of the group felt the same excitement from the same sights and experiences that past *Bowdoin* sailors had felt and others would feel in the future, but Mac admitted at the time that leaving Boothbay in his reborn schooner was the greatest thrill of his life. The vacationers had their share of adventures, though. The first was rescuing a pair of young and very nauseated stowaways from the crow's nest on the way to Monhegan Island.

Helga remembers clearly the white faces of the stowaways. They weren't just seasick, they were limp, they were so weak. It was a job to get them down from the crow's nest, and the barrel had to be cleaned up. "The young men did that," Helga says with relief, "the very young men." (A few years ago, Helga was at a cocktail party and a man came up to her. "I think we've met before," he said. She didn't remember him. "I was one of the stowaways on the *Bowdoin* in 1946," said he.)

Helga and Miriam shared Miriam's bunk on the port side of the after cabin. "It was almost a double," Helga says. "It was a little close, but that was all right." Miriam kept calling to Helga to come see this iceberg or that one, but to Helga, who had grown up in Greenland, icebergs weren't worth putting down her book for. Helga remembers going fishing at St. Mary Harbor: "The salmon were making their run—they'd go up and bash their heads against the stone—there were dead ones coming down. It was fascinating." She remembers the mosquitos, too. The people in the fishing party were covered from head to toe with insect-protection clothing. "We were four mosquito-people," she says. "You could look at one of us and say, 'I think that's so-and-so....'" Despite all the precautions, one of the company had an allergic reaction and became very ill from being bitten.

The trip was the inspiration for much doggerel verse that celebrated, among other things, the captain, seasickness, and the over-exuberance by members of one watch who were not properly respectful of the other watch's desire for sleep. The trip had surprisingly little foul weather, although they met the ice pack further south than Mac ever had at this season before, which limited their northern range at two-thirds of the way north along the Labrador, 58° 30', Saglek Bay.

About their return to Maine, Clayton Hodgdon says, "It was the first time I'd come in on a ship and not been glad to get the hell off it." And, in fact, he was a fixture on the rest of MacMillan's trips with the schooner. But the significance of the trip was that it showed that the *Bowdoin* was ready to go back to work.

NINE

Dr. Edward Morse

*S*OON AFTER SHE RETURNED from her trip on the *Bowdoin* in
the fall of 1946, Helga Knudsen and Ed Morse were married. Nine months later, Dr. Morse left for Greenland on
the *Bowdoin* himself, as Ship's Physician. MacMillan always wanted
to offer something to the communities he visited; medical exper-
tise was one such offering. He had taken a doctor or pharmacist
with him on some earlier trips for the same reason.

Ed's father gave him a crash course in field dentistry and
supplied him with a set of extraction instruments and elevators.
Morse packed a surgical kit adequate for emergency appendecto-
mies, first aid supplies, and medicines: antibiotics, novocaine,
ether, ophthalmic ointment and sulfa drugs.

The scientists in the ship's company included a botanist, a
geologist and two ornithologists. Of course, Miriam was also
along. There were to have been four professional crew members,
but the first mate didn't show up at embarkation time; MacMillan looked at his watch, said "We go," and go they did. At first the
engineer doubled as first mate; later, one of the others took over.
There were a few college students aboard, as usual, for a total
of fifteen.

As always, every member of the group pulled his share of
ship duty. Even though few of the men had much sea experience when they came aboard, they all became sailors with Mac's

119

support. When each man stood at the wheel for the first time, Mac stayed close by and, without appearing to pay any attention, quietly gave guidance when necessary. Morse says Mac never raised his voice in anger, even when a serious mistake was made—and in return, the boys did all they could to earn the captain's respect. "Every once in a while," Morse says, "you meet someone who's such a good teacher you just don't want to do anything to make him unhappy. If Mac clammed up, if he didn't speak to you for a day, you knew you'd done something wrong."

Dr. Morse tells one of many stories about Mac's intimate knowledge of the Labrador coast. Passing through a bay, with a chain of islands outside them and the mainland to port, there was a single rock visible in the middle of the bay. As he went below, MacMillan told his helmsman, "Watch for the ledge."

"Right," said the helmsman, but after a moment he wondered why Mac would have mentioned such an obvious hazard. Perhaps there was another one, less visible. He called down to the captain, "Where was that ledge you were talking about?"

Crack!

"You're on it!" came back the response.

A common evening occupation for the men in the fo'c'sle was thinking up a controversial question about Greenland or perhaps a previous voyage and then to call on Mac to come forward to set things straight. Once the skipper was in the fo'c'sle, it was easy to keep him talking, and there was no better way to pass time aboard ship. Mac was a dramatic story teller. His hands became World War II planes landing on the ice field, represented by the butter sitting before him on the table. Without particularly noticing, he wiped the grease off his hand and continued his tale. Another of his stories was about ships during the war; the ketchup bottle on its side became a part of the action. One of the boys, seeing ketchup running out onto the table, tipped the bottle back up, but Mac immediately put it back on its side; it was part of the story, and ketchup one place or another wasn't important.

The first of Dr. Morse's medical calls was on the way up the

Labrador in early July. The *Bowdoin* was at anchor when a couple of fishermen rowed over from a nearby schooner. "Have you a doctor aboard?" they asked—a 12-year-old boy on their vessel had a metal splinter in one eye. They weren't going home to Newfoundland until September and they were worried about the boy. Dr. Morse went back with them to the fishing vessel; below, the stench of fish was strong, the light was poor, and there lay a young boy, eyes shut. The boy's eye was inflamed, and the pain was so bad he couldn't move his eyeball. There was nothing Dr. Morse could do where the boy lay, so they took him back to the *Bowdoin*, and lay him down in the after cabin. Miriam held a flashlight, they anesthetized him, and with a scalpel Morse removed the splinter. He was concerned about the filthy conditions the boy was returning to, but gave him a tube of eye ointment, and told him to keep putting it in his eye until the tube was gone.

A couple of years later, the *Bowdoin* was again anchored in a cove on the Labrador near a fishing schooner. Fishermen again rowed over in a dory asking if there was a physician aboard. In the dory was the boy Dr. Morse had treated; he had recognised the *Bowdoin* and wanted to thank the doctor and let him know he was fine. Mac accepted the message on Morse's behalf and passed it along when he got home.

In Greenland, Dr. Morse treated a newborn baby for an infected navel, an ordinary enough problem, but the baby was extraordinary; it was Matt Henson's grandchild. (Matt Henson was the African-American dog-sled driver who had accompanied Peary on his final assault on the North Pole in 1909.)

Morse recalls that the 1947 trip had its share of sailing adventures, too. One clear day, the *Bowdoin* was under way well off the coast of Greenland. Dr. Morse was in the galley with some of the others when, out of nowhere, they heard a distinct "thump." Another wave and another "thump." One more "thump," and then it was over. They went up to see what had happened, but there was nothing to see. They had struck a submerged ledge. The fathometer had shown plenty of water before and after, but there it was. "Mac just marked it on the chart," says Dr. Morse.

Crossing the Arctic Circle was celebrated as usual with whistles and fog horns and shotgun rounds; Miriam dropped a sealed bottle overboard from the Arctic Circle with a note in it. The following May, the note was returned to her from the Orkney Islands off northern Scotland, 2,200 miles away.

They stopped at Refuge Harbor, where the schooner had spent the winter of 1923–1924. Miriam was thrilled to find the foundation of the scientific station, as well as cutlery and tin cans left from the expedition so many years before. She even found the record Mac had left in a cairn that year.

They kept on northward. In Melville Bay, which Scotch whalers called the "dreaded" bay—between 1819 and 1853, 210 vessels went down there—with at least subdued light even in deepest night, they were able to travel around the clock despite bergs, growlers and pack ice, until fog descended upon them. They ran the ice anchor out to a close iceberg to await clearing. But the fog let up before long, and they were off again.

The *Bowdoin* got further north on this trip than she ever had previously, to 11 degrees from the North Pole, but Mac was disappointed that again, as in 1923, he couldn't make Cape Sabine. The ice pack in Smith Sound was solid for 20 miles. Indeed, escaping the ice took more than two days, as it seemed to be coming in on them from all directions. The midnight sun no longer with them, they had to tie up to an ice pan overnight; in the morning, Mac calmly said, "If the wind had turned easterly. . . we might have been in Baffin Bay for some time to come."

As always, the *Bowdoin*'s crew enjoyed their contact with the Inuit. Morse describes a night at Nugatsiak when a few of the schooner's crew were ashore wandering around by themselves. They noticed people straying into a wooden building, bigger than the few others in the village. "What's going on here?" they wondered, and walked in. It was a big, barren room with only a few Inuit standing around; at the far end there were some musical instruments. The men from the *Bowdoin* stood at one end and the Inuit at the other. No one said anything, so the *Bowdoin* people started singing songs. They sang one after another, with the Inuit watching them, deadpan. They sang everything they could think of, including Christmas carols and even the Halo shampoo ad song, all with no response from the Inuit. Finally, they sang "Old MacDonald Had a Farm," complete with quacks and oinks and moos. Their audience cracked up. They doubled over in laughter, holding their stomachs because they were laughing so hard.

Then it was the Inuits' turn. One stood up in front of the rest, holding out his hands like a formal conductor, and they broke into four part harmony. It was absolutely beautiful. They sang several songs, and the *Bowdoin*'s people applauded each one.

Miriam and a couple more of the fellows from the *Bowdoin* came along as the Inuit picked up their instruments and started playing lively dancing music. Everyone danced, Inuit and *Bowdoin* people alike, changing partners constantly and bounding about joyously.

When the *Bowdoin*'s company left for the schooner, all of the Inuit filed out after them and lined up along a high cliff overlooking the harbor. From there they sang and sang and sang to the schooner, until the people aboard wondered if they would ever stop. The ship's company waved and cheered from the deck and then went below. Only then did the Inuit stop the serenade and go home.

Two Inuit from Thule were aboard the schooner for a couple of weeks, Kahda and Sorkak. During their stay, Morse says that one of the scientists found what he considered to be a true treasure and brought it back to the schooner, where he showed it all around. "Look, an Auk embryo," he said proudly. The scruffy little dead thing was recognisable as a bird, its feathers visible, wet and matted down, but Kahda kept making some kind of unintelligible and negative noise. The professor took the embryo over to Kahda, and tried to explain in very simple English what he had found. "Look. Baby Auk. Not born yet."

Kahda still was not impressed. Finally, quietly, the Inuit man went to one person after another, saying clearly and in English, "Fox shit!" Morse says it was the only English he ever heard Kahda speak.

Miriam used the latest recording technology, a wire recorder, to record the language of the Polar Inuit, providing much amusement for both the *Bowdoin*'s people and the Inuit, as well as documenting their speech patterns for MacMillan's continuing dictionary work.

Morse reports being impressed with the Inuit ingenuity in fixing things. He saw a fellow with a pair of Navy binoculars which had been thrown away because of a broken part; that part had been replaced with ivory, and the glasses looked as if they had been originally designed with that ivory piece.

But as he reflects back forty-five years later, the most impressive aspects of the trip to Dr. Morse were the history and geology of the land. It's all very well to know that Owl's Head, Maine, where he now lives, used to be under a half mile of ice, or to look around at the effects of the glaciers on New England, but in Greenland, Morse was awed to see the glaciers still at work. The boulders were still coming down. In one place he saw three levels of beaches, each separated from the next by rock formations. Huge dikes rose up where mountains had split and igneous rock erupted through.

It was hard enough for Dr. Morse in the 1940s, when the radio didn't work half the time, and there was no one coming to rescue you if you got in trouble, to imagine the hardships faced by the early Arctic explorers or even the *Bowdoin*'s early days. But from the perspective of the 1990s, even the difficulties he faced in 1947 seem real. "You felt as if you were really getting to the frontier. It's hard for a young person to do today," Morse says. "The *Bowdoin* is a symbol, and shaped my life."

TEN

The Last Years Together

The 1950s

*I*N THE SUMMER OF 1950, the *Bowdoin* finally reached Cape Sabine. For more than 25 years, Mac had wanted to take the schooner to the site of the Greely party's last habitation. The coast looked different in summer (Mac had only been there in the winter), but the schooner had little trouble approaching through the moving ice. Mac, then 75 years old, guided the vessel in from the ice barrel and came down to the deck by sliding down the throat halyard to the foreboom. They landed at the remains of Greely's hut, 67 years after the Greely party was rescued. The ground was still littered with reminders of those soldiers' lives: boots, clothing, tin cans, camping equipment. The bronze tablet Mac had installed in 1924 looked like new.

As Mac and Miriam stood looking at the tablet, thinking of the few piteous men who had been rescued from this very spot so long ago, a whistle was heard from the *Bowdoin*. They rushed back to the shore.

The schooner was surrounded by an ice pack which extended as far as they could see. It had moved in on her in just 20 minutes. Mac jumped from ice pan to ice pan until he reached the schooner, with Miriam behind him and the boys who had gone ashore behind her, dragging the dory. It was clear that the *Bowdoin* might be crushed against the rocky shore. As they clambored up the side, Mac ordered, "Give her full speed, cramp your wheel to port." The schooner crept forward. Mac brought her in as close to the shore as he dared, in the lee of a little point. There they dropped anchor again, with the engine still turning over, and swung the *Bowdoin* one way and the other to avoid the heaviest pans as they came in on them.

Low tide brought another worry—a ledge appeared just off the port quarter. If the wind switched to the northeast, the *Bowdoin* would be gone. Would she join the *Polaris*, the *Proteus*, the *Advance*, the *Windward* and the *Fram*? Mac hummed, which Miriam knew he did only when he was worried. But they were saved by an iceberg, of all things, which grounded on a ledge just to seaward of the *Bowdoin*, protecting her from the rest of the pack.

They made one unsuccessful attempt to get out, took a break for one watch to have supper, and tried again. This time, with the engine again fully revved up, the *Bowdoin* slowly pushed her way through the ice. She took one good whack—down below, Clayton wondered, "Who in hell is at the wheel?" but he kept dishing out food. The schooner's hull sprung so there was a six-inch gap between it and a bulkhead—but in a few days she had brought herself back into shape. Mac knew no steel vessel could have made such a recovery.

The rest of the trip was less exciting, although they couldn't get into the usual harbors along the Labrador coast because of ice. Mac had to keep the *Bowdoin* outside and head south in Davis Strait, unprotected. The sea was rough; everything not tied down crashed from one side of the boat to the other, eggs broke and people were banged black and blue. But the *Bowdoin* got home ahead of schedule. As the schooner lay safely at the dock in her winter berth in Boothbay Harbor, Mac and Miriam relaxed in the after cabin listening to the radio. They heard that a full gale off the northern coast had taken the lives of several vessels.

Jim Stevens of the Goudy and Stevens boatyard in East Boothbay was five years old when the *Bowdoin* was launched at the Hodgdon Brothers yard next door. He was closer to thirty when he first became involved with the schooner when, after the war, his yard started doing repair work on the *Bowdoin* for Mac-Millan. Although MacMillan was well into his seventies, Jim says that MacMillan still had the same routine with the schooner he'd always had. When he came back from the north, Mac would leave the *Bowdoin* just as she was for the winter, and he would scurry around fund-raising for the next voyage. It wasn't until he had gathered enough money that he would arrange to get the boat ready. "He'd make all the schedules and plans and wouldn't know the bottom of the boat wasn't there," chuckles Jim. "By the time we hauled her, his schedule had gotten narrower and narrower."

Before one of Mac's last trips, Jim relates, "we hauled the *Bowdoin* to discover that the shoe, three-quarter-inch plate iron, was bent right around flatwise, the hard way, at right angles, sticking six feet off to one side. And all the wooden shoe and keel underneath was gone." Stevens was surprised that the schooner hadn't taken on water after she ripped off so much of her bottom. He remembers being up in the blacksmith's shop in the middle of the night, pounding that piece of iron back out. "We hauled her late in the afternoon — there were five of us working then — and the next morning, there was a new piece of wood back in, the shoe was straightened around, she was ready to launch again. MacMillan got his money's worth, that time."

Clayton Hodgdon

Clayton Hodgdon says he doesn't know how he'd feel, seeing her again. "Wouldn't be the same, I'm sure. You know, there at Hawkes Harbor, Labrador, they had that whaling station there, flensing them whales out, it was an awful odor, and you'd get it on your feet and come aboard. Well, that smell never left the *Bowdoin*, not even over the winter — we said then she had the flavor of the Arctic. She wouldn't have that now."

Clayton sailed as steward on all of MacMillan's trips north after the war; he sailed on more of Mac's *Bowdoin* voyages than did anyone but Miriam. "It got to be a habit," he says. "I couldn't think of the boat leaving the dock without me." He talks of Mac-Millan: "He was good to sail for—the first trip, we sailed from Boothbay and headed eastward for Cape Sable. It's hard to make Cape Sable, a strong tide sets you in, and sure enough, just as I was serving out breakfast she struck. She struck hard. Well, I'll tell you, it didn't bother me, I'd ridden on a minesweep and felt those mines detonate right underneath, but she struck hard. I stuck my head out—and right over there," he tosses his head to show us where, "there's sheep blatting at me in the fog. Sheep! I could hear Seal Island blowing, Seal Island fog horn, and I said to the engineer, give her all you've got, and she'll come off, and he did, he gave her all she had, and she come right off."

Clayton describes MacMillan appearing and saying easily, conversationally, "Clayton, we could have lost her," and Clayton thought to himself, "Well, if you're so easygoing, I'll sail with you." And Mac truly was easygoing. "Had to be, to get him out of trouble—he was in trouble a lot, rocks and ledges and all. . . ."

He admits that he thought Mac was a little too casual about things sometimes. "One time, we were heading for Halifax Light Vessel, it was midnight and foggy, and suddenly you can hear this big wheel turning—there was a big Belgian freighter running for that light too, damn near run us down. If she'd gone down, she'd've gone down like an arrow, all that weight forward," he says. "I always thought if she struck an iceberg, what I'd do, I'd run on deck, cut the lines off those dories and get in one." Did they have abandon ship drills or any kind of drills? "No, we didn't do drills. Those boys were good, they become seamen just a few days out to sea, standing watches and all, they learned the ropes."

Clayton smiles as he remembers Mac's storytelling talents. "He was quite a storyteller, bullshitter. Yes, he kept everybody happy, kept them looking, they might see a polar bear or something. . . . We did see a polar bear swimming one time, a mother bear and her cub. They swam right along beside us, miles out to sea—we could tunk that cub on the head with the log line—he'd swim along, we'd tunk him on the head. . . ."

Storms didn't bother Clayton on the *Bowdoin*. "She'd ride up on those waves, and she'd come down — she'd ride those seas like a duck, God, guess they must have been 20 or 30 feet — 'Course nobody ate anything, so I got a vacation."

Miriam was always aboard when Clayton sailed. "It was good to have her aboard. She was a good sport." After 1946, she stood duties like everyone else and even took her turn as galley slave. "Everybody was alike on board," Clayton says. Everyone but MacMillan and Clayton, that is. Clayton was left to himself to run the galley — he was always below, cooking all the time, "six meals a day, three meals in two shifts each, and those boys, they worked hard, they were hungry. There was hardly any stovetop — that first year, the stovetop was all taken up with the water, and the oven was so small you could only bake two pies at a time. It was a coal stove — burned 3,200 pounds of coal — and on one tack you got quite a backdraft. God, that was an aggravation, you know." Clayton eventually made Mac switch over to an oil-fired stove, which used only a gallon or two of fuel oil a day. He also had a second stack put on, so the backdraft wouldn't bother anyone regardless of which tack the schooner was on. Even so, "That was a lot of cooking. Bake all that bread, pastry, pies, a lot of pots and pans to wash — 'course I had a galley slave, they were all good boys — but that's rugged, day in and day out, I'm telling you, seven days a week, six meals a day.

"You couldn't cook by a menu very well, it might be rough or something — I just cooked for myself, cooked things I liked to cook and things I liked to eat. Just Down East cooking, nothing fancy. Roast turkey, fried chicken — we got a side of beef in Nova Scotia and hung it in the rigging, covered in canvas — 'course the temperature out at sea's ideal to hang a beef, about 30 degrees, and I cut it up when we got to Greenland. Aged just right."

Ed Morse remembers the beef on the '47 trip. It was completely green when it was taken out of the rigging, and most unattractive. "But Clayton scraped it all down — God, he had a know-how. It was delicious."

Clayton says, "We ate a lot of fish: salmon, trout, codfish, halibut, Arctic char. We had a 12 cubic-foot freezer, ran off batteries; as the meat went down I'd fill it up with fish. Yes, I cooked seal, I cooked all that stuff. I cooked a baby polar bear haunch once—it had a real strong smell. We had a couple of Eskimos on board once, they harpooned a walrus, and they cut it up, ate the undigested clams right out of the stomach. Eskimo clam chowder, we called it. I didn't do that. So I cooked a piece of that walrus, the boys tried it—'course it was pretty tough."

Morse describes the "experiment" Clayton pulled, cooking up some whale steak and some beef, and challenging each of the two watches to tell him which they had been served. "None of us guessed we'd all had some of each," Ed says.

Did the boys do what he told them? Clayton says, "Damn right they did. 'Course we was always on the rocks. The milk cans back aft weighted down the stern, so the usual thing was to carry the milk cans forward, weight down the bow, we'd slide right off. So this one time, early in the trip, we ran on a reef someplace, and I stuck my head out of the hatch and said, 'Well, boys, get the milk cans forward,' and one of them said, 'Listen to the cook give his orders, will you? Do we have to do that?' And then along comes the captain, and he says the same thing as me, uses the same words, and after that, they began to respect me."

Did the kids know what they were getting into?

Clayton laughs. "Hard to say. But they knew they'd been somewhere when they got back. . . ."

Clayton sums up: "It was a cold, rough, wet ride, but it was a good experience. We had those scientists, the best in their fields, giving lectures and all—you see, that was the thing, interesting people."

Mac's Final Voyage

MacMillan made his last trip north in 1954 when he was eighty years old. He took the *Bowdoin* to Labrador, Baffin Island, and North and South Greenland. Botanist Rutherford Platt was along for a third trip, as well as Miriam and the usual group of students. The end of that trip, along the Labrador, was perhaps the most dangerous. In a routine check, Mac saw that in a single hour the barometer had dropped an inch. Hurricane Carol was coming.

The *Bowdoin* moved along down the inside passage, though the the wind and seas were high. Surf crashed on the rocks on either side of the narrow passage. At twilight, Platt was at the wheel. Mac quietly gave the command to turn hard to starboard. Despite the apparent suicidal nature of the course, Mac was the captain and obediently, unhesitatingly, Platt turned to starboard, directly into the breakers. Then came an order for hard to port. And again hard to starboard. Through a narrow gap in the rocks that no one but Mac knew was there, the *Bowdoin* passed into a tiny, peaceful little harbor. Mac had been there before, starting 41 years earlier, on his North Pole expedition with Peary, aboard the *Roosevelt*. This was the site of Captain Bob Bartlett's camp. Mac told the boys to look on the rocks; there would be ringbolts they could tie up to, where Bartlett used to tie the *Roosevelt*. And sure enough, there were the rings.

A number of fishing schooners went down that night. But the *Bowdoin* lay peacefully in West Turnavik, waiting out the worst of the hurricane, which had already caused the deaths of 68 people and $500 million of damage as it passed along the New England coast.

Retirement

MacMillan had long been well-respected as being among the most knowledgeable about the local waters on both sides of Davis Strait. It is said that more than once, he led fishing schooners to safe harbor in storms on the Labrador. The *Bowdoin* brought him through one horrific situation after another, and she always was ready for more. Over the years, MacMillan had brought a wind-powered generator to Nain to provide the first electrical power to the village, organs for both the school and the church, a dentist's chair, and 20,000 false teeth. He gave the missionaries the

40-foot power boat *Seeko* which allowed them to travel the coast. Each year she sailed north, the *Bowdoin* brought supplies for the school and the village. But it was time for him to retire.

He wanted to see his schooner taken care of, even though he wouldn't be sailing her. For the next few years, he and Miriam tried to find a suitable home for their beloved vessel. The continuing expense of maintaining her was very difficult for the MacMillans, even though Hume MacDougall of MacDougall Shipyard in Falmouth, Massachusetts, was doing what he could to help. Miriam, in particular, wanted the schooner to be tended for all time. At least one friend of the MacMillans', a long-time supporter of their Arctic work said, "Let her go, she's just an old slab." But they wouldn't give up.

Finally, the curator of Mystic Seaport Museum, Edouard Stackpole, said he wanted the schooner—the museum had recently opened an Arctic exhibit which the *Bowdoin* would nicely complement—but the museum had no money. After a concerted fund-raising effort by a group of the MacMillans' friends and concerned Bowdoin College alumni, enough money was raised to help Mystic with the purchase, and the schooner was sold to the museum in 1959.

Before delivering her, MacMillan replaced a mast, put his sextant and other navigation gear aboard and, in general, fitted out his little schooner as if she were preparing for a trip north. He was determined to give the museum a perfect exhibit. The *Bowdoin*'s presence at the museum would remind visitors of the days when serious exploration and scientific study was done in sailing vessels. In addition, the *Bowdoin* would be maintained.

MacMillan sailed the *Bowdoin* from Falmouth to Mystic himself. Miriam, of course, was aboard, as were Clayton Hodgdon, and Don Mix, the radioman from the 1923–1924 trip. Mix operated his ham radio during the delivery, contacting people all along the coast. At every stop, the *Bowdoin* was honored. In Newport, in the pelting rain, a hundred well-wishers greeted her, including the mayor, the chief of staff of the Newport Naval Base, and all the members of a local boy scout troop. The *Bowdoin* was escorted by a Coast Guard vessel, and by the visiting

Boston Yacht Club Commodore E. Ross Anderson, in his beautiful Alden schooner *Lord Jim*. (Tragically, after the stop in Newport, the *Lord Jim* went onto a reef in dense fog and sunk. MacMillan made sure the people got off, but not much else was saved.)

When the *Bowdoin* arrived at Mystic on June 27, 1959, she was welcomed to the Seaport Museum by a marine parade nearly a mile long. Bands played and speeches were made. "We haven't lost her; we haven't lost the *Bowdoin*," Mac said. "The *Bowdoin* remembers it all, and will be glad to entertain and do what she can to make all comfortable aboard. She knows she is not going out of our life. She is still ours in a way, for we may visit her at any time, go below to our quarters, sleep in our bunks, light up the galley stove, put on the coffee pot, plug in music from home as we did night after night, and imagine that we are again at sea bound north, or returning home following a long trip, with Monhegan again in sight and friends who thought enough of us to come out to sea to welcome us back."

Mystic seemed the perfect home for the schooner.

PART TWO

After MacMillan

ELEVEN

Rescue

Jim Sharp

A T MYSTIC SEAPORT in 1968, priorities had changed since the *Bowdoin* had arrived nine years earlier. A new director was spending the museum's limited funds to emphasize its shoreside aspects; a sail loft and rigging shed had been acquired, and other displays were being developed to illustrate the shorelife of a seaport in earlier days. The Arctic exhibit had been dismantled.

The schooner *Bowdoin* was rotting where she floated. She had been an old lady when she arrived at Mystic, and there had been little or no maintenance performed on her during her time at the museum. She hadn't been hauled in seven years. As her caulking disintegrated, rainwater permeated her interior. The museum closed off sections of the *Bowdoin* as they became too rotten to show, until a woman's spike heel went right through a deck plank. Finally, they closed the *Bowdoin* altogether and covered her in plastic. The cover was left in place all summer, and her timbers steamed and rotted beneath it.

MacMillan was as unhappy as his schooner. She was dying, and he was 93 years old and couldn't do anything for her. He went to the press, letting it be known that if he could liberate the *Bowdoin* from the museum, he would give her to someone who would care for her.

Among the people who became interested in the schooner was Captain Jim Sharp. He was running the old fishing schooner *Adventure* as a windjammer. He had just bought his waterfront property in Camden, Maine, where he wanted to set up a small shipbuilding museum. He was looking for a historic vessel to display on the pier. He and Mac went to Mystic to look at the *Bowdoin*. They found a dismal sight.

The *Bowdoin*'s engine had been removed and was sitting on the shore with the wind blowing through the manifolds. The masts lay in the sand beside a shed, one of them broken. Anything salvageable had been stripped from her. There were holes in her bulkheads where a couple of young men who had been living aboard had "vented" the cabin with a chainsaw. The cabin top had been cut off with a chainsaw when the engine was removed. But although the museum people said she wasn't sound enough to make it across Mystic harbor, Jim and Mac agreed that there was enough left solid on the *Bowdoin* to be worth rebuilding and that she would tow just fine. Her bottom was good; salt water is an excellent wood preservative. The museum, however, was uncomfortable about releasing the vessel directly to an individual.

In the meantime, a group of people in Maine who had sailed on the *Bowdoin* or cared for her over the years had gotten together to try to bring her back to Maine. They didn't know where to take her, or what to do with her, but she wasn't going to be scuttled at Mystic if they could help it. They appointed officers, with Ed Morse as president, and Ed contacted Waldo Johnston, then the director at Mystic. "We have an organization which would be willing to accept the *Bowdoin*," he said.

"What's the name of your organization?" asked Mr. Johnson.

They hadn't considered a name. Ed said the first thing that came to his mind: "Schooner Bowdoin Association." The next day, Ed went to a local printer and had a few pieces of letterhead stationery printed. The officers and members of the organization were listed down the side, and it looked very official. Morse wrote the museum director a letter outlining their proposal. Johnson was impressed. "Little did he know that stationery was all we had," says Ed.

The now-formalized Schooner Bowdoin Association considered another man's proposal for the schooner, but rejected it because he suggested putting a topmast on her. One of the Association members said that would be like putting a mini-skirt on Queen Victoria. Mac was happy with Captain Sharp's plans, and the Schooner Bowdoin Association decided to work with Jim, officially leasing the *Bowdoin* for a dollar a year, with the understanding that Jim would fix her up. Jim paid ten dollars up front for a ten-year lease. He found himself more excited by the prospect of having the *Bowdoin* sailing again than he ever could have been by having her ashore as a museum piece. (Today he realizes his first plans would have been disastrous. He believes that for a wooden vessel to stay healthy, she must be sailing.)

Many of the *Bowdoin*'s bits and pieces were again rounded up, much as they had been after World War II. Her rescuers closed up the holes, installed big pumps aboard, and towed her north.

John Nugent Comes To Town

In the fall of 1967, a few months out of the service, a lanky young man with unkempt-looking hair drove his raggedy-topped Karmann Ghia convertible into the parking lot at the public landing in Camden. He lived there, in his car, near where the *Stephen Taber* was berthed. He had sailed aboard the *Stephen Taber* a number of times as a high school student.

"All my life, I'd been running," John Nugent says today. "I was a timid kid. I had this teacher in fifth grade who would ridicule you if you didn't know an answer, so I started studying hard so I wouldn't make any mistakes. Then, of course, the more tired you get the more time it takes to learn anything, and I was doing sports after school, and studying till one in the morning, and

I ran and ran all my life, until finally it just caught up with me."

When John's mother died, it was the last straw for him. "I didn't tell my father or anyone, I just left. I was going to do or die," he says. A month or so before he showed up in Maine, John had parked—and lived—in Provincetown; when the police started hassling him, he came to Camden, fondly remembering the weeks when he had sailed from that town. He had little money—he budgeted 25 cents a day for food. For breakfast he ate shredded wheat; his other daily meal was a can of hash. "I used to get these headaches, not all the time, but they'd hit me sometimes. My brain would crackle and snap and my eyes ached so I couldn't move them. I'd just have to get out by myself, but sometimes I'd sit in the car and I wouldn't even have the strength to turn the key."

Orvil Young, skipper of the *Stephen Taber*, recognised John, although he didn't look much like the tidy young man who had sailed with him a few years earlier, whose sweaters were always neatly folded in his cabin. "He'd had a kind of a reversal," Orvil says. But it was starting to get cold, and Orvil didn't like to think of him trying to winter in his car, so he asked him to stay on the *Taber*, and John moved aboard.

"That was when I grew my beard," John says. "I didn't trust myself with a razor, and I stopped shaving." This was a time when long-haired young men were looked at with suspicion. John withdrew more and more.

Jim Sharp, whose schooner *Adventure* berthed alongside the *Taber*, remembers how John would stand in the companionway of the *Taber*, the hatch just barely cracked, looking silently out across the harbor, hour after hour.

It was early the following spring, in 1968, that the schooner *Bowdoin* came to Camden, and into John's life.

Family Yacht

Once the *Bowdoin* was in Camden, Jim hauled her to remove the steel plating that Stuart Hotchkiss had applied in 1942 which, after seven years without paint, was rusting and coming loose. Jim scraped off years and years worth of barnacles, too, and Stu's extra sheathing. John Foss, then a student at Bowdoin College and now skipper of his own schooner, the *American Eagle*, remembers volunteering to help. He and a couple of other people wooded the topsides, took off the metal plate where the anchor bears, and helped remove fuel tanks. He says he enjoyed the work, though the specific detail he remembers most vividly was trying to cook lobsters in an electric coffee pot. "Every time it came to a boil, it shut off. It took three hours for the lobsters to turn red. Extended the cocktail hour out a lot."

The next step was stripping a couple of planks from the side to let air pass through the hull. Jim covered the hole with canvas, and over the course of the summer, she dried out so she floated a full inch and a half higher in the water.

John Nugent started doing a little work on the *Bowdoin*, but he would never take any money. "I was too depressed. I didn't want to get into the hassle of taxes and all that—and I didn't feel I could honestly take money, when I didn't know if I could give a day's work. Sometimes I'd get started on something, and I just couldn't keep myself going, I had to stop."

With the advent of the summer sailing season, Jim and the *Adventure* and Orvil and the *Taber* went to sea each week. Jim asked John to stay aboard the *Bowdoin*, as a kind of ship's keeper. John moved onto the *Bowdoin*, taking care of her at the dock until the season was over and the frantic work began.

Jim wanted to get the schooner sailing before MacMillan died. Orvil had worked as a shipwright much of his life, and had always been able to do magical things with wood. A third man, Cappy Quinn, was also on the crew. Cappy had come into Jim's life three years before when Jim was scarfing a new piece of buffalo rail for the *Adventure*. "That's not the way to do that," said an older man walking by.

"Then you come up here and do it yourself," Jim snapped. Cappy Quinn did just that, and worked for Jim on and off for fifteen years, bringing a lifetime's experience with him.

The crew was filled out by John Nugent, who still wouldn't accept pay. He couldn't have had any better teachers in boat building. Together they built a new foredeck and housetop, and replaced the break beam, which runs across the break in the deck. They made a new mainmast, starting by traveling up to Aroostook County to cut a huge Maine spruce. Although the mast was only 72 feet tall, it had to be of such a diameter at the top that a 100-foot tree was required. The tree they found was 185 years old and three and a half feet across at the butt. The crew shaped the mast by hand, first four-siding it with a two-man chain saw, then eight-siding it, then sixteen-siding it, and so on, until it could be smoothed round. After the chainsaw phase, the rest of the work was done by hand.

The original engine was cleaned up and put back into service. Although it was 25 years old, and had been neglected during its stay at Mystic, Jim says, "It never missed a beat."

In 1969 the *Adventure* again called Jim away for the summer. She returned to Camden harbor from her week-long cruises on Saturday mornings. Although most of her crew went home and enjoyed a hot bath and a day away from schooners, one member, Bill Elliott, was cutting out ratlines for the *Bowdoin*. "Come down out of there," Jim would holler to him up in the rigging. "It's your day off!"

"I'm having a good time," Bill would yell back.

"He got her all rattled down during that summer on his days off," Jim says. (Bill, then just out of school, has since gone into full-time shipwright's work. With another man, he runs Bay Ship and Yacht Company in California, the "Boatyard in a Box" from which he has worked on such large vessels as the *California* and the *Sacramento*. He built the 116-foot brig *Niagara* over the course the summer of 1988, a feat unheard of in this day.)

That fall, Jim and his family and Orvil and John and other friends sailed to Provincetown, headed for MacMillan's. "We were coming in through the fog," says Jim, "running a compass course — of course there was great anticipation, we all knew the whole town was just beyond that fogbank. Pretty soon we saw a boat or two at anchor; we knew we were right there, but we still couldn't see anything. MacMillan knew we were coming; he was watching for us all the time, too. All of a sudden — it was like it was God-given — we were running our time out, and the fog just parted like a curtain and we dumped out into the clear blue sky. And we were wing and wing, running towards his house. He came out onto his porch, we jibed the mainsail over and let her luff there a minute, and gave him three long blasts on the horn."

Mac and Miriam were thrilled to see the schooner; tears ran down Mac's cheeks. Jim took the *Bowdoin* into the town dock, where MacMillan and half the town came down to see her. Jim finally had to stop people coming aboard until some got off — "the vessel was going down in the water, you know, and there just wasn't any room on deck to move around."

Within a year, MacMillan passed on.

Back from the trip, Captain Sharp was pleased with how the *Bowdoin* had performed. The schooner was such a handy little vessel, Jim and John could sail her alone. To raise the main, they would each take a halyard and haul until they stalled out. Then they'd cleat the peak off and gang up on the throat halyard, and finally jig it up. Then they'd finish off the peak the same way.

There was still a lot of work to be done, though. Below, she was a mess. They finished off the main cabin enough to set it up as a dockside museum with Arctic artifacts (and a donation box). Jim, Orvil, Cappy and John kept working, and after three years, they finished the interior. The *Bowdoin* was looking good.

By now, John had moved to a barn in Camden, and in the winter of 1969–1970, he started working on the *Mary Day*. He still didn't take money, but the owners of the *Mary Day* arranged for John to get food at a local restaurant. "I'd go up there and get something to eat, and then I'd go to the library and sit there until they closed, and I'd go to the Y and have a swim and a shower, and then I'd go back to my barn, and I'd crawl under my electric blanket — that's all I had for heat — then later I got a light bulb, and I'd study for my Coast Guard license test there, under that electric blanket." In the summers he worked as relief-crew on the Camden schooners the *Mattie*, *Mercantile* and *Mary Day*. He finally contacted his father, who then cancelled the Missing Persons Report he had filed three years before. A 13-state alarm had been out for John, but this was the first he knew of it.

Before and after the *Adventure*'s season each year, Jim took his family cruising on the *Bowdoin*, with John along as crew. They eventually covered most of the coast from the Chesapeake to Halifax, Nova Scotia. They sailed late every fall, coming home around Thanksgiving. The *Bowdoin* had become a family yacht.

Jim speaks of the schooner with great respect and affection, though he doesn't describe her as always being a restful boat. "She was like a young colt in a seaway," he says, "but she'd always bring you home. I remember when my son Zeb was about six months old, we were crossing the Bay of Fundy. The *Bowdoin* was like a bucking bronco, kicking up her heels, and there's little Zeb below, as green as he can be, but there's nothing you can do for the little feller." His boys, though, grew up on the *Bowdoin*. "Topher, he learned climbing the rigging. He'd climb the ratlines all the way up to the masthead on the main, jump on the peak halyard when the sail was furled, and slide back down. My heart was in my mouth, but you can't stop them."

The Sharp family and John sailed the coast of Nova Scotia, stopping at every little harbor along the way. "We came to Lunenburg on one of those perfect days," says Jim. "We had the wind offshore, and we were under full sail; I had the engine in neutral just ticking over, just in case something happened, and we sailed the whole length of all the old fish docks, where they used to have all the sailing vessels. 'Course there weren't any sailing vessels any more, they're all draggers now, but all the old fishermen remembered the days of sail. So we sailed up along the docks, skimming right by the pierheads, one right after another, looking at all the boats and all the sights, all the way to the head of the harbor, and we spun her around and sailed her back again. Well, we had so much fun doing that we turned around and did it all over again. And then weren't they buzzing, all the old fishermen on the docks. And they came down and said afterwards, 'Oh my God, I ain't seen a sight like that for 35 years.'"

On one trip to the Chesapeake they broke the main gaff in

an accidental jibe. The nearest safe haven was the AFL-CIO trade school at the mouth of the Potomac River. There were signs all around warning people to stay away; the school was fenced and patrolled by dogs. It was not a welcoming dock. But there they were. Met by a fierce-looking fellow, Jim explained his emergency. "You better go see Tony," he was told gruffly. Jim went to see Tony. Tony was a big, tough, well-dressed Italian with a big belly and a big cigar. Jim again told his story. And Tony told Jim to go down and see Lou at the shop and "tell him Tony said 'fix-a dat gaff.'"

"They treated us like kings," says Jim. "Not only did they fix the gaff, and they did a beautiful job—they used stainless steel bolts and stainless steel angle iron—but they wined and dined us for two more days."

Jim used the *Bowdoin* as a work vessel as well as a pleasure yacht. She towed the engineless *Adventure* and *Stephen Taber* to and from their winter berths, and while Jim was also working on his wharf, he used the *Bowdoin* to salvage flotsam out of the bay. He knew just where everything would float onto the islands off Camden after a storm, and he'd go out, tie a hitch around a few good heavy salt-soaked logs, and drag them home to use in the wharf. "She was so handy you could pound nails with that boat," he says.

In 1971, Jim hired Alan Talbot to take private charters on the *Bowdoin* during the summer season, and for four years the *Bowdoin* brought in a little money to keep herself up. But the relations between Jim and the Schooner Bowdoin Association weren't easy. In 1975, Orvil Young and Jim bought the schooner *Roseway*, and Jim let the Association take the *Bowdoin* back; they returned the three or four dollars prepaid on his lease. But Jim and his family had had a wonderful time aboard the schooner. "If she'd been mine," he says, "I'd be sailing her to this day."

TWELVE

The Interim Years, 1975-1979

Dismasting!

ROGER BRAINARD AND his partner, Carl Chase, having just bankrupted their schooner *Nathaniel Bowditch*, chartered the *Bowdoin* for the 1975 season to do their scheduled weeklong educational programs for youngsters. Carl's younger brother, Andy, was first mate. Looking back on it, the highlight of the season for Andy was the dismasting.

"We were off Isle au Haut with a load of passengers one sloppy, rolly sort of a day," Andy says. "There wasn't all that much wind—but the mainmast broke right at the cross trees." It was the mast Jim Sharp had so painstakingly built not so many years before. "There was a defect in the wood, there—you couldn't see it," Andy explains.

"The top of the mast fell down, and hung up on a piece of rigging. The main boom came down WHANG right between some people—and a serious chunk of wood fell right near Roger, he was near the base of the mast—but nobody was hurt." Andy was sent up the mast as far as he could climb. "I set some spikes in the mast, and tied mooring lines aft and forward onto the windlass—we cranked those up to secure it so we could get in someplace. We went into the harbor at Isle au Haut and unlaced the foresail from the gaff. Then they hoisted me up in a bosun's chair dangled off the gaff, with the main sheet tackle." He went up as if he were on a derrick, until he could reach the broken top of the mast. He attached the tackle to it, which was then led forward to the windlass. "It was a one-inch line, and we hauled on it till it stretched so much it was almost unrecognisable, but the mast didn't budge, there was so much weight on it with all the rigging pulling on it." But it did seem that the mast wasn't going to fall further, so they steamed in to Billings Marine at Stonington. "They almost maxed their crane out, taking that out. With all the rigging and everything it was phenomenally heavy," Andy says.

Roger hired a lobster boat for the rest of the week, and took the kids out to islands to investigate natural life there. Andy says, "Roger was very pleased that he could keep the program going. But more amazing was how fast Billings fabricated a new mast. They made up a steel mast, it was just a steel pipe, half the diameter of the real mast—it looked like hell, but it worked. And I think they had it ready for the next week. Maybe we missed a week—but I don't think so." It was everyone's intention to just get through the season with the steel mast, but when the schooner returned to Schooner Bowdoin Association the following spring, there wasn't any money to replace it, so the *Bowdoin* kept that ugly mast Billings had made so quickly.

Schooner Bowdoin Inter-Island Expeditions

In 1976, the Schooner *Bowdoin* Inter-Island Expeditions was formed under Ed Morse's leadership to run educational programs. Morse asked Jim Sharp if he knew someone who might suit as skipper of the *Bowdoin*. "John Nugent," said Jim.

John had by then obtained his captain's license and had run the little windjammer *Mistress* for a couple of seasons. He certainly knew the *Bowdoin*, and the Morses liked him. "There was something about John," the Morses say. "He was just aces." John accepted pay for his captaincy of the *Bowdoin*—it wasn't much, but it was more money than he had seen in years.

The program brought students aboard the *Bowdoin* to sail and introduce them to marine biology, botany, and ornithology. For a time, part of the program took place on small, isolated Butter Island in Penobscot Bay, where the youngsters learned about self-sufficiency, too.

One of the educators aboard the *Bowdoin* was Wes Hedlund, who later would be the runner-up for Christa McCauliff's spot on the ill-fated 1986 Challenger space flight. "We would pull into a harbor," John says, "and Wes would dive and bring up all kinds of stuff you never knew existed." He also could take advantage of circumstance. "We came into Campobello Island with the kids — we were doing some educational thing on the dock — and a couple of fisherman come over asking if we wanted a sturgeon. It was eight feet long. I didn't know what a sturgeon was. Well, first Wes dissected that thing on the dock. And we had a freezer, so we ate sturgeon steaks for three weeks."

After a season with the steel mast that had been installed at Billings, someone convinced the Weyerhauser Company to donate a proper mast for the schooner. The company produced a western spruce log; Potlatch turned it on their lathe, and it was delivered to Thomaston, Maine, along with some other masts for schooners in the area. John made the spreaders and the hardware for the rigging. The *Bowdoin* had a new mast.

Maintaining a wooden boat is a constant endeavor. One sunny day on a layover between programs, Cappy Quinn was working with John, just as he had when Jim Sharp had the *Bowdoin*; Cappy was working on staging over a float on the dock side, replacing some bad wood around the hawsepipes. John was on another float on the water side of the vessel. He heard a thud and climbed up over the schooner to see what had happened; he found Cappy very upset because he had dropped a hammer — it had fallen onto the float and then into the water. "No big deal," says John. "I got him another hammer, and we went back to work. Pretty soon there's another thud. 'There goes another hammer,' I thought — maybe I'd better go see if I can console him." When John stood up to peek over the rail, a couple of women on the dock were looking straight down into the water. Cappy had fallen in the water—and Cappy couldn't swim. John could see Cappy a foot or two below the water, spread eagled and flailing around helplessly, so John pulled off his shoes and jumped in. When John came up alongside him, Cappy grabbed frantically at the younger man; John was afraid they'd both be dragged down. John backed off and then dove underneath Cappy to push him up for air. John's clothes weighed him down so that he had trouble staying afloat, but somehow he dragged Cappy back to the float. A couple of guys on the pier had stripped down and gone in to help by then, and they hauled Cappy out of the water. Cappy said later if John hadn't pushed him up for air, he wouldn't have made it.

John always kept his personal life private. He never told anyone his age, or when his birthday was. But one day between trips, John brought the *Bowdoin* into the Morses' dock at Owl's Head, and Ed, Helga and Miriam surprised him with the proclamation that the day was his birthday, and they gave him a party. Every member of the crew was given a T-shirt; John's was marked "Captain Perfect." Wes, who rarely wore anything but his bathing suit, was the "Handsome Mariner," Dana, the mate, was "Pun Sailor," and Brenda, the cook, was "Burning Brenda." "Brenda Littlefield was a live wire," says John. "She had learned somewhere how to fall convincingly. She would come up to the boom and there'd be an awful clunk, and she would fall down as if she were dead—we'd go running over to her, and she'd be laughing." Brenda still ships out on supply ships.

Not long after a major drug-smuggling boat had been sunk on the coast of Maine, John sailed the *Bowdoin* to Canada. Along the way she was observed carefully by the Coast Guard, first at Petit Manan and again further on. Finally, a helicopter hovered above them for a few minutes. When they returned to the States, a jet shot across the bow; it returned, waved its wings at them, and was on its way. They hadn't sailed much further before they were stopped by the *Point Hannon*, a Coast Guard cutter. "It took forever for them to come over—I offered to send someone to pick them up, but they didn't say anything." Fully armed, they came aboard and checked the *Bowdoin* out. Of course they found no contraband. Brenda had just made cookies, and as they finished their search, she asked John if she could give them some. "As long as they don't consider it a bribe," he said. The Coasties were getting back in their boat and cramming cookies in their pockets when Wes leaned over the side. "You'd better watch out for those cookies, they're full of marijuana."

John's heart stopped. He had been on the wrong side of the police too often. Now what? But the Coasties just laughed and went on their way.

Jim Sharp introduced John to Jack Crowell, who had sailed with MacMillan so many years ago and was now living on Isle au Haut. Then, whenever he went out to Isle au Haut, John stopped to say hello to Crowell, or Crowell rowed out to greet John. One year, John and a group of Crowell's friends took the *Bowdoin* out through the densest of fogs to celebrate Crowell's birthday. "I couldn't believe it," Crowell said, "thick o' fog, and all of a sudden there are those masts. I knew right away what it was."

When the television version of "Captain's Courageous" was filmed, John was skippering the *Bowdoin*. "It was a lot of fun," he says. "I never had done anything like it—we had to dress up in different clothes, and there was one scene where the *Adventure*—she was playing the *We're Here*, of course—was supposed to be the first to leave the fishing grounds, so we all had to holler out to her as she left, 'Say hi to my kids' and all that kind of thing. But it didn't make it into the movie.

"That scene where there are all the dories running around, they were all launched off the *Bowdoin*, because we were the only one with the right kind of dories. And in the harbor scenes, we were in the background—we had our sails up, to block some people's boats that the owners wouldn't move—and we had people running up and down the rigging.... They took the whole parking lot, they had oxen there, and they shut Wayfarer Marine down completely. It was quite something. I had dinner with Karl Malden once, at Yorkie's—'course that's not there any more."

John ran the boat for Schooner *Bowdoin* Inter-Island Expeditions for four seasons, maintaining her himself. He bought an aging yellow Beetle (his Karmann Ghia having stopped running years ago), and with a loan from his father he purchased a small house in Camden. He had come a long way from the sad young man who had driven into town nearly 12 years before.

After the 1979 season, Ed Morse and the directors wanted to extend the educational program, but the *Bowdoin* needed a great deal of work to meet increased Coast Guard requirements. The watertight bulkheads which MacMillan had insisted upon in 1921 had been adulterated over the years; pipes and wires were run without nipples, and the lazarette was wide open, with no watertight door. "There were some structural problems as well," John reports, "and since all that work had to be done anyway, we thought we might as well get her right while we were at it. And we wanted to do it before Miriam passed on."

In the fall of 1979, the *Bowdoin* went home to East Boothbay, to Goudy and Stevens. The long saga of the rebuild began.

Song for the Bowdoin

Well, you sailed the cold waters
Of the great northern bays,
Ice thick on your rigging,
Lee rail under the waves,
And the snow on your canvas,
Like a winter gull's wing.
Oh, all the times you've been through.

> *And now you've got hard times,*
> *And now you lie still,*
> *And you're fast to the anchor and chain.*
> *Broken and tired,*
> *Summer winds pass you by,*
> *But you're bound to go sailing again.*

Well, you cleared out of Boothbay
On a gentle south swell;
With the breeze on your quarter,
How that bow rose and fell.
There are those who remember
So much more than they'll tell;
Oh, all the times you've been through.

Greenland and Baffin,
And the white Labrador,
In the winds and the terrible snow,
When they carried their ice picks
Just to bring you about
In the light from the lanterns below.

And now you've got hard times . . .

So rest, lady, rest
From the fog and the gales.
Let the harbor protect you
Let the sun dry your sails,
Let a hundred old sailors
Tell their saltiest tales
Of the hardest of times you've been through.

And we'll see your masts mingle
With the spruces and pines,
And we'll bow as we all pass you by.
For a boat is more patient
Than a sailor can be
When the sun and the wind fill his eyes.

And now you've got hard times . . .

—Words and Music by Larry Kaplan,
© 1976, Hannah Lane Music, BMI

THIRTEEN

The Rebuild—
Part One

Getting Started

GOUDY AND STEVENS HAD maintained the *Bowdoin* during the last years MacMillan sailed her north, and John had been with her since her rescue from Mystic; no one knew her better than Jim Stevens and John Nugent. Together, they surveyed the schooner. "She needed to be scrapped," says Jim. "The building plans were in existence; they should have built a new one." Clayton Hodgdon agrees. "They shoulda just encased her in cement and let her go." But Miriam and the Schooner Bowdoin Association wanted to rebuild the old vessel. John believes that, had things gone smoothly, it would have been far more economical to rebuild her than to start over. In any case, rebuilding was the route chosen.

While the schooner was at the Goudy and Stevens yard, John Nugent lived in Jim Stevens' house, and worked in the yard part time and on the schooner part time. The yard provided a crane to help him unstep the masts, but he stripped the greenheart sheathing and the interior himself, saving cabinet doors to rebuild around.

Although the Schooner Bowdoin Association wanted to leave the schooner at Goudy and Stevens, they couldn't guarantee regular payment and the yard couldn't afford to tie up the ways without a commitment. However, the ways at the Maine Maritime Museum (the old Percy and Small yard) were available, and the museum would benefit from the ongoing display the restoration would provide.

David Short had decided that he wasn't much of a student after a couple of semesters at the University of Connecticut, but he wasn't sure what he'd like to do instead. He had been a winter maintenance volunteer aboard the sloop *Clearwater*, which sails the Hudson River with environmental educational programs, and just when he was searching for an alternative to the classroom, he read in the *Clearwater* newsletter about the Shipwright Apprentice program at the Maine Maritime Museum in Bath. The apprentices would pay no tuition and be paid no wages, although housing would be provided. They would receive training in shipbuilding techniques in return for their labor on the restoration of the *Seguin*, a big steam-powered, wooden tugboat built in 1884 that had worked on the Kennebec River and the coast of Maine until her retirement in 1969.

David joined the apprentice program in the fall of 1979. But due to unforeseen circumstances, the *Seguin* project was first cut back and ultimately dropped, and the apprentices were left with no long-term job. The *Bowdoin* came along at a good time.

While the *Bowdoin* was still in East Boothbay, with the help of men and equipment from Goudy and Stevens, the apprentices at the Maine Maritime Museum prepared for the haulout. They dismantled the huge cradle initially built for the *Seguin*, with its two extra-long steel shoes, and reassembled it for the *Bowdoin*. They sunk a huge deadman in the ground at the head of the ways to rig the hauling tackle.

In September 1980, on the neap tide, two big National Guard bulldozers came to haul the schooner up the skidway. But there wasn't enough water to float her onto the cradle, so she had to stay in the water another month. During that time, David and the other apprentices started working with John Nugent, who became their instructor. Together, they took the lines off the *Seguin* and laid them in the mold loft, where they remain today. In

October, the higher tide allowed the *Bowdoin's* haulout; "She just squeaked out," John says. The month's delay was minor, compared with what was ahead.

John built a plastic cover over the *Bowdoin* by himself, portending times to come. The schooner was rough when she came out of the water, and nearly all of her planking and timbers were to be replaced. John and a gang of apprentices and men from Goudy and Stevens tore the deck off, leaving a few beams and the bulkheads in place for strength; then they started removing frames. With hammers and chisels, the crew pounded and chopped and slashed and ripped, taking out cement ballast and removing every other frame. These were replaced with white oak as originally built, and then the intervening frames were removed and put back anew. David remembers very well being deep in the bilges in the raw cold of midwinter, dressed for the Arctic, digging away at structural materials. Every timber was removed, save those low in the engine room, which were thoroughly oil soaked.

Through the winter they worked, and into 1981 — a paid crew from Goudy and Stevens, John Nugent, David Short and the rest of the apprentices. In the spring, David's apprenticeship was over. He asked to be put on the Goudy and Stevens payroll, but they didn't take him, and he moved on to work in another boatshop.

John continued on the project with the rest of the crew.

That summer David's hand developed serious problems. It turned out that he had broken a bone in his wrist during the winter's demolition on the *Bowdoin*, though with the cold weather and general discomfort at the time, he didn't realize it. After a couple of operations to rebuild his hand, and a period of convalescence, in September of 1981 he returned to the *Bowdoin*. This time he was taken on, technically working for Goudy and Stevens although he never worked in their yard. There was still a good-sized crew of eight or maybe more. They were bending in the sheer clamps, and doing the heavy structural framing and the carrying deck framing.

Whenever Jim Stevens came along, he would create a whirl-wind of activity. "He'd get everyone fired up or aggravated, one or the other," David says. Despite his misgivings about the project, the *Bowdoin* was important to Jim, and he put a lot of his own time and care into the project.

But by November, the Schooner Bowdoin Association was running out of money, and they had to lay off most of the crew. The only people left were John Nugent and, from Goudy and Stevens, David and an older shipwright named Dana McClain. David remembers Dana remarking, "This leaves nothing but a skeleton crew for this job, and I'm the skeleton." Following Dana's lead, John and David had gotten out the shear planks, and the three of them just tried to get by, short-handed as they were.

One Monday in January, Dana didn't show up. He had had a heart attack while shoveling snow. He was dead.

Today, David describes this time as a personal turning point. He was but a novice, and though John had developed considerable skill working on the schooner fleet, he didn't have the lifetime of building experience that Dana had. The job was left in John and David's hands alone, and even if they weren't yet as knowledgeable as they would have liked, they were both committed to the vessel, and they stayed. For nine months, the two of them carried on, planking.

Each plank was heavy white oak, 22 feet long, 2¾ inches thick, and a foot or more wide. Each had to be spiled, shaped, steamed, spiked into place, and treenailed. They'd lay a batten into place along the hull where the next plank would go, marking it as they went along so it stayed straight, and then transpose their marks onto a planed plank. They'd cut the shape of the plank on the band saw, and put it in the steam box.

For every inch of thickness, a plank had to be steamed one hour; therefore, it took nearly three hours to steam each plank. When the plank came out of the steambox, John says it would sag like a noodle. With gloves on to protect their hands from the heat, they would grab the plank and run it into place and spike it as fast as they could, hurrying to get it positioned before it set up. The two of them struggled with plank after plank. When one plank was spiked in place, they'd start the next one steaming and begin shaping the third. They'd crank the yellow pine ceiling planks into place, drill for treenails and, if they had any time left before the next plank was steamed, they'd treenail.

Captain McCorison of Islesboro found locust for treenails on the island, and Ed Morse and John brought it across on the ferry. On weekends John turned the treenails out himself so they always had a supply. John and David treenailed the whole works, pounding each sturdy dowel through holes drilled through outside plank, rib, and ceiling, and wedging it inside and out. (Normally, a half a dozen or so workers would be on a project that extensive.) Day after day, week after week, John and David drove uncountable numbers of treenails. One was driven from the lower side of each plank into the forward timber of the double sawn ribs, and another from the upper side into the after timber. Two treenails every eighteen inches of each plank. Then they finished the deck framing, cut out the covering boards for the bulwark stanchions, and started laying the deck.

"Because it's a boat, which people are going to entrust their lives to, you take any extra care you can," David says. "Day-to-day it's just work, but you do put a lot of thought and energy in that you wouldn't on a house."

But by the end of November, there was no money left. David had to leave. However, the *Bowdoin* had given form to David Short's life; he went on to make his life as a shipwright. He says that before he worked on the *Bowdoin*, he might have chosen an easier profession. Although his hand has never been 100 percent right since his time with the *Bowdoin*, he has since worked on several other vessels: *Spirit of Massachusetts, American Eagle, Natalie Todd* (his first time running the job), *Niagara,* (where he was the owner's representative, overseeing the work of builder Bill Elliot, who had worked on the *Bowdoin* on his days off from the *Adventure* under Jim Sharp), *Mercantile, Mattie/Grace Bailey,* and the *Lettie Howard.*

John stayed on with less than minimal pay because the *Bowdoin* was his life. He had plans for her; they had a future together. (John and David had talked all during their work about taking the *Bowdoin* back to the Arctic when she was finished, with John as captain and David as mate.)

Through the winter of 1982–1983 John worked alone. Although his father had helped him to buy the house in Camden, John couldn't afford to keep it going, so he rented it out and camped in one room of an empty house that belonged to the museum. He finished up the foredecking, getting help where he could. Ed Morse, still president of the Schooner Bowdoin Association, occasionally took time off from his surgical practice to hold the set while John beetled oakum into place. Leaving the *Bowdoin* only a couple of weeks to sail as relief-mate on *Adventure* and *Angelique,* John kept on alone through the summer of 1983, picking away at what he could.

Ginny Sides

Ginny Sides retired to Maine just as the *Bowdoin* rebuild was being planned, and although she had known of the schooner most of her life (she was born in 1922 while the *Bowdoin* was frozen into the ice in the Foxe Basin, during the schooner's first trip north), she became involved through happenstance. Her own path and that of Ed Morse had crossed periodically, first in Waban, Massachusetts, where they both grew up, and later when Dr. Morse was her parents' physician in Maine. Her fund-raising experience included thirteen years of seeking support for Wellesley College. She had also, at one time, led a private girls' school in Pittsburgh, where she chose to be called Head-mistress; the archaic quality of the title amused her. "Everywhere I've been," she says, "I've felt great delight in being able to do something they said couldn't be done, or finding how to do old things in new ways." Ginny Sides was just what the Schooner Bowdoin Association needed.

For four years, while John Nugent shaped and sawed and pounded on the schooner, Ginny Sides and Helga Morse ran the office of the restoration project. Just as if it were a paying job, they went to work every morning. At first, they camped out in the Morses' kitchen, then in the summer living room of Ginny's house, and later in the basement of a bank. They were often helped by two other women, Toni Walter and Vera Hill, but Ginny and Helga, and of course Ed, were the regulars.

Ed says that the application for a matching grant from the National Trust for Historic Preservation was Ginny's work. Ginny, however, takes little credit, pointing to the efforts of Miriam, who dug through her late husband's journals and other writings to find just the right paragraph, just the right thought for each part of the application, and to Helga, who put it all together. It took them several weeks to complete the grant application, but Ginny says it was as if MacMillan himself had written it.

In any case, in 1979 the National Trust gave the Schooner Bowdoin Association $95,000 in matching funds, which spurred on the organization to raise its share. Week after week, Ed Morse and Ginny traveled all over the state of Maine, speaking to Kiwanis Clubs, Rotaries, Garden Clubs, Historical Societies, "anywhere anyone would listen." They showed movies or slides of the *Bowdoin*'s Arctic trips and, Ginny says, "Ed gave very good speeches." They visited individuals, too. Miriam, Ed and Helga went to New York, Washington and Boston, telling the story. Some of Mac's "Boys" from the Portland area gave cocktail parties for potential donors; later, Ginny and Helga wrote to the guests, asking them to consider a contribution. They combed lists of potential donors wherever such lists could be found — people who had made gifts to other local endeavors, or people who had sailed on the vessel, or who had heard MacMillan speak, or who knew the *Bowdoin*'s history, or who were interested in maritime history in general. All in all, they exposed hundreds and hundreds of people to the *Bowdoin*'s story, and many of them contributed, in varying amounts. "What keeps the fund-raiser going," Ginny says, "is not the money, it's the spirit behind the gifts, the belief in something which the gifts represent.

"Fund-raising is just common sense," she continues. "It's not frightening if one has a good story to tell, one can document a need, and one can demonstrate that the project is fiscally responsible and the money will be used for a purpose in which the donor has special interest. It's just matching the interest of a potential donor with the cause. You have to realize that if there is a mutuality of concern, people are willing to help."

Ginny takes pleasure in seeing the mutuality of causes. She approached a widowed friend of hers from Rhode Island. "Her husband had been interested in things nautical, and flags specifically." Although neither the friend nor her husband had a particular connection with the schooner, "I suggested she might like to donate signal flags to the *Bowdoin* in her husband's memory." The proposal pleased Ginny's friend, and the *Bowdoin* received the flags. Larger gifts were solicited with the same approach.

Ginny and Helga also took care of all the day-to-day business of the restoration. "We'd come in at 9 in the morning, often earlier, and read the mail. If anything needed answering, I'd dictate letters and Helga would take them down. We had our own shorthand; I would say 'insert the mari heri paragraph here,' and Helga would put in the maritime heritage paragraph. I'm a lousy typist, so Helga did the typing." Helga managed the finances, too, paying the bills and keeping track of the money. Toni and Vera did some typing and the filing. "Toni kept us organized."

"It's fascinating to me how much the *Bowdoin* experience meant to so many people," Ginny says. Donors came from 39 states and several foreign countries. Although Ginny would never say so, it must have been discouraging when it was clear that the *Bowdoin* needed more money than was coming in. It certainly was exhausting for all concerned. In 1984, 15 years after he had helped the *Bowdoin* return to Maine from Mystic, Ed stepped down as president of the Association, becoming President Emeritus. Not too long later, when the decision was made to borrow the funds needed to finish, Ginny left the project.

And then the *Bowdoin* came into what was probably the most difficult period of her life.

FOURTEEN

The Rebuild—
Part Two

The Irish Mafia

*B*ILL COUGHLIN WORKED FOR *The Boston Globe*, but his father had been a master mariner, and he himself was interested in the sea and in history. "I was always a sucker for schooners," he says today. He was particularly intrigued by the fishing schooners that worked the Grand Banks. He was friendly with Leo Hynes, who had owned the *Adventure*, the last dory trawler fishing the Grand Banks and now Jim Sharp's windjammer. Bill had sailed on the *Adventure*, and had written several articles about her for the *Globe*. He became good friends with Jim Sharp, and aboard the schooner he met John Nugent.

It was Jim who suggested that Bill should take a look at the project John was involved with down in Bath.

So in the fall of 1982, Bill Coughlin drove to Bath to see John and the *Bowdoin*. "I couldn't believe my eyes. All she was was bones. John had built this sucker himself. When you walked up on her everything wobbled and wiggled—she was just frames." John was putting in the horn timber, which was at least twice as long as he is tall. "Here's this 12 by 12 piece of solid oak, handcut with adzes but with perfect precision—he's jury-rigged swings and slings and blocks and tackle to get it in over her rudder all by himself. This is a job that would have taken 30 or 40 men in

160

the original days," says Bill. "I just couldn't leave him there alone. And thus began the odyssey."

Bill started driving up to Bath from Boston on weekends, on his days off and any other time he could manage. "I was head over heels in love with the project and all the people involved in it," he says, and he determined to do whatever he could for the *Bowdoin*. He helped cut covering boards and frames. "John showed me what to do—I was just an overgrown kid who never got boats out of his eyes. John was not only willing to accept your help, but he was also a teacher, kind and gentle, a throwback to the original shipwrights. He was dedicated, honest, truthful, you could trust him in every direction. He was hand-carving the *Bowdoin* back to original condition, based on the original drawings."

The time came, though, when no more progress could be made without a new engine and fuel and water tanks. But Bill had been working his connections, folks who came to be known jokingly as the "Irish Mafia," and to whom he gives more credit than he will take for himself for the effort they made for the schooner. The head of the machine shop at the *Globe*, Jack Quinn, knew someone who had a brand new, 190-horsepower Cummins diesel engine, still in the crate. It was worth $28,000, but Jack and Bill persuaded the owner to give it to the schooner for $4,000. Although it was more powerful, the engine's dimensions were identical to the one that had been in the vessel since 1946, so the transmission and drive shaft would connect easily.

The old engine sat beside the schooner's plastic house; Bill, Jack and John shoveled snow off it to cannibalize parts which they cleaned and fixed up before reinstalling them on the new engine. They reconditioned the transmission. Bill says he wore out a Chevrolet just carrying stuff back and forth to Boston. The completed engine was brought to Bath in a *Globe* delivery truck. But before the engine could be set in place in the schooner, the water tanks had to be put in their place in the bilges underneath the engine.

A company in Taunton, Massachusetts, donated the stainless steel for the tanks, and another of Bill's friends, Paul Martin, built the two new tanks.

It happened that when they were ready to lower the engine in place, the Percy and Small wharf at the museum was being rebuilt and a hoist was there for the job. The operator spent a lunch hour lifting the engine from the newspaper delivery truck and lowering it into the schooner, his boss perhaps never the wiser.

Next came the oddly-shaped fuel tanks which were set in under the afterdeck. Bill and his friends hadn't the skill to replicate the fuel tanks, so John borrowed an old truck, which barely ran, and took the tanks to another friend of Jack Quinn's, Billy Moore, who ran a machine shop in South Boston. Moore built — and donated — new fuel tanks.

By now, the entire Irish Mafia was helping John Nugent with the rebuild. (The "Irish" Mafia also included a Greek, a Boston Brahmin, an Italian, and a German. But the good Irishmen Bill Coughlin and Jack Quinn were the ringleaders.) The gang would drive up on Friday nights in the Buick with which Bill had replaced his dead Chevrolet, and they'd all sleep in John's house in Camden. On Saturday morning, John would wake everyone up at 3:30 or 4:00 and they'd drive back to Bath to go to work on the *Bowdoin.* "Our wives thought we were crazy," Bill says. "They were pretty unhappy about it. Banana-headed husbands." And perhaps that's just what they were. It's how they ended up feeling.

While Jack was scheming how to put the various systems together, designing bilge systems, figuring out how the wiring would be installed as the engine room progressed, and working weeknights on the project down in Boston, other plans were being made of which none of them knew a thing.

One day after a month or two without a visit they came up to Bath and their engine was gone.

They were stunned.

(Ed Morse explains that when the Cummins Diesel Company learned of the existence of the *Bowdoin*'s original engine, they thought it was the oldest Cummins engine still operational, as well as the first to have been adapted for marine use. Its illustrious career was an attraction, too, and they wanted the engine for a museum they were establishing. They offered the *Bowdoin* a larger, brand new marine diesel, for which it would be easier to obtain parts, and they offered to install it for free. The Schooner Bowdoin Association was thrilled with the opportunity, and Ed says that it wouldn't have been possible if they hadn't had both the original engine and the *Globe*'s replacement to give to Cummins. In 1994, he is surprised to learn that no one had ever explained this to Coughlin and his friends.)

No one had told John, either. One day, a truck appeared beside the vessel. "Here's your engine," the driver announced.

"What engine?" John asked.

"Your engine."

John called Ed Morse, who told him indeed, this was his engine. But the deal wasn't as simple as the Schooner Bowdoin Association imagined. The new engine required major structural changes to the vessel. Ballast had to be jackhammered out to make room for it and the motor mounts had to be torn out and new steel ones welded in. The old gearbox had to be taken out. The Association hired a welder who worked several weeks to make all of the changes. Just as they had in 1946, the Twin Disc Company donated a new gearbox and power take-off, though no one told Bill Coughlin and his friends about that either. When Bill and Jack came along, the new engine had already been connected to the shaft, but the connection hadn't been trued up; just eyeballing it, Bill could see the shaft had been bent to fit. Unbuttoned, the flange jumped up two inches, Bill says.

This was a time of change within the Schooner Bowdoin Association. The new president of the Association let John go. Someone else within the Association told John, however, that there were internal discussions going on, and suggested he shouldn't disappear, that things might turn around.

Sue

John had met Sue Chapman during the summer of 1983, aboard the windjammer *Angelique*, when he relieved the mate for a week's break. Sue says he brought his sextant aboard, and spent time showing the passengers how to take sightings. "I was fascinated by his knowledge — but the twinkle in his eyes is what caught me."

The following summer, in 1984, she worked as mess cook on the *Angelique*. Leaving her teaching job in New Mexico early, Sue joined the *Angelique* as she embarked on a two-week trip to a Tall Ships get-together in Halifax, Nova Scotia.

The *Angelique* sailed across the Gulf of Maine into Halifax, and, Sue says, "There was John on the dock to greet us. My heart was just a-pounding to see him." John helped them tie up, and a little later, as she sat below peeling potatoes, he came down and said hello. But he was soon gone again.

The next day, Sue was on deck whipping cream and again, John appeared. "He was very shy, you know, but he got courage up to ask if I'd like to go out to eat when we got back to Camden. 'Sure, I'd like that very much,' I told him. It seemed to surprise him. Off he went, and I didn't see him again." John had driven all the way from Camden to Halifax to ask Sue for a date.

"I had a devil of a time trying to ask her out, to find her alone," he says. "If she'd said no, I guess I wouldn't have ever seen her again, but she surprised me and said yes. And then, on our first date I stood her up. I was out on one of the schooners, and we were supposed to come in early, but we didn't make it."

Sue says one of her friends told her she might as well write him off, but their next attempt to get together worked out better, and before she returned to New Mexico at the end of the summer, they were seriously involved with each other.

To Boston

Bill Coughlin was very concerned about the work being done in John's absence, and was relieved when a shakeup within the Association brought John back. He and the welder and the Irish Mafia all kept plugging away. Fall came.

Finally, although there was still a great deal to be done, in late October 1984, the *Bowdoin* went overboard. Mae Fogg, MacMillan's niece, now in her late seventies, showered flowers upon the *Bowdoin*'s bow, just as she had done as a young girl at the *Bowdoin*'s original launching in 1921. Miriam was also on hand, along with a large crowd of well-wishers who stood in the cold rain under brightly colored umbrellas, cheering as the schooner floated off her cradle.

John kept working. Ray Quirnbach, of Associated Diesel Company in Boston, got the generator running and showed John how to pipe fuel into the main engine. Jack and the Bath Iron Works Pipefitters designed the exhaust system, which BIW donated. They also loaned a crane for installation.

Through the efforts of George Collins of the Boston Globe Foundation, which had become interested in the project through *Globe* employees Coughlin and Quinn, the *Bowdoin* was given a berth behind the U.S.S. *Constitution* at the Charlestown Navy Yard. The Association hoped that the increased exposure there would generate more money and that the systems work would come along more easily.

In January of 1985, Jim Sharp towed the schooner to Boston, charging far less than market price. "I never did get rich from the *Bowdoin*. She was a piece of my soul at the time," Jim says. The overnight trip down to Boston was miserable. "It was colder than hell," Jim describes. "The hawser dipped into the water now and then, and it would freeze before it had a chance to shake itself. There's two or three guys on the *Bowdoin*, supposed to be steer- ing. Soon they're sitting behind the house, still trying to steer, then they're lying on the deck, and pretty soon they're all below." (John, who was aboard, says that even if Jim couldn't always see them, there actually was always someone on the wheel; they took half hour shifts. "It wasn't fun. Water was freezing on the decks and we were slipping all around.")

"There was a little tiny pilot house on my tug boat," Jim says. "We had two electric heaters, and there were three or four of us in there. You'd think the body heat alone would have kept us warm, but it didn't. Neal Parent was with us, and he kept us in stitches the whole way down. That's the only thing that kept us from freezing." Bill Coughlin was on the tug too. "Neal told the longest, funniest jokes. His jokes last an hour and a half," Bill laughs.

The schooner hadn't taken on much water during the trip, and after tying her up behind the *Constitution*, with plenty of slack in her lines to accommodate the tide, the crew set up an electric bilge pump with a plastic pipe leading through a porthole onto the deck. Their work done, they all headed back to Camden on the tug, including John, who needed to get his car. The return trip was just as cold. They travelled through the night again, the tug icing up all the way, and arrived in Camden the following morning to find ice so heavy at Jim's slip that they had to dock the tug on the other side of the harbor.

That first night that the *Bowdoin* spent at the Navy yard there was heavy snow and rain and sleet and ice in Boston. Bill Coughlin was worried about the schooner, and about midnight, he stopped by. "Instinct," he says. "She goddam near sank. She was well over her waterline." The deck had filled up with water, her scupper holes had frozen solid, and because there were no freeing ports in her high bulwarks, there was no way to let the water off the deck. In addition, the automatic bilge pump kept dumping more water on deck through the open porthole, and because the porthole was lower than the caprail, water from the deck was flowing right back down below.

Bill saw that the water below was half way up the side of the engine, four or five feet deep throughout the schooner. He climbed aboard and tried to work the deck pumps, but by himself, in the cold, he couldn't do anything.

He went ashore to call Jack Quinn (who probably wasn't thrilled to be awakened in the middle of the night, and who had the flu, to boot). But Bill told him to get a pump down to the schooner. Before long, a colleague of Jack's from the *Globe* arrived with a pump. They took it below and Bill stood beside it in the water when they started it. "I'm lucky to be here today," he says; something was shorted out, and he got a tremendous jolt. But eventually, they emptied the schooner out. When Jack and Ray came to the pier in the afternoon, Bill was still there, pumping by hand. "It's a wonder he didn't have a heart attack," Jack says.

Changes

In February, John took a week's trip to New Mexico to see Sue. Her third-graders were excited to see John because they'd heard so much about him from their teacher. They had been following the progress of the work on the *Bowdoin* all year, with photographs John had sent to Sue and a videotape of the launching. When they met him, they adored him. He brought them all T-shirts marked "Crew of the Schooner *Bowdoin*" and told them about the vessel. Through John and Sue, the *Bowdoin* once again had a little cache of school-child enthusiasts just as she had had when she sailed north in the early days, and her skipper had a following like Mac's. The children played chess with John, "concentrating so hard that the sweat just ran down their faces," he describes.

When he returned to Boston, the Irish Mafia helped John build the watertight bulkhead by the captain's cabin, with a double layer of matched boards. Jack studied the Coast Guard regulations and designed watertight fittings for the piping to pass through the bulkhead. But while he was working on these fittings at home at his own expense, the Association hired someone else to build them.

In May, Sue came back east. She accompanied John aboard the *Bowdoin* while the schooner was towed from Charlestown to Rose Marine in Gloucester. There, the *Bowdoin* was hauled to correct planking that was done while John was gone. The repairs were to be made by carpenters from the boat yard, and a rigger had been hired to do the final work on the rig.

While that work was progressing, John wanted to go to New York to see his father, who was very ill and in the hospital. Even though he volunteered to drive back and forth between New York and Gloucester to oversee the ongoing work, the Association wouldn't grant him leave. "In a big company, no one gets leave for personal matters," they told John. When he said he had to go, they asked him to resign. He wouldn't. But he packed all his tools and all his personal gear into his yellow beetle, Sue squeezed herself in on top with her feet against the dashboard, and they drove to New York.

John made sure his father was home and had nursing help before he returned to Camden several weeks later. He opened the door to his house to find a termination check, dated the day he had left Gloucester.

Bill Coughlin, Jack Quinn and the rest of the Irish Mafia were disgusted and abandoned the project. Jack still has some of the stainless steel fittings he made. More than $100,000 of services and materials had been donated or produced by the group, but not one of them has ever sailed on the vessel nor, since the rebuild, has John Nugent.

Small Gifts and Large

During the course of the rebuild, individual supporters of the *Bowdoin* gave $25, $50 or $100 each to the project and the support of the vessel. A few gave significantly more. In addition, many donated items in kind or their labors: the Irish Mafia, the Cummins Diesel Company, the Twin-Disc Company and others all gave large in-kind contributions, and the dockage in Boston behind the *Constitution* was donated, but smaller gifts like Ginny Sides's friend's flags were of just as much importance.

While the *Bowdoin* was on the railway in Gloucester, cabinet maker Roland Blanchet was working on a steam yacht in the same yard. Like so many people his age, he had read about Mac-Millan as a boy, and knew about the schooner's adventures in the Arctic. Because he wanted to make a half-model of the old schooner, he asked for a set of plans. He happened to have a couple of pieces of lignum vitae at home, and somehow, he ended up turning her belaying pins. He never got the plans, and he never made the half-model, but his belaying pins are on the schooner today.

Joy Wilcox was doing the *Bowdoin*'s books during the last several years of the rebuild; her friend, Otis Albee of Rockland, Maine, made more than a hundred ratlines and gave them to the vessel.

All in all, Joy says, well over 1,500 people gave time, materials, energy or dollars to the rebuilding of the *Bowdoin*.

FIFTEEN

Sailing Again

*I*N JULY 1985, ON THE occasion of her eightieth birthday, Miriam stepped up to the microphone at the Boston Yacht Club in Marblehead and began speaking. Not everyone was paying attention. She started again. "Mac was in love with another woman."

Suddenly, her audience was quiet. Everyone looked at everyone else, afraid that Miriam was going to tell them some horrible story. Jody Latimer, a crew member on the *Bowdoin*, wondered if Miriam had lost her mind. But she hadn't. "There she is," said Miriam, pointing out the window at the *Bowdoin*.

The Cowans

Jody Latimer and her fiancé, Captain Bill Cowan, had recently returned to Rockland after having crossed the Pacific. Bill had skippered the steel cargo ketch *Edna* on a six month voyage, they were tired, and they were looking forward to a spell ashore. But within two weeks, a friend called to tell them the *Bowdoin* needed a captain. The *Bowdoin*! For Bill, who had been to the Arctic on the *Regina Maris* in 1982, this was not an opportunity to miss. *Regina* had given him a great year, combining sailing, sail training and scientific research, and a feel for exploration in the north. The *Bowdoin*'s history epitomized this life. Everyone knew the *Bowdoin*. The *Bowdoin* was special. Perhaps he and Jody could be a part of bringing her back, getting her sailing again and even ready to go north. It didn't take them long to sign on with the famous old vessel.

Bill and Jody joined the schooner before the end of May of 1985, while she was still hauled in Gloucester. She had no electricity and only part of her plumbing and interior was completed. Her new engine wasn't fully hooked up. Her masts were in, but the shrouds were not attached. Her sails and other gear were scattered all over the coast of Maine. The first order of business for the Association, its Executive Director, Renny Stackpole, and for the new skipper and crew, was to get the schooner rigged and back to Maine as soon as possible. Bill and Jody moved aboard and, because the *Bowdoin* had once been a Navy vessel, she was given a berth for six weeks alongside a battleship at the Charlestown Navy Yard, again near the *Constitution*. There, Bill and Jody and two other carpenters worked long hours; the initial project for them was to build their own bunks. Tourists visiting the battleship gawked at them at all hours of day and night. Bill rented a truck to collect the sails and other gear and hauled it all back to the schooner. The sails had been new when they were stored, but who could have known that they would be in storage for five years? They now had mouse holes and needed major repairs—and were just one in a long list of projects that had to be completed before the *Bowdoin* could go home.

Finally, after the reception at the Boston Yacht Club in Marblehead, the first of many fund-raising events scheduled for the summer, Bill, Jody and two others readied the *Bowdoin* for the trip home. In Gloucester, they happened upon George Nichols, whom Bill had known on *Regina*; George, now on the *Rambler*, saw that they were short-handed, and released two of his sailors who volunteered to sail with the *Bowdoin* to Rockland.

Dr. Pete Rand, who had sailed with MacMillan in the 1950s, was then president of the Schooner Bowdoin Association. He wrote of his 1985 Fourth of July:

*After a sunny noontime of clan festivities on a seaside lawn
in Cape Elizabeth, I had the first morsel of my mother-in-law's
delicious salmon and peas just off the plate when a glance out the
window made me drop my fork. There she was, running in from
the light buoy, wing and wing to a gentle southerly. Home again
in Maine waters, the* Bowdoin *glided by Portland Head Light
and into the harbor. The sight was a real heart-stopper.*

When the *Bowdoin* arrived in Penobscot Bay, the annual
Great Schooner Race was just finishing off the Rockland breakwater. As the *Bowdoin* joined the fleet of windjammers, skipper
after skipper greeted her with cannon salutes, each of which her
crew cheerfully returned. Bill sailed her into Rockland, where a
berth awaited her.

Bill, Jody and her other crew members alternated between
finishing the schooner's systems and interior, and sailing to
fund-raisers up and down the coast. On the weekends when she
was in Rockland, the *Bowdoin* shared her dock with the *Nathaniel
Bowditch*, another schooner designed by William Hand and built
at Hodgdon Brothers in the early 1920s, now operating as a
cruise schooner. But the *Bowdoin* was more likely to be in Portland or Cundy's Harbor or North Haven or even way up the New
Meadows River at a tiny dock, surrounded by ledges. "That was
your best docking," Jody reminds her husband today. "You got
quite an ovation, that time." But Bill says that he could do anything with the *Bowdoin*. "I don't know if it's the design or her per-
sonality, but I could go anywhere with her. I had the most fun
docking her of any boat I've ever known—I could make her spin
around in circles—you could try things you'd never even think
of doing in another boat. There was something about her that
said 'it's OK.'"

Everywhere they went, Bill and Jody say, they felt like celebri-
ties. "Always a crowd greeted you, always there was fanfare,
respect." Bill, dressed in his blue blazer and white shirt, became
accustomed to explaining to people what the next step in the
process would be, what piece of equipment was most needed at

that moment, what their next obstacle was. People came down to the schooner and told their own stories about her. One woman brought flowers to the *Bowdoin*, along with a photograph of herself standing in the bow, holding flowers during sendoff festivities years before. Another woman told about being brought aboard the boat by her father when she was a baby. It was only rarely that someone came along who had never heard of the *Bowdoin*, but even they could feel the schooner's appeal. At one reception in Portland, a man was so impressed he went home to get a hundred dollars for the donation box. "He wasn't the kind of person who would necessarily have a hundred dollars extra to spend," Bill says, "but he did it."

And always, there was Miriam. When people's steam ran low, as it did again and again during the lengthy project, she was there; she would attend one more reception, meet with the governor one more time, come down to the pier one more time. Although it was becoming difficult for her to negotiate the rail, whenever she came aboard, "she lit up," Bill says. Miriam would head for the wheel box, sit down, and look around. And something she saw would remind her of a story, and soon everyone would be huddled around her, listening to her talk of trips north and MacMillan and the schooner's earlier days. "But she wasn't living in the past," Jody says. "She was definitely in the present. She was the mother of the whole situation. And she was a role model for me, to think she made all those trips, so young."

The money came in, although not as fast or as much as the project required. "There were times," Bill says, "when the Association didn't have the money to pay us. And we stayed on, we felt committed, we still worked, we felt that strongly. We were going to make it happen." But it was exhausting. Living aboard, there was no fixed work schedule; they might work until ten at night. And, because the vessel was always open to the public, people were always dropping by. During the winter of 1985–1986, Bill and Jody moved ashore. They were married in April and lived in a seemingly palatial one-room apartment in Camden.

It became clear that, in order to finish the job, the Association would have to borrow money and get additional professional help. With the help of Key Bank and the crew at National Sea Products, an intense push to get the boat certified was made. Bill Cowan met with the Coast Guard in Boston, and later in Portland, to work out the plans and details of the new Sail Training Vessel standards; because the *Bowdoin* was the first vessel to be certified under this standard, it was a long and difficult process. The type of wire, fuel hose, valves, lights, fire sprinkling systems, hardware—even the size of the lettering to mark safety features—all had to meet specific criteria. The vessel had to have life rafts and EPIRBs and an air compressor for a fog horn. There were backup systems for backup systems, or so it seemed, and the Coast Guard kept a careful eye on the actual installations as well, to be certain that all was up to standard. Negotiations took place on such details as the midships hatch and the placement of a watertight bulkhead. Bill says the Coast Guard was thorough and careful, but also respected the historic integrity of the *Bowdoin*. In a few cases where following the letter of the regulation would have compromised the vessel, agreements were cordially reached.

Finally certified, the *Bowdoin* spent the spring of 1986 working out of Boston on a *Globe*-sponsored program, taking students on day sails and introducing them to seamanship and oceanography. On June 22, a number of guests boarded the schooner for a special cruise from Boston to Martha's Vineyard, Nantucket, Woods Hole, and Newport, culminating in the Statue of Liberty's centennial celebration in New York on the Fourth of July.

Bobby Edwards

When Bobby Edwards was a child in Pasadena, California, in the late 1920s, her father took her to hear MacMillan speak. The *Bowdoin* was a frequent subject of discussion at the family dining table—Bobby wonders if perhaps her father wished he could go north with MacMillan himself, though he wasn't a sailor. By the time Bobby heard MacMillan speak a second time, she was hooked on sailing and on the *Bowdoin* too, although it would be forty years before she first saw the vessel.

At fourteen, Bobby was a regular member of the crew of a forty-one foot yawl, the *Corola*. With five young men, classmates at school, she sailed as often as she could, sometimes skipping school. "'The *Corola* Corew,' we called ourselves. To use the engine was a disgrace," Bobby says. "One time we went to Catalina — in those days you could sail with young men, but you couldn't stay on the boat overnight — my mother had a friend on Catalina, so I had stayed with her. We were coming home the next day, and we got into a dense fog — it never occurred to us to kick on the engine, and it got late. There were six sets of worried parents, and when we finally got in and they realized there was nothing whatever the matter with the motor, they were very upset."

The day after Pearl Harbor, every young man Bobby knew enlisted. *Corola* was put in dry dock — there was no one left to sail her except Bobby. Two of the young men died in the war, but in 1990, at their fiftieth high school reunion, the other three were waiting for her. "Friendships are richer, more important as you get older," she says.

Bobby's husband was a cattle rancher, and for many years she didn't sail at all. After his death, Bobby moved to Santa Barbara and became interested in sailing again. When she started thinking about transplanting to the east coast in 1979, she subscribed to *Down East* and *WoodenBoat* magazines, and there she read again of the *Bowdoin*, who was then just beginning her rebuild. Bobby was intrigued, and looked forward to learning more.

She moved to Maine and happened to meet Renny Stackpole. "We hit it off right from the start," she says. She was fascinated with Renny's knowledge of all the big and old vessels — "I'd love to climb inside his mind," she says. She saw the Stackpoles a lot, "and suddenly, Renny became the Executive Director of the Schooner Bowdoin Association." Renny's father, Edouard Stackpole, had been curator at Mystic Seaport when the *Bowdoin* retired there; it was after he left that the *Bowdoin*'s days of sorrow began. It was fitting that Renny should become involved with the rebuild of the schooner.

Bobby, too, became involved in the *Bowdoin* project. "For some reason, I was relatively flush right then," she says, "and I could contribute a little — when they got tight they'd come to me and I could write a check to help pay a bill or meet the payroll or something." When it was time to move the *Bowdoin* up to Camden from the National Sea boatyard at Rockland, Renny asked Bobby if she'd like to sail up on the schooner. She certainly would.

It was a terribly cold day. "I'd dressed for it — I was the only one on board who had," she says with a little pride. "They gave me the wheel — I was on the wheel of the *Bowdoin*! I was thrilled. But they were all just waiting. They were telling me to go to this buoy and that one, and I knew my way around there really well by then, and that was fine, but when we came around Curtis Island, and then you're in close quarters — and I couldn't see over the bow. You know how her bow's so high, because of the ice — well, no one can see over her bow, even tall people. I certainly couldn't. They were all just waiting to laugh at me. Of course in tight quarters MacMillan would be in the ice barrel signalling to the helmsman."

While the *Bowdoin* was in Camden being worked on, Renny and Bill and Jody Cowan were over at Bobby's all the time. And she kept making contributions to the project. "I was just really grateful that I could help out."

Then word came that the *Bowdoin* was being invited to the Op Sail festivities in honor of the Statue of Liberty Centennial. Renny was excited by the honor being given the vessel — and so was Bobby, particularly after Renny asked if she'd like to go along. She had read how much money people were paying to be on one of the ships in the parade, and realized that this was a money-making opportunity for the *Bowdoin*. "I'd love to go," she told Renny, "but give me 24 hours and I'll sell the four forward berths in the foc'sle for $5,000 apiece." That was in the morning. A phone call to a close friend and college-mate, Emilie, sold one immediately. Another friend also accepted without hesitation, and knew who would purchase the third. Bobby purchased the fourth herself. By afternoon, the foc'sle was promised to four graduates of Mills College, classes of '44, '45 and '46, and $20,000 had been promised to the *Bowdoin*. It wasn't long before Renny had also sold berths to four men who had contributed substantially to the project in the past.

They all came aboard at Boston, where the *Bowdoin* had been working that spring with school children. "The men didn't know at first how to deal with us," Bobby says, laughing. "We were old enough to be their mothers—grandmothers of all the crewmembers." But it didn't take long for everyone to settle in, and soon they were having a fine time.

The first stop was Provincetown. "Renny knew just where to go; he took us to the MacMillans' house, and we had a party. Renny was really good at PR. He had photographers and the newspapers there, and of course there were a bunch of what Miriam called her '*Bowdoin* Boys' there." When they came aboard, the Mills women felt out of place, and went off exploring.

At Woods Hole the same thing happened. "It was very impressive. We got off there as fast as we could—the *Bowdoin* Boys there had lots of authority. The head of the lab there was a *Bowdoin* Boy—everywhere we went, it was as if *Bowdoin* Boys were the power structure of America."

Nantucket, the next stop, was Renny's home port. Then on to Newport for three days, where the schooner was "overrun with admirals." Newport was a rendezvous point for a lot of the tall ships coming across the Atlantic. "It was so exciting to see them all coming in," Bobby recalls. "We were tied up right ahead of *Matador*, who had just won the Bermuda race, and when she left, *Shabab Oman*, the Tall Ship from Oman, came in—it was her first landfall. She had all these tough-looking Arabs in turbans, and the boat looked terrible—there was a steady stream of briefcase-carrying penguin-people going on and off—oil deals, I suppose." The *Shabab Oman* got cleaned up while they were in Newport, readying herself for the parade.

The Mills women wanted to get out of the way of all the visiting dignitaries and let Renny and Bill do their public relations work. One of them had once met someone from Newport at a wedding, who had told her if she was ever in Newport to give her a call, so she did. "It turned out that the woman, Countess Szpari, was a Vanderbilt, and she lived on the top floor of The Breakers. She was charming, a wonderful woman. She was just starting up the Newport Yachting Museum at that time. The rest of the Mills girls weren't sailors, but they were just gaga," Bobby says. "The top floor of The Breakers was our home base for the rest of our visit.

"There was sadness all around at that time, too," Bobby remembers. "The *Pride of Baltimore* had just gone down. And it was intensified on the *Bowdoin* when she was asked to take the *Pride*'s place leading one of the files of Class B vessels, beside the *Eagle*. It was particularly emotional for Bill—he knew people on the *Pride*."

From Newport, the organizers of Op Sail gave each participating vessel her route. The *Bowdoin* spent one night anchored off a little village in Connecticut; the next day they moved to a yacht club further in Long Island Sound, and finally into the city. "Going down the East River, of course we all had binoculars, but at first we couldn't understand what we were looking at—it was mass humanity. It was hard to realize there were that many people. Once we got past Hell's Gate, every window, every balcony, every street was full—there were Tall Ships before and after us—and every kind of private vessel, and all the Coast Guard people—the procession was kind of quiet, imbued with a sense of how choice it was, how privileged we were."

The *Bowdoin* was berthed at South Street Seaport. "We were rafted up with Sea Education Association's *Westward*—she caught on fire, and the smoke was terrible. The New York Fire Department came, dressed for dire disaster, and everyone was clashing over our decks carrying huge pickaxes—we had horrible images of the mayhem they could cause. But there wasn't any serious damage." From Rockport, Maine, Lance Lee's Atlantic Challenge boats, *Egalité* and *Liberté*, were also at South Street Seaport. "It was fun to have people from home right there," Bobby says.

The fireworks were on the night of July 3. "One of Emily's sons had an apartment on the Battery, so we had a front row seat for the fireworks. We could see everything—all around the Statue of Liberty the private boats had to stay behind an imaginary line, and the Coast Guard was cruising up and down, patrolling.

"There were so many people, the New York City cops had

brought in more cops, but there was no crime that weekend at all. No murders, no burglaries, no robberies. Can you imagine? But it was scary, with so many people."

Early the next morning, the morning of the parade, 25 more friends of the schooner came aboard for the day. "They paid through the nose, too," says Bobby. The *Bowdoin* and more than a hundred other vessels rendezvoused, 30 Class A vessels and scores of smaller schooners, sloops, yawls and ketches, old and new. "It was a huge staging area, and they were all given orders about exactly what to do—we had to be out there long before we started parading—it was really exciting," Bobby says. "The huge spectator yachts were all over on one side, and little ones on the other side, all around the Statue of Liberty, and there was an enormous channel in between where the parade would go. There was a nice wind, and there were some near calls, tempers going, with those big things tacking back and forth.

"Finally the word came. *Eagle* started out; we started out. I just can't tell you how exciting that all was. Your heart was in your throat, you had chills down your back. *Eagle* makes you so proud—well, I hate her history, I wish we'd built her, and she wasn't spoils of war, but she's beautiful. And down we went to the George Washington Bridge, and what was really exciting was that we went back down beside all the tall ships, and we could see each one coming in."

Back to Work

Once back in Maine, Bill and Jody were thrilled that the *Bowdoin* had finally returned to her life's work of education. The first program, a two-week archaeology and sail training program for high school students, took the schooner to Canada and back. The crew was looking at archaeological digs and sites and sounding harbors, looking for other potential dig sites in order to investigate the days before the cove bottoms were submerged. But the entire two-week period was foggy. The students were great, the Cowans say, full of energy, but they never got to see the extraordinarily beautiful places they were sailing. Bill and Jody were happy, though; he was teaching navigation, and she was using her zoological background, and the youngsters loved the experience anyway. And the *Bowdoin* had come full circle.

The *Bowdoin* soon undertook a research program with Bigelow Labs of Boothbay Harbor, in conjunction with Texas A&M, which took the schooner into deep water, measuring water temperatures at different depths and testing salinity. The *Bowdoin* provided a satisfactory platform for doing the research; she was far steadier and quieter than other research vessels the scientists had used. Bill was amused — and very pleased — by the computers aboard for this work; despite her age, the *Bowdoin* was able to keep up with the times.

For Jody, the bridge between generations which the *Bowdoin* represents is one of her most significant features. "You had MacMillan, the old age of exploration, and then Miriam, she was a different generation than her husband, and then the students." And during the rebuild, Mac's boys had become the older generation, while the younger people were actually doing the work — John Nugent and the Cowans and so many others. "John's energy fed us," Jody says. "We worked very hard for the *Bowdoin* for very little, because it meant that much to us, and it still does. She was our whole life for two years, not a job." And the Cowans use John Nugent's very words: "We put our heart and soul into her. We can step back, now, and can say we're really proud of what we did." But the older folk were always with them. "Particularly living back aft, I'd look around, and know that was where Miriam slept, and Mac, and that was Mac's chart table," says Jody. "We brought Miriam and Mac with us in spirit."

SIXTEEN

Outward Bound

Cate Cronin

WHILE A COLLEGE STUDENT in 1975, Cate Cronin took a summer job as assistant cook on the *Adventure* under Jim Sharp. She knew nothing about sailing, and only a little more about cooking. She had no idea how her life was about to change. The young men on the crew teased her about her interest in getting involved on deck, going aloft, and generally learning how the schooner worked; she was reminded that this was brawn work, where there was no room for women.

She returned to the *Adventure* the next summer, and that fall she worked with the *Clearwater* in New York, which, with her strictly educational mission of creating environmental awareness, was a little more receptive to women's involvement. "At least there I was allowed to throw docklines," she says. The following summer she returned to Maine, on the *Nathaniel Bowditch*, moving up to cook, but due to the smaller size of the *Bowditch*'s crew, she helped on deck, too.

Cate then spent a couple of years instructing at Outward Bound. She also worked aboard the *Harvey Gamage*, doing both educational programs and passenger trade in the Caribbean, to gain enough time to qualify for her U.S. Coast Guard Captain's license; although a lesser license was sufficient for Cate's work with Outward Bound, she received a 100-ton license. But still, she had no intention of using it other than with Outward Bound students in pulling boats. Cate thought of herself as an educator, not a sailor.

But the skipper of the *Clearwater* was leaving, and Cate was asked to take over. She was completely green as a captain, but she had a capable crew, all working toward a greater goal than simply running the boat. The *Clearwater* operated on a group-effort basis of mutual respect. Although when Cate first came aboard the crew was predominantly male, they helped her in every way. Sometimes her crew was asked by journalists how they liked working under a woman, and they always seemed a little startled, as if they hadn't thought of her in any different way because of her sex. And when "Good Morning America" came aboard they remarked that the crewmembers that day were all female. "Oh, are they?" asked Cate, and looked around. Sure enough. "I didn't think about it, I just hired people I thought would do well."

Although over the VHF radio Cate was called by nicknames like "Captain Cupcake," she encouraged a more professional attitude aboard the *Clearwater*, which was only just growing beyond her casual hippie-and-folksinger image. Gradually, Cate became respected by the professional sailors of New York. On the Hudson, she often acted as an intermediary between tug boat captains and yachtsmen, who weren't able to communicate so easily directly with one another. "*Clearwater*," a tug captain would call, "will you tell that sailboat that if they're not drawing thirty feet like I am then would they please get out of the middle of the channel?"

Cate finally left the *Clearwater* to go back to school, although she still worked occasionally aboard the sloop and on other vessels. She received her master's in education in 1986. Cate is not sure that had she simply come up through the ranks of the windjammers and become a captain in Maine at the time, she would have been so easily accepted in the schooner world. But once she had commanded the 76-foot sloop *Clearwater*, in the most heavily trafficked waters of the United States, she received respect wherever she sailed. That fall, her connection with the schooner *Bowdoin* started.

A Mission for the Schooner

At this time, the Schooner Bowdoin Association was looking for someone to take responsibility for the schooner. No private organization was willing to assume the large debt she had accumulated, and someone had to come up with a scheme to make her self-sustaining. Ken Shaw, then captain of the schooner, contacted Cate because of her experience with educational sail programs and together, with the help of several others committed to preserving the coast of Maine, they came up with a plan. Under the umbrella of Outward Bound, the *Bowdoin* would host a wide variety of programs with many different organizations. Outward Bound was sold on the idea because of the package deal of the boat and the people involved—the "fire-eyed people behind the program who were going to make it work," as Cate describes herself and the others. Outward Bound agreed to lease the vessel for 18 months, from spring 1987 through fall 1988.

Under the auspices of Cate Cronin as Program Director and captain, more than 2,000 people participated in short or extended programs aboard the *Bowdoin* in the next 18 months along the coast from Maine to the Chesapeake. The schooner wintered in the Chesapeake in order to extend her working season; she was only laid up for three months during the winter.

It was an intense time for the *Bowdoin* and her people; every few days they faced an entirely different program with entirely different students. They would work with inner city youngsters one day and corporate executives the next. The schooner carried emotionally disturbed children, educators, women's groups, and mixed groups of people who signed up specifically for a *Bowdoin*-based Outward Bound course. She carried day-tripping Bowdoin College alumni, and visited coastal festivities like the Lobster Festival in Rockland. She had an irregular schedule and no lay-up time. Following the Outward Bound personnel's model of intense work during a course followed by time off, her core crews, mostly Outward Bound people with experience in large sailing vessels, were rotated frequently, and the *Bowdoin* kept going. In addition to Cate and Ken, who had stayed with the schooner, there was another set of skippers during the period, Captains Chris Mays and Candy Kane, who had experience with adjudicated youth, and specialized in those courses. A set of regular procedures were agreed upon by all, but it was difficult to maintain consistency. Some programs were based on day trips; others were multi-day or a week or even two in length. Often the professional crew would be minimized in order to make room for participants; the *Bowdoin* would have two of her own people aboard, along with Outward Bound instructors specific to the particular program (for example, those who worked in signs for the deaf), who might never have sailed before. It took fast communication among captain and crew and the instructors about what exercises and possibilities for learning were available aboard. They developed various programs, based not only on the basics of running the ship—navigating, steering, engine-maintenance, sail handling, cooking and dishwashing—but also on climbing aloft to recreate the trust and teamwork of the traditional Outward Bound rock-climbing program.

Cate describes one trip when a heavy, blustery man said he had bad knees and couldn't go aloft. Two teenaged girls, small of both frame and stature, climbed up, and afterwards, told the older man he should do it. Still concerned about his knees, he agreed to go aloft in a bosun's chair, hoisted by the two girls. The experience built a deep bond between the unlikely trio; he had entrusted himself into their young hands, and they all recognized the importance of this step.

All Outward Bound programs aim to instill a sense of each person's importance to the success of a job, and also to build a person's self-appreciation by letting the students surprise themselves by accomplishing more than they expect. The staff's job is to foster a sense of urgency and accountability; they put a person in a position, on the wheel of the *Bowdoin*, for example, and then let the person figure out how to handle it. First, the new helmsperson has to learn which way the boat turns when the wheel is turned left and right—trial and error is always encouraged. Then they learn to use the compass to follow a straight line. Then comes decision-making. "When will you tack?" a staff member asks. The student has no idea. "Well, how will you decide?" and the student starts to think about the shore, the rocks under the water, the importance of the chart and therefore the role of the navigator, and so on. And then there are the consequences of a decision—who else will tacking effect? "Oh. The sail trimmers. And anyone whose head is in the way of the boom." The interconnectedness of the vessel and of the team operating her becomes clear.

The ideal is that the questions come early enough for participants to puzzle out the answers, but Cate and the staff would often seek out crowded situations, in order to force multiple and instant decisions. Sometimes they could assist quietly without taking away from the students' sense of having solved a problem themselves, perhaps by subtly backing the jib to get a little push off the wind, and at all times they had a backup plan. Only once does Cate remember having to start the engine to get the *Bowdoin* out of a predicament the students had gotten her into.

Part of the success of a program was in the staff's quick assessment of the participants. Often they would put either a trouble-maker or a particularly quiet and shy individual on the wheel, where he or she would have to devote full attention to the job at hand, thereby learning something to pass on to the rest of the group. They involved that person in the team and sometimes even developed a leader from a person who had never been in that role before.

There was one significant mishap during the eighteen month period. After all the groundings she'd suffered and survived in the far reaches of the Arctic, she was done in by Sunken Money Ledge at the mouth of Blue Hill Bay. (There were those who thought hitting that particular ledge was an apt commentary on the whole rebuilding project.)

At the time of the accident, Miriam MacMillan was seriously ill. Ed Morse remembers thinking, "It's a good thing Miriam doesn't know about what's happened to the *Bowdoin*." Miriam died on August 18, 1987, three days after the crash.

The schooner needed major repairs to both her rudder and keel. She was hauled at Goudy and Stevens while Cate frantically rearranged the schedule. The *Bowdoin* was out of commission for several weeks.

Cate feels that her own contributions to the *Bowdoin* lay in the people and program aspects; she left the mechanical skills to others who were stronger in those fields. Her leadership style has always been to find people with the right abilities so that all aspects of a project are covered—and not necessarily by the captain. (She laughs at herself being known as "Captain Telephone," claiming she knows the location of every pay phone between Rockland, Maine, and Norfolk, Virginia.)

Again and again, while with the *Bowdoin*, Cate was reminded of the schooner's past. At dusk one day, the *Bowdoin* was coming down the Delaware River from Philadelphia, and an upbound ship came on the radio to announce its approach around the next bend. Following protocol, Cate responded, "This is the schooner *Bowdoin*, I will keep on the western shore." The ship's captain came back, repeating the words "schooner *Bowdoin*. . . schooner *Bowdoin*" in awe, several times. Then he described meeting MacMillan when he was a boy in Portland.

But Cate wasn't merely recreating the *Bowdoin*'s past, she was building her future. Cate was teaching the *Bowdoin*'s students— students of the electronic age—the human factor in sailing. When the scientific frontier had moved on, MacMillan had done the same thing, working with young men. If the *Bowdoin* were to have a healthy future, what could be more fitting than to be part of an education program?

"It took a hundred percent—no, ten hundred percent of my energy," Cate says, but she is proud she could demonstrate that the boat could meet the triple accomplishments of paying her own way as an educational platform, doing good things for the world and for people, and staying in good shape.

At the end of the eighteen month commitment, Outward Bound didn't renew their lease, deciding instead to concentrate on their existing programs. But their involvement with the schooner had been a catalyst for the *Bowdoin*.

SEVENTEEN

Maine Maritime Academy

Arrival

THE *BOWDOIN* FOUND a new home: Maine Maritime Academy. She came into the Academy's Castine dock at noon on the Friday after Thanksgiving, 1988, skippered by none other than Andy Chase, the *Bowdoin*'s first mate thirteen years earlier and now a licensed captain and Assistant Professor of Nautical Science at Maine Maritime. Cate Cronin and others from Outward Bound joined a crew from the Academy and sailed the *Bowdoin* from Rockland to Castine. The day was frigid, and it was blowing hard—"a *Bowdoin* breeze," Cate says, "and Andy was smiling from ear to ear." Cate knew that the *Bowdoin* would be loved in her new home.

The Outward Bound crew stayed aboard the *Bowdoin* through the afternoon, along with ten people from the Academy who were so excited that the schooner had come to them that they gave up their Thanksgiving weekend to put her to bed for the winter. By dark, they had her stripped. Castine residents came by throughout the weekend to admire the schooner and watch the winterizing process; those who visited the dock on Friday and didn't come again until Sunday afternoon were astounded to find the schooner fully wrapped in her winter cover.

It had been a long process getting the *Bowdoin* to Maine Maritime Academy. A couple of years earlier, an Academy student,

186

Chris Kluck, knowing that the schooner was looking for a permanent home, approached Andy with the idea of the Academy taking her on. Andy, then a fledgling professor, hadn't much time to give to the project, but he gave Chris his support, and Chris mounted a campaign. He circulated a petition which he presented to MMA President Ken Curtis with more than 200 signatures. "He got some of those under duress," Andy admits. "He passed the petition around the dorm courtyard during a fire drill!" Although the schooner had already been leased by Outward Bound, the petition did get President Curtis's attention. During this time President Curtis became not only aware of the *Bowdoin*, but of schooners in general. He happened to sail on the *William Albury* in Miami, and was impressed with how much attention she drew. "There were any number of 200-foot megayachts tootling around the harbor," Andy reports that Curtis noticed, "but everyone wanted to see the schooner."

By the time the Outward Bound lease was up, Curtis was convinced that the historic schooner had a great deal to offer the Academy, both because of the public relations potential and for the training possibilities she offered cadets. The Schooner Bowdoin Association leased her to the Academy with an option to buy; the lease fee was to make the loan payments. The price of ownership was simply to assume the entire debt.

Some years before, the federal government had confiscated a large sailing yacht in a drug case and given it to the Maritime Academy. Although they had sailed her occasionally, she didn't fit into any program so, not long after the *Bowdoin* came to the Academy, Ken Curtis sold the yacht and used the proceeds to pay off the schooner's debt and take full title. "Ken always says it was drugs that bought the *Bowdoin*," Andy remarks.

Learning the Boat

In the spring of 1989, Andy and the *Bowdoin*'s crew, led by first mate Elliot Rappaport, scraped, sanded, primed and painted the entire vessel, inside and out, tarred the rigging, varnished the spars, slushed the masts with Vaseline, and installed a new stove, a coal-fired Aga. The first Coast Guard inspection was a joke—

much of the schooner's equipment was late in coming, and no one seemed to know if the *Bowdoin* was certified as a Sailing School Vessel or not; the wording on the certificate stumped both the inspector and Andy. The *Bowdoin* sailed her first ten days for the Academy as a yacht, uninspected.

The Academy created a Marine Advisory Board to guide the use of the schooner. Among others, John Nugent was appointed to the new board. Now skippering the *Olad*, his own day-sailing head-boat out of Camden, John sailed to the first meeting, which was aboard the *Bowdoin* in Gilkey's Harbor, where the *Bowdoin* had stopped at Seven Hundred Acre Island to visit Charles Dana Gibson in 1921 on her first trip north. John rafted up with the *Bowdoin* and the *Mary Day*, whose captain, Steve Cobb, was also on the Board. Three other members of the advisory board had sailed in on the *Bowdoin*. This was but the first of many business stops the *Bowdoin* made during her first summer hailing from Castine. The Academy mounted a capital campaign and, once again, as in 1985, the *Bowdoin* made appearances all up and down the coast, from Eastport to Portland, on Mount Desert Island and inland as far as Bangor. She took groups daysailing and was open for public inspection at many stops along the way.

The other important business for Andy and the schooner their first summer together again was Andy's learning the boat: developing routines, trust, understanding and expectations of her, and seeing what changes needed to be made before undertaking more significant voyages.

A large part of Andy's job also was training the less experienced members of his crew in seamanship. Again and again during the summer, Andy challenged the *Bowdoin* and her crew with close-quarter maneuvering. In mid-June Andy wrote in his journal of one harbor approach: "The entire job was done by the mate and the crew with no fuss or fumbling. It was extremely satisfying to see that the break-in phase for this group is essentially over. We now have a capable and handy crew of schoonermen, any one of whom I feel I can rely on."

Leaving that same anchorage the next morning: "We hoisted sail, broke out the anchor, and backed *Bowdoin* out of the harbor under sail for about a quarter mile. She handled nicely in reverse, with Elliot tending the foresail, backing it from side to side as needed."

And later that day, entering Boothbay Harbor: "Once again *Bowdoin* impressed us with her willingness to tack in virtually no wind, with only a half-dozen boat lengths to get way on between tacks. Her headway was all but imperceptible, yet she never failed to tack, and the result was we were able to work our way dead to windward up a crowded and narrow harbor under sail."

Two or three weeks later, Andy again tested the schooner, this time in the islands of Penobscot Bay:

> *By late afternoon we had a light southerly breeze and a fair tide once again so we sailed in beside Brimstone and the East shore of Vinalhaven to Winter Harbor.... We just kept poking in further and further under sail, until we had come far enough so we couldn't bear to turn on the engine. In the end we managed to beat up a channel that was at its narrowest just 3½ boatlengths wide. It was incredible to see her actually pull it off. This boat will sail into anything. We managed to squeak, squeeze and wriggle our way all the way up to the head of Seal Bay, to drop the hook under Hay Island, in what must be the most protected anchorage in the world.*

Aboard the *Bowdoin*, navigation was a primary subject of instruction and practice, high- and low-tech alike. Andy wrote in his journal of an early day off the Georges Islands: "Will was the navigator for the day, and it kept him busy. There are a lot of off-lying ledges both marked and unmarked that require close attention. Most of this navigating is done by eyeball—lining up a buoy with a point of land, or a ledge with a hill. It's a knack to learn to use everything available without needing to rely on buoys, radar, and bearings."

And later: "The system for making speed checks by throwing a piece of paper over the side and timing the run from the anchor davit to the quarter bitt was worked out." Andy also taught electronic and celestial navigation techniques.

Andy wrote that right there at home in Maine, they faced some of the navigational difficulties the *Bowdoin* had seen in the north with MacMillan. "A calculation of the current in Goose Rock Passage, and a warning that it has been clocked at nine knots, has set us up for an early morning to make our exit at slack water." And at Machias Seal Island: "There are unmarked shoals there, and swift currents, not to mention a local magnetic disturbance. But it was a clear day, and we had several different methods of checking our position, so in we went to within a few tenths of a mile for a good close look."

Despite Andy's meticulous care, the *Bowdoin* maintained her historic tradition of harmlessly running into things, providing more learning experiences for her crew. Andy described the first grounding, in Atkins Bay in mid-June: "It makes a good anchorage, if you don't get past the range formed by the old state pier remains—which I did. I was just rounding up when *Bowdoin* took a very gentle heel to port and stopped. We were well parked, and only gently, with a coming tide, so we held a grounding drill. The kedge anchor (a 75-pound Danforth) was got into the boat with two docklines bent on, and run out to windward. Taking it to the windlass, we were able to heave her bow into the wind slowly, and in 20 minutes we were afloat again."

Andy says that an important part of a watch-officer's training is psychological:

> *I decided to turn the watch over to Zach completely at this point and left him with instructions to be off Nancy Head at 0600, and call me then, and I turned in for an hour's nap.*
>
> *I wanted him to have the watch really to himself, to get that first feeling of knowing you're it. It never comes as long as there is another higher ranking person up and around, and you never know the feeling until the others go below and go to bed. Even then it may not sink in right away, but sooner or later a decision has to be made, and there is no one there to ask, and you realize that you're it. It can be scary, or it can be thrilling—depending on the circumstances and your own state of mind.*

*But whatever he did or thought, Zach woke me at 0600 and
we were right on target.*

The people-training didn't always go as smoothly. Two
groups of pre-Academy seminar students sailed with Andy on
successive weekends. These youngsters were put ashore on an
island overnight as part of their experience, forcing them to
think things through for themselves as a group. Before the
second group was left ashore, Andy lectured them about fire,
and said that the first group had disobeyed instructions and had
lit a fire. They were absolutely not to follow suit, he told them.

But in spite of their orders, the young people built a fire.

*I was very upset by this situation, and made it quite plain. I
told them that the fire hazard was real, and the consequences of a
fire on an island were total.*

*But I explained that the fire risk was the lesser of the two
problems. The worst was that they disobeyed a direct order of
mine—a serious order that was plainly and directly given. I
explained that this had taken a swipe at the very heart of what
MMA was all about, and that they had just seriously jeopardized
their application for admission. It was a very grim bunch that I
left on deck when I dismissed them and came below—I could have
heard a mackerel sneeze when I got back aft.*

(Andy reported that the students did enter MMA as scheduled. But he hopes they learned something from their island
experience and his lecture.)

The Halifax trip was the climax of the summer. Andy's journal outlines the talk he gave to the crew, covering the details of
the routine aboard. Safety issues included having watch members wear harnesses on deck after dark and carry knives, and be
fully prepared for watch—including wearing proper clothing
and using the head before they reported for duty. The routine
was a three-watch system, with a single person as galley slave all
day. (One of the students on the 1991 trip says: "Everyone would

prefer to be on deck in rain, piss and cold, rather than down as galley slave.") The watch rotation was ritualized: "Watch Officer relieves the lookout, but stays aft. Lookout goes below for coffee (5 minutes) then relieves helm. Helm takes 5 and goes forward." On-coming and off-watch ate first, with idlers (those who didn't stand watches) and off-going watch eating second.

Standing orders for the on-duty watch included calling the captain if approaching land or other vessels, if there were indications of squalls coming, if the wind shifted, or if visibility dropped below two miles. Sun lines were to be taken three times a day, azimuths twice a day. After dark, the watch officer was to check the radar at least half-hourly. They were to monitor weather reports on the SSB radio and record engine room information. At the change of watch, the on-coming watch would conduct the "Boat Check," which included checking all halyards, the running rig for possible chafe or fouled leads, navigation lights at night, and the engine, if running. They were also to check all the bilges, make sure that everything on deck was securely lashed, and finally, pick up loose gear and coffee cups.

Underway at 1000 hours on July 25, they motored past Isle au Haut in flat calm, giving the captain opportunity to give his talk based on the notes in his journal. The watch schedule started at 1300, and a nice southerly breeze came in, but at 1700 Andy was made uneasy by a "most peculiar wind fluke... it must have been a mini-micro-burst. We were sailing along with about 10–15 knots from the southwest on a reach when out of nowhere she jibed. A puff had sprung up from the northwest—just one puff. Then it went calm. Then she jibed back—a new puff from the southwest. Within a minute or two we were back underway as before, but we were all a little nervous. I stayed that way all night." Andy was well aware that it was just such a burst which had sent the *Pride of Baltimore* down only three years before.

They ran a few sun lines on the first day, but faced fog the rest of the way into Halifax. They didn't use the Loran, however, relying instead upon the traditional dead reckoning and soundings, and arrived only a mile and a half off. "I think the watch officers are impressed," Andy wrote. Like Lieutenant Hotchkiss forty-seven years earlier, they sailed on into Halifax, surprising Halifax Traffic, which told them that they had gotten east of the channel. "I explained that I needed the sea room to jibe over and fetch the next run. They came back: 'Oh, I see, *Bowdoin*; we didn't realize you were under sail.' They must've figured us for crazies — storming in through the thick-a-fog under full sail."

In Halifax they were made to feel welcome. They enjoyed a jazz festival which happened to be going on at the time, and they visited with the *Bluenose II*. (Finally seeing her under sail as they left, Andy was awed by the sight of the 143-foot schooner whose total sail area was more than four times that of the *Bowdoin*.)

A stop on Roseway Bank produced a pair of enormous cod, 43 inches long and weighing perhaps 40 pounds apiece, which the steward turned into the most delicious dinner Andy had ever tasted, some of it blackened cajun style and some simply broiled. Everyone had their fill, and there was enough left for a chowder. "I guess it's safe to say the fishing gear has been paid for," Andy wrote.

They had more fog coming home:

> We made a smuggler's entrance into Bar Harbor at 0200 this morning — in a dungeon fog and pitch dark. Visibility was somewhat less than zero, but the Bay is a good one for that kind of run. We passed Egg Rock light (a 13-mile light), less than $^1/_{10}$ of a mile off and never even saw a glow. We groped our way right up into the harbor and dropped the hook just outside the line of anchored boats, and hit the sack. It had been a fast trip across, as the breeze kept dying and the sea became dead flat.
>
> This morning we had to wait for Customs until 11:30 — they don't have an office there as I had thought, but have to come down from Bangor. Finally we were cleared and got underway. It was sunny and windy — a smoky Sou'wester — but the fogbank was hanging out just offshore, and shut in anyway as the afternoon progressed. I headed back out to sea — to get outside the traffic and rocks, and also to try to get back the rhythm of the voyage. I wasn't really ready to give up the trip just yet. . . .

The end of the Halifax trip brought more public relations trips, to Bangor, Medomak and Seal and Southwest Harbors, with day sails from Castine as well, and another grounding on a single rock at the opening of Eastern Bay off Great Wass Island, which embarrassed Andy as it was right in front of a friend's house. "The only harm done ... was to the sensitive parts of the mind."

Finally they finished the promotional trips: "We are ever so glad to be done with the Capital Campaign trips ... it's exhausting, being polite all day to strangers," wrote Andy. But the summer was over, too. The effort had produced a million dollars for the Academy—ironic, considering that the schooner had been in such dire economic straits in the last decade. Of course, that money was given to the Academy, not to the schooner, but they acknowledged she had helped produce it. Andy returned to the Nautical Sciences classroom, and the *Bowdoin* was put back to bed for the winter.

EIGHTEEN

Labrador Again

FROM THE START OF their involvement with the *Bowdoin*, MMA President Ken Curtis and Captain Andy Chase knew the importance of taking her north again. The 1989 trip to Nova Scotia had been a token trip; Andy had never sailed north himself, and wanted to make a cautious approach. "Halifax is only inches north of Castine—it's about the same as Bangor," Andy says, "and I thought we'd go a little further each year." But reading the old accounts of MacMillan's trips, he realized that it had only taken the *Bowdoin* ten days to reach the Labrador coast. After the Halifax trip went so smoothly, Andy decided that in 1990 the *Bowdoin* would return to Labrador, with Mac's northern home, Nain, the objective.

First, though, the *Bowdoin* needed a new galley. Elliot spent the winter working in the schooner, taking out the steward's berth and installing the new equipment. "It was a hell of a job," Andy says. "We got it in our heads we wanted a stainless steel refrigeration system. It would have been much easier with fiber-glass, but we didn't think we wanted the smell of fiberglass in the food. It turns out everybody in the world has fiberglass refrigera-tion. But Elliot did an extraordinary job," says Andy. "He and John Steer, who had just graduated from the MMA Yacht Design Department, both worked like dogs on it." Once the refrigera-tion was installed, 10 cubic feet of refrigerator and 15 of freezer,

Elliot had to put back the steward's berth. While they were at it, they tweaked the midships cabin around to make room for an extra berth. They worked through four weekends, until midnight twice during the final week, and "by the skin of our teeth," Andy says, "we made our first commitment to sail on June 8."

After a quick round of visits from one end of the Maine coast to the other, followed by a week's preparation, the trip to Labrador began in style. A Saturday night lobster bake drew thirty or forty of the *Bowdoin*'s old friends, including Stu Hotchkiss, who came up from Connecticut. At noon on Sunday, the first of July, the *Bowdoin* departed Castine.

The first day, Andy put his crew through all the drills, including fire, "Gumby" (survival) suits and abandon ship. When it came time for the man overboard drill, "I threw a pillow overboard and we never did get it back. I think it was sobering for all, how easily we lost track of it. We got our ring buoys and MOB [man overboard] pole back fine, but not the Oscar."

Andy had certainly "learned the boat" in the prior year. He describes a docking at Baddeck, Nova Scotia:

> I went over to the marina and sounded their dock. I found 9½ feet at one end, and 7 in the middle, so I decided to go for it, since it was our only hope to get fuel and water. We made it, by backing her in through the anchorage, and letting her blow down sideways to the wharf. I used our Avon and the marina's to help out, and in the end we tied up about 2 feet off the dock, touching bottom. The fuel hose made the reach, with an inch to spare.

The rigors of Labrador introduced themselves early, as the schooner left Red Bay:

> We left Red Bay about 1600 in a veritable gale. It was a Katabatic wind off the mountain — just as warm as could be, and blowing about 30. We steamed up into the Basin and set sail (full main) and came out past the wharf doing about 8 knots. Hardening up, we set out through the channel and got a gust that buried our rail completely. It was quite a thrill for all, and the

The *Bowdoin* sails to her new home, the Maine Maritime Academy in Castine, November 1988. (Tom Stewart)

As a little girl, the woman on the right had been aboard the *Bowdoin* during MacMillan's days and Mac had given her a gift of chocolate. Here, in 1990, the *Bowdoin* has returned to Labrador, and the little girl, now a village elder, gives chocolate to Captain Andy Chase. (Tom Stewart)

Captain Andy Chase, inside Bowdoin Harbour, Labrador, 1991. (Tom Stewart)

First Mate Elliot Rappaport, Disko Bay, Greenland. (Today, Elliot is captain of the *Bowdoin*.) (Tom Stewart)

Deborah Harrison, steward, and a galley slave prepare a meal. The infamous Aga stove is in the background. (Tom Stewart)

The *Bowdoin* off the coast of Labrador. (Tom Stewart)

The *Bowdoin* at anchor, Eclipse Harbor, Labrador. (Tom Stewart)

Andy Chase and crew, the coast of Labrador. (Tom Stewart)

Crossing from Canada to Greenland. (Tom Stewart)

Stuart Hotchkiss back aboard the *Bowdoin*, 1991. (Courtesy of Elliot Rappaport)

The *Bowdoin* off the west coast of Greenland with a typical sail configuration for the northern waters, 1994. (Tom Stewart)

first real test of the rig. Once outside we swung off and ran before
it, making about 9 + knots. The minute we cleared the harbor
entrance, in the span of a few seconds, the temperature dropped
about 40 degrees.

Off Battle Harbor, through the St. Anthony Coast Guard, Andy called Ed and Helga Morse to report their arrival on the Labrador. "I hope we made their 20 years of effort worthwhile," he wrote.

It was Andy's original idea to stay offshore going up, because he was picking up a lecturer in Nain who could pilot them back down through the inner passages. "But I started looking at the charts, and realized that coming in to Nain from the sea would probably be more difficult than staying inside all the way up. And by the time I had gotten to Labrador, I'd gotten a little more brazen." So up the familiar passages went the *Bowdoin*.

She continued her tradition of finding unsurveyed and unnamed harbors. The naming conventions have changed over the years, however; 'Wicked Decent Harbor' is the name the 1990 group gave to their own found hole. But, just as the students had done in 1934, they built a cairn and left their mailing address in a bottle.

Approaching Hopedale on July 17, Andy noted that sunset was at 2200, it didn't start to get dark until nearly midnight, and it never did get fully dark. "By 0400 it was light enough to come back up to full speed."

There certainly had been changes from MacMillan's day. When they ran out of Barge Cement, used to mend sails, Andy called back to the Academy and arranged for it to be shipped to Nain. And the technological advances for navigation would have astounded Mac.

To determine his present location, MacMillan had depended upon celestial navigation; navigating was by compass and dead reckoning. Of course, charts were little better than nothing, too. The barometer and his own knowledge of weather patterns and weather signs, what he could see, and what he heard from other travelers about the ice conditions along the coast all helped

MacMillan choose a course. In his later trips, he had radios (so big they filled most of the midships cabin) and a recording fathometer and, in part due to his own research, charts were a little better, but he still had few other tools.

Today, radios and depth sounders are installed even on the average 20-foot pleasure boat; on larger boats, radar is commonplace and provides a tremendous amount of information. By reading signals from satellites, a Global Positioning System (GPS) makes it possible to locate oneself anywhere on the planet, and is accurate within feet. Satellites also provide maps of both surface and atmospheric weather, which can be printed out in a vessel's navigation station by a weatherfax machine. The Canadians create ice maps, updated twice daily, and these, too, are available on weatherfax. A radio-link medical call-in service is now available. The *Bowdoin* was equipped with the latest and best electronic equipment, although not all of the equipment functioned all the time.

But the Labrador landscape hadn't changed. Andy wrote:

> *This morning we got underway by 0430. The weather is poor — colder'n hell (about 40°), drizzling and threatening rain and fog. The cold goes right through you to the bone. We have a long day ahead — the whole trip up the inside from Hopedale to Nain is one big brickyard. Many of the passages are a few tenths of a mile wide, others are wide open spaces spotted with starred rocks. Depths range from 50 and 100 meters to zero, in an instant. The fathometer trace looks like an EKG. My good radar is still down, but the little one is carrying the day. I sure hope he keeps on ticking. . . .*
>
> *Also I have to consider that any of the islands or rocks could be mis-charted . . . . There are 2 buoys on the chart that covers about 1,000 square miles — there is one can and one nun inside Hopedale harbor. There are also 2 whole lighthouses.*
>
> *Yesterday as we came through a very tight hairpin turn entering Hopedale Run, Mark was on the wheel. As we approached what appeared to be a cul-de-sac, with islands surrounding us just a few tenths of a mile off, Zach asked Mark*

*what he was steering. Mark's reply was classic. "3-2-5 degrees, but
Jesus Christ, has anybody looked up ahead?"*

*I can count 13 islands surrounding us. Only one of them has
a name—Nepatalik Island, to starboard. It actually has some
short trees on it. These may be the only trees we've seen in 2 days.
The rest is about 50% bare rock, 50% lichen and tundra.*

The variation here is 32° W. . . .

*I wish we had a geologist aboard—there is a long story told
in the patterns of those cliffs.*

The next chart only covered 875 square miles, but had
no buoys marked and just a single lighthouse. "And about a
billion islands," Andy wrote. Soundings were only marked on
one path through the middle of the chart. Andy stopped the
Bowdoin for the night 18 miles from Nain "in a prehistoric cove. . .
It would be no surprise to see a Cro Magnon Man come down
the rocky slope, or a troll, or a dragon," he wrote. "If this isn't
the end of the world, it's as close as I want to get," said one
student.

Sails up, they headed toward Nain. Andy was again and
again surprised to see how accurate the charting of the approach
was, his depth-finder recording each change shown on the chart.
Much of the research for the charting was done by MacMillan
himself, on the *Bowdoin*, so many years ago; although he is given
no credit on today's charts, undoubtedly his data is used.

Approaching Nain, photographers from *The National Geographic* and a film crew from the Canadian Broadcast Company
came out to meet the *Bowdoin* in a speed boat hired by a local
man, Winston White. Winston pointed out the sights as they
passed them—where Mac's camp had been, where the *Bowdoin*
wintered one year, and the harbor where he himself had grown
up. Winston told Andy that a crowd was on the dock waiting to
spot the *Bowdoin*'s mastheads coming round the point, just as
they always had done in the past.

The excitement on shore was no greater than that on deck.
"In my mind," Andy wrote, "and others I'm sure, was the
knowledge that so many people had invested time, energy and

money in this moment, and how privileged we were to actually be here." The *Bowdoin* herself was suitably festive:

> *We took it all in. I don't recall a lot of talking. We bore off and ran wing and wing straight toward the public dock where a crowd was indeed gathered in the cold and damp. Showing off, we ran straight up to the dock, jibed over about a boatlength off the dock and rounded up, striking sail as we rounded to. I let go a cannon blast as we swung past them. We were flying the big maroon* Bowdoin *pennant at the mainmast head, the MMA flag at the main crosstrees, and at the fore crosstrees we flew a string with the Canadian flag at the top, the Provincial flag of Newfoundland and Labrador in the middle, and the Labrador flag at the bottom with its blue, white, and green, with a green spruce sprig. The US ensign flew from the peak of the main gaff.*

Although Mac would never have made such a showy entrance, the *Bowdoin* and her followers on deck and ashore all appreciated the flair.

The rain started in earnest, but the dock was abuzz. Andy climbed onto the dock and introductions began. One woman burbled cheerfully away at Andy on the dock, but it wasn't until later that he understood that it was she who was pictured in one of the *National Geographics* they had aboard.

Nain had changed since Mac's day. His school was no longer operating (the building now houses the Okalakatiget Society, which produces radio and television for regional distribution). In the late 1950s, the government resettled the northern Inuit, more than doubling the population of the town. No one now winters north of Nain. It had even changed since the year before, when the *Bowdoin* crew would have had to buy fuel in drums and deliver it themselves. Now, fuel was delivered to the vessel by truck!

The four-night stay at Nain was filled with visits and programs and adventures. The *Bowdoin* crew were shown films about the area's history and given a big festive dinner at the hotel. They took a few of the village elders sailing, all of whom were thrilled to be aboard the schooner. The group visited a local sculptor and climbed Nain Hill to build another cairn. The town was out of alcohol when they arrived, but the coastal steamer came in during their visit and took care of that. Although they were cautioned to stay clear of the bar, some of the crew did stop by and had a good time. It was obvious, however, when it was time to return to the vessel. Alcoholism and accompanying domestic violence are common in Labrador today, as is teenage suicide. The Inuit have lost not only their traditional home ranges but much of their identity as a people.

On Sunday, July 22, a good crowd gathered to bid the *Bowdoin* goodbye. Andy raised sail at the dock, and the crew set off a cannon salute as they departed.

The trip down the coast was made "exponentially better," according to Andy, by the presence of Tony Williamson. Tony was a friend of a friend of Andy's, teaching at Memorial University, St. Johns, Newfoundland, who had spent a number of years working on the coast of Labrador for the Labrador Development Council. He had friends all up and down the coast, and he explained many local historic and social topics to the *Bowdoin*'s people along the way. Tony himself enjoyed the trip, although he says the weather was too good—there was only wind enough for one good day of sailing.

They saw many whales on their journey and for a time they took lots of fluke pictures while following a humpback whale. "Late last night Bill Carson said that with his ear pressed against the hull he could hear one singing," Andy reported.

On down the coast they ran, meeting mosquitos and visiting villages along the way. At Hopedale, which Andy describes as a "dead-feeling" town, they were taken to the local museum, and a little further on they went into West Turnavik, where Bob Bartlett, captain of the *Roosevelt*, had his fishing camp and base. Tony Williamson remarks on the sense of history going into Turnavik; the *Bowdoin* had been there so often before. This was the skinny harbor in which she had ridden out Hurricane Hazel in 1954, her last trip north.

"What a spot!" Andy wrote. "Skinny is right. Once inside I

had just enough room to spin around, backing and filling. But I had two fathoms all around. And they talk about having 5–10 schooners in there together. I understand there are ringbolts in the rock to tie up to." (The *Bowdoin* herself had been tied to them in 1954.)

At Makkovik they visited with Rupert MacNeil, "who is one of the old guard of entrepreneurs and hard workers of the area, and who had very fond memories of *Bowdoin* and MacMillan."

While they sailed further south, they saw three yachts in two days. Andy wrote, "Getting crowded."

The little harbor known as the Punchbowl surprised Andy:

> *We knew it was a gathering place for fishermen, and a supply spot for them, but the effect of entering the place was bizarre. As we got up to within a half-mile of the entrance, there was nothing yet to be seen, and we anticipated nothing but a few shacks and perhaps a collector boat or two. On the chart it was not even named, and was only shown as a half-mile wide, enclosed salt-pond, with a 1/10 mile opening and just one sounding, showing one fathom. A place no one but a small boat would enter. As we came around the point we saw a lighted green buoy — a surprise enough — then a lighted red one, then 2 more green and another red. This was the most buoys in a single channel we'd seen since Nova Scotia. And beyond them was a blaze of lights like a small city, and a modest-sized (200 ft.) freighter, alongside a big wharf, unloading cargo, surrounded by 15 or 20 fishing vessels also tied up to the wharf. Here was a huge commercial fish plant complete with all services, store warehouse, processing plant, big cement wharf, forklifts bustling all around, all under stadium lights. It looked and felt for all the world like a James Bond secret harbor. . . . A mile away, you would swear you were 100 miles from any civilization. Here, there were fifty or more houses, and a large-scale commercial operation in an uncharted harbor.*

The *Bowdoin* spent a night in this odd harbor, her crew taking advantage of the telephone, free showers and laundry facilities.

They couldn't leave the north without trying out their ice

anchors, so before Battle Harbour they attempted to tie onto a particularly beautiful and interestingly shaped berg. The berg had a little harbor in it, into which Andy tucked the *Bowdoin*. From the crosstrees, Andy estimated that the berg stood another twenty feet over his head, making it 75–80 feet tall. Tying on wasn't successful, however. "I wasn't comfortable with letting Chris climb up on the berg," Andy says. "It was too slippery, too stupid."

The last day of July they met up with the *Corwith Cramer* off St. John's. The *Cramer* is the second large sailing vessel belonging to Sea Education Association, for whom Andy had sailed the *Westward*. "They were a fine sight, bearing down with everything flying," Andy wrote. A threatening hurricane passed south of them while they stopped at St. John's, where Tony left them.

On the final legs home, Andy put tape over the face of the GPS and had the students take over navigation duties using dead reckoning (DR) and the fathometer. They could get an occasional sun line, too.

On Monday I decided to run over to take a look at Sable Island, since we were ahead of schedule. But that didn't pan out. About 0200, I was up and struggling with the DR. By 0330, I was losing my nerve and flicked the tape off the GPS. The depth contours showing up on the fathometer weren't looking quite right, and though we were still (theoretically) about 25 miles north of the island, it was thick fog, the Loran was not working, one radar was down, the other was questionable, and even the RDF was looking suspicious. So I peeked at the GPS and it said "Error — see manual." I lost my nerve and changed course due west and away from "the Graveyard of the Atlantic."

I reinitialized the GPS and snoozed a bit. In an hour or two it produced a new position and we found that in fact our DR had been just right, but somehow our fathometer hadn't picked up on one big hump, and had picked up a deep hole not shown on the chart. Goes to show you never can tell.

So we came on along. Will got a fuel sounding in between swells, and guessed at our fuel remaining. It was apparent that

we needed to put in to Halifax for fuel, so that's where we headed.
It stayed socked in with fog the rest of the way, and by 0600 we
were entering the Halifax Traffic area. Again our fathometer
readings seemed a little out, though by my guess they were just
showing us to be a little south. So I peeked again, and sure
enough, we were about 2 miles south of our DR. Not bad for
4 days on DR.

On the way back from Labrador, Andy had started thinking
about the following year. It had been so comfortable taking six
weeks and going to Nain, he says it almost seemed more frightening to go further. He thought perhaps they'd take a year off. But
the first thing President Curtis said to Andy upon his return to
Castine was, "This is wonderful, you've got to go north again." At
first they thought about Frobisher Bay, Baffin Island, and then
Andy realized if they went to the top of Frobisher Bay, they
would be in pack ice, close to the Arctic Circle, but unable to
cross it. "That would be silly. Then I started thinking about the
ice charts, how they always showed ice on the Baffin shore, but
Greenland was all clear, saying 'Hey, come here!'

"In nine weeks we could do Disko. What Nain was to
Labrador, Disko Island was to Greenland—Jakobshavn—that's
where Helga was born—and it was feasible. We would make a
first stop at St. Johns, bypassing Nova Scotia, then take fairly
long leaps to Nain—we knew people there, we could get supplies
there—and then we'd hop across Davis Strait to Nuuk. Coming
back, the ice should allow us to go to Cape Chidley and *Bowdoin*
Harbour."

So it was decided that in 1991 the *Bowdoin* would return to
Greenland and to Northern Labrador.

NINETEEN

Back to the Arctic

Provisioning

EBORAH HARRISON IS FROM Alaska; her mother is
Yupik (Eskimo) and Athapaskan (Indian); her father
is white. She was raised with Yupik customs and
values, living sometimes in her mother's Yupik village, and sometimes (in the summer) at the ancestral fish camp, where she
learned about cooking for a group. She got her pilot's license at
age 17, it being more useful where she lived than the driver's
license she obtained in preparation for going to Smith College.
While at Smith, Deborah headed up the Smith College Native
American Students Union, which had three members in 1993,
all of whom were graduating. "I don't know if it will continue,"
Deborah says sadly.

As a young child, Deborah read *Treasure Island* and *Sinbad*
and wanted nothing more than to be a pirate; at Smith, she
couldn't pass up the opportunity to spend a semester at sea on
the brigantine *Corwith Cramer*. She was hooked. Looking for time
at sea during the summer of 1991 to count toward her Able
Bodied Seaman's License, and with no knowledge whatever of
the *Bowdoin*'s history, she applied for and received the steward's
position on the *Bowdoin* for the Greenland trip.

As steward, Deborah's job was clear: all she had to do was provision the vessel for ten weeks, store and keep track of all the provisions, provide food for everyone aboard throughout the voyage (three meals each day, two sittings each, plus three official snacks each day), and see that the schooner was kept in order at all times. That's all.

A few short sails up and down the Maine coast in June with the professional crew and a few guests gave Deborah a chance to practice her menu-planning and stowage skills; even the provisions for that short period took her a couple of days to store. Big containers had to be broken down into smaller packages which could then be crammed into little corners. And, she had to plan in advance what would be used when, so she could pack everything to be accessible when needed.

Before they sailed for Greenland, Andy and the chief mate, Elliot Rappaport, sat Deborah down for a heart-to-heart. After significant throat clearings to announce the importance and delicacy of the question, they asked, "Have we discussed the chocolate supply?" They recommended that $300 to $400 of the budget be spent on that important commodity, and they let her know that the most important job of the steward is to ration the chocolate.

Deborah devoted a full week to planning menus. Nutrition book in hand, and scheming about stowage, she came up with ingenious uses for tiny spaces. The food was delivered the day before they were to leave; it made a huge pile on the dock. The mates informed Deborah that it was a tradition that, at this moment, the steward burst into tears. Deborah suspects that her subsequent problems with the galley stove were due to her failure to follow this tradition. Tradition is very important to sailors, and she says it would have been easy to have succumbed.

But she was left to store the food, and no one was supposed to come below and bother her. Kiirsten and John wandered in, and Deborah grabbed them. "Are you students on the Greenland trip?" They were. "Good, sit down," she instructed them, and put them to work filling baggies with blueberries. Evenually, little bags of blueberries filled all the odd nooks in the freezer.

She packed frantically all night. In the morning she was

joined by Bill Carson, the steward from two years before, who was aboard for the first day's sail; he also cooked supper for the crew before leaving the schooner. (Perhaps the tradition of the steward bursting into tears was a short-lived one. Bill was a widely respected professional merchant mariner who gave Deborah the impression of being in control of everything.) Deborah says that Bill's help that day was invaluable, as much by his emotional support as by his concrete assistance. "He went out of his way to show me that this was *my* trip, *my* galley, asking permission to put something away or to use supplies for dinner. For the expert to say 'you can do this'—it meant a lot."

Deborah packed flour, sugar, oatmeal and the rest of the dry goods in fishboxes and crammed them three layers out, four high under the second mate's bunk and her own. "The containers were rectangular, so I put split peas and beans into baggies, and worked them into the corners. It took three or four little bags for a stew, but it would have been wasted space." Although they were expensive, Deborah chose boned chicken breasts because they were efficient in terms of both space and waste. The eggs remained good all the way to Greenland, stored in a cool location in the "Projects," as the midships cabin, the old hold, had been dubbed in 1990 in recognition of its less-than-posh accommodations.

There was a padlock on the refrigerator, installed to save on cooling energy. Deborah planned each day's meals around one or two openings of the reefer daily, and installed the padlock initially as much to keep herself from opening the door without thinking as to keep others out. Later, she was glad for its presence to protect the precious resources from visitors and fellow shipmates. She stowed as much of the chocolate as possible in the refrigerator. The balance was under her bunk, with a board above it, a cache that was not discovered until it was no longer needed. Although some members of the crew tired of Hershey bars before the *Bowdoin* returned to Castine, Second Mate Zach, in particular, required regular chocolate fixes. There were times when Deborah was mightily tempted by his offer to stoke the stove in exchange for a Hershey bar.

"I was especially proud," Deborah says, "because stowing that much in the *Bowdoin* hadn't been done since Mac's day, and no one really knew how to do it." Of course, the job wasn't made easier by Andy's informing her after she stowed the canned goods in the storage boxes on deck that it wasn't safe to have done so. In a big sea, he told her, they might come loose and be dangerous missiles on deck, or they might be lost overboard. So, Deborah unpacked them all and put the cans below, much to the displeasure of the first day's galley slave, who came aboard with a hangover and didn't enjoy spending the day with his head in the bilge, stowing cans. The deck boxes were filled instead with fresh vegetables.

Deborah hoped to buy milk and fish locally as they travelled, and indeed was able to do so, although she couldn't depend upon it; her plan was to make the *Bowdoin* self-sufficient "unless we were grounded and had to spend the winter," she says, smiling. She knew full well how close the *Bowdoin* had come to that predicament in the past. She packed 50 pounds of salt so she could salt down the meat and not lose it if the freezer quit. And, she planned not to be dependent upon fresh goods for vitamin needs.

"We should have had more emergency rations, and I would have ordered everything to be delivered a few days earlier, so I would have had more time to stow it all," Deborah says in retrospect. "But assuming the stove had worked right, the provisioning was good."

Underway Again

From first mate Elliot Rappaport's journal:

> *June 30 — Departure Day — Mayhem. . . . I have twelve hours since lost the ability to decide what I'm going to do next, and now wander aimlessly amidst the wellwishers, amidst piles of food cartons, flour sacks, fuel drums, clothing, deer rifles, exposure suits, cans of paint. Down below, I sidestep bananas. Duck to pass under bulging hammocks filled with potatoes and onions.*

Pirouette past cases of coffee. There cannot possibly be room for
all of this. There is enough to supply the siege of Troy. To feed the
Pittsburgh Steelers for an entire season. There is enough to
provision an Arctic expedition. Hmm.

By evening we are anchored in Orcutt's Harbor, around the
corner from Castine. If we actually left the dock there to come here
I have no recollection. Ashore, the spruces breathe silently beside
summer cottages just opened for their season. By all reckoning we
will be skipping summer this year. The skiff goes ashore and
emergency, secret, last-minute runs are made for forgotten
essentials. Eyeglasses. Foul weather gear (compliments of L.L.
Bean). Toothbrushes. Aboard, and in several hours of relative
calm, the students try to learn the routine: When to wake up for
watch. How to make coffee. How to set sail. Where to find the
main peak pennant. The after bilge. The man-overboard pole. The
Barograph. They are told to carry their knives at all times, like
residents of some nautical DMZ. To keep the log in black ink. To
beware of lines under strain, and to flush the heads with twenty
pumps of the long brass handle.

On June 30, 1991, with the traditional noisy fanfare from a
flotilla of well-wishers, the *Bowdoin* left Castine bound for Greenland. Her first day's sail was but a short hop to initiate those
aboard who had never sailed offshore before. Thirty days and
two thousand miles later, the *Bowdoin* crossed the Arctic Circle
and was cruising among icebergs in Disko Bay, Greenland. For
the first time since before most of her company had been born,
the *Bowdoin* was back in the seas she was designed for.

In addition to Andy Chase as captain, Elliot Rappaport as
chief mate, Zach Thomas as second mate, Chris Cluck as second
mate/engineer, and Deborah Harrison as steward, the schooner
was taking nine students north, whose ages ranged from 21 to 42;
eight were from Maine Maritime. Two berths were available for
visitors, which at one time or another included lecturers and
paying guests. Steve Kloehn, a reporter from *The Bangor Daily
News*, and photographer Tom Stewart each spent five weeks
aboard. One of the guests was Stuart Hotchkiss, who had not

sailed on the vessel since 1943. Andy's plan was to sail outside Newfoundland, up the eastern shore of Labrador to Nain, and across to Greenland.

As he had the year before, Andy established a Swedish watch system, with three watches working five shifts a day: the day watches were six hours each, the night watches four. This system allowed the crew twelve consecutive hours off every third day, a luxury which would have astounded the *Bowdoin*'s earlier Arctic sailors. Classes were held each day, "on deck in nice weather, below when it was rotten, and cancelled when it was really rotten," as Josh Smith, one of the students, described them. Subjects included: meteorology, seamanship, anchoring, magnetic variation, provisioning, Arctic whaling, whale populations and identifying whales, Arctic culture.

Deborah prepared crepes with strawberries for the *Bowdoin*'s first breakfast underway, and a soup made of cornish game hen, mushrooms and celery for lunch. Good food combined with a perfect sailing day — it was sunny with gentle winds from the west — how could life be any better?

An early start allowed the *Bowdoin* to sneak up on Andy's nephew aboard the nearby schooner *Alamar*, still at anchor. The *Bowdoin* fired a cannon shot at close quarters, awakening the other party if not scaring them witless.

With a northwesterly breeze sending them along easily, Andy brought out the video camera to record Cadillac Mountain dipping over the stern. "Last time we'll see that till we've been and back," someone remarked.

Because there wasn't room to freeze both of the turkeys Deborah had purchased, she planned to roast one while it was still fresh. Apparently, though, the bird was already spoiled when she bought it. It was given a formal burial at sea. Andy covered it with a dish towel and spoke solemn words of benediction as two men carried it ponderously to the rail and allowed it to slide gracefully into the deep. (However, the dead turkey didn't have the grace to sink; the carcass floated along after them.) The towel was duly and ceremoniously folded and presented to Deborah, the grieving widow. Andy told her not to feel too sad. "He was a kind of a turkey, after all."

The good weather held all the way to Newfoundland, allowing the crew a look at Sable Island, known as the "Graveyard of
the Atlantic" and often unapproachable. The island is a sandspit,
twenty miles long and very narrow, with 50-foot dunes and its
own climate, smack in the middle of the Gulfstream. The Canadian Coast Guard maintains a station there, manned by a half a
dozen people, and the only other inhabitants are the huge packs
of seals, flocks of sea birds, and a herd of feral ponies, descended
from ponies on a ship wrecked on Sable around the turn of the
century. Wooden remnants of wrecks litter the beaches.

Captain Andy Chase had a more formal approach to teaching seamanship than had Mac. Emergency drills made up the
first lessons, followed by lectures about the specifics of gear and
the *Bowdoin's* rig: reefing the main, setting and tacking the trys'l,
and sail maneuvering, the latter broadening the scope to the
concept of balance under sail.

Five or six days out, as the sun was setting, everyone was
hanging around the afterdeck, eating little cheesecakes made
with the last of the fresh strawberries. They were chatting about
nothing important, enjoying the warm evening, when Deborah,
who hadn't had a chance to steer since they began the trip, took
the wheel. "I was steering with my rear end, still eating cheese-
cake," she says, "and Andy said, 'Before this trip is out, we'll all
learn cheek-steering.' There was laughter all around, but then
there was silence. I looked around and realized we weren't
strangers anymore."

Recurring jokes had developed already and would continue for the whole trip. Zach, although he had grown up in
Maine, now lived in New Jersey. Everyone on board agreed that
real people didn't come from New Jersey—and certainly not
schoonerpeople. "New Jersey is the land of the Big Hair," they
said. With that, "Big Hair" became the symbol of not belonging
to the new community of the schooner *Bowdoin*. If anyone came
to breakfast with their hair askew, someone would be sure to
remark, "My, what Big Hair you have today," and everyone would
laugh.

Nor was anyone ever allowed to forget any silly little mistake
they made. Josh was harassed for the entire trip because early

on, he had gone below while still very sleepy, turned on the coffee spigot, and missed his cup altogether.

Music became a large part of each day's enjoyment. Andy and Elliot often would play their guitar and banjo in the evening, and others joined in. Zach had a Japanese flute. "He played beautifully," says Deborah, "but he was the schooner clown. He is very sharp, and was always making observations in a reflective tone as if lecturing about the Nature of the Planet, and he'd have us rolling in laughter." One night he was sitting crosslegged in his bunk, playing a lovely song. There was a hush. Then a long silence. Dave, whom Deborah describes as "rough-and-tumble, manly Dave," spoke. "That was really beautiful, what's it called?"

"That was a song I wrote in dedication to my true love, entitled 'Spank Me In The Dark,'" said Zach. So much for quiet reverence.

Whale and dolphin displays at sunrise and Northern lights capped the crossing to Newfoundland. Andy worried in his journal: "I only wonder what the payback for this might be. . . ."

The schooner approached Newfoundland on July 7. From Elliot's journal:

> *David Ames spotted our first ice of the trip at first light this morning, a small bit just a mile away that I'd been watching as a suspicious little dot on the radar for most of the early morning.*
>
> *By 1000 the bergs have become almost routine, as they march by in a monolithic parade of white shapes — immense haystacks, meringues, sugar cubes, crystalline elephants, wrought with blue veins of re-frozen water.*
>
> *The ice is an indescribable, almost implausible shade of blue. This afternoon, a berg that we had just passed split in two with a huge crack and dropped a garage-sized piece of ice into the sea. In the still water the splash produced a perfect curling wave of jade green. It looked like a surfing poster. The Newfie Pipeline . . . not for the faint of heart.*
>
> *Later, a pod of 8–12 Humpback whales blew and sounded close by.*

The Canadian Coast Guard makes ice maps available to ships over their weatherfax machines. Andy knew as they approached St. John's, Newfoundland, that Belle Isle Strait and the whole coast of Labrador was still closed with ice. The unusually heavy ice conditions were forcing fishing vessels to stay offshore well into their normal inshore season. A few days layover in St. Johns showed no improvement in the ice conditions. Reporter Steve Kloehn and Tom Stewart, the photographer who had sailed to Labrador in 1990, were supposed to join the schooner for the Greenland leg at Nain, but it didn't look as if the *Bowdoin* would be able to make Nain. In 1937, when Miriam went to Nain to meet Mac, she had no way of knowing if the *Thebaud* would be coming to get her or not, but by 1991 it was a different world; Andy called Steve and Tom, and they made arrangements to meet the *Bowdoin* at St. Anthony's, Newfoundland, instead.

Andy had planned a surprise man-overboard drill in Conception Bay, but Elliot lost his hat over the side, providing the same exercise. Andy announced that they should assume it was he who was overboard, and climbed to the ice barrel to observe. Elliot, first mate, was the only one who could see the hat, so he had to be lookout, leaving the second mates in command of the schooner. The exercise was successful, and the group retrieved the hat in short order.

The *Bowdoin* sailed along the northeastern Newfoundland coast, passing through a field of icebergs of all sizes and shapes. Elliot described the Canadian Ice Patrol's terms:

> Pack ice, or frozen seawater, is distinct from glacial ice—bits of broken-off Arctic icecap that patrol the ocean as icebergs, bergy bits, and growlers. The latter items, the ice patrol tells us, are categorized by size. If you encounter a chunk of ice the size of your ship, it is an iceberg at which you are looking.
>
> As a berg moves through changing conditions of climate and water temperature, it is in constant flux. It melts under the warm sun until its faces shimmer under a skin of flowing fresh water. As the melting process removes weight from its exposed portion,

its equilibrium is disturbed, and it rotates to compensate. Often
a berg will tilt gradually and imperceptibly, slowly basting itself
like a turkey on a spit until its sides are ridged with dozens of
uniform striations — waterlines of days past. The average iceberg
has about a fifth of its volume exposed at any given time.
Occasionally throughout the process of decay some point of cosmic
balance is exceeded and the whole works overturns, upending
with thunderous booms of stress relieved and mini-tsunamis of
displaced water. You do not want to be nearby when this happens.
Often as not the new orientation cannot meet the structural
requirements necessary to remain as one, and it breaks into pieces.
Two. Ten. A hundred.

The ice patrol has names for these pieces as well. A two-car
garage of glacial ice floating slowly by is a bergy bit. Growlers,
warns the patrol, are most dangerous because they are small and
hard to spot, floating just above the surface. A growler is the size
of a grand piano.

The schooner encountered pack ice on the way toward St.
Anthony's. Elliot saw it first on the radar "as a blight of electronic
smallpox. . . and then a long low line of ragged whiteness, seemingly solid and just below the horizon." Then they got into the ice
itself, "an incredible checkerboard of floes melted into Dali-
esque shapes of all sizes, in what seemed to be about two-tenths
concentration." Andy said the low concentration, being easily
navigable, made a good learning experience. He bumped a piece
"just to see what we were up against," and found the ice was
rotten and soft. "It just went mush."

Elliot's journal showed that the other navigational hazards of
MacMillan's days had not all disappeared, despite the increased
identifications and descriptions of some of them:

July 15. Made the run from Lumsden to Twillingate through
a Middle-Earth landscape of black hills and poorly charted tickles.
The chart coverage has begun to break down somewhat as
unsounded areas become more prevalent and chart margins fill

with terse warnings to the effect that "Snooks Is. is reported to be considerably to the East of its charted position."

Elliot described St. Anthony's as "a crack in the rocks, a fish plant, three crumbling wharves. The Sir Wilfred Grenfell Mission Hospital. Two hundred houses. Blue icefloes aground in grey rain."

The Job of Steward

The stove aboard the *Bowdoin* was an ongoing challenge for Deborah. It was a coal-fired Aga, a wonderful stove to be sure, but not constructed to go to sea. "It never worked reliably after the second day; the shifting around scrunched the thermostat," Deborah explains. She described the stove in a letter to a friend:

> *Her name is Baby Aga. She is the captain's child, really, but I am her nursemaid for the duration of this voyage. Baby Aga is a big, blue-enameled cookstove, our only source of heat for cabin warmth and for cooking. But like a spoiled and petulant child, she insists on being at the center of my attention at all times, night as well as day. My shipmates, men who, for the most part, are not given to flights of fancy, often wake me in the night to inform me solemnly that "Baby has a fever." I get up and feed my child, for her thermostat does not work, and when she gets enough draft, she must be fed constantly or she will burn herself out. Have you ever known a fever so high that it melts steel and scorches asbestos? Baby Aga had one such fever not long ago, melting a hole clean through her lid.*
>
> *When Baby is not feverish, she is usually chilled. Long days and nights have I spent feeding chunks of coal to her, one at a time, coaxing heat from her until her fire dies despite my efforts. Even when we hit shore and others go exploring or take showers, I never leave Baby for long, and then always in the hands of a*

*capable sitter, lest she feel neglected and pout. Do not think that
I have taken leave of my senses, or at least that I have done so
alone. There is not one person aboard who has not sidled up to me
and whispered, to keep her from overhearing, "How is Baby Aga
today?" I've seen the captain pat her gently and ask how she is
feeling, and I have had other shipmates offer to make prayers to
the God of Agas that she may be in better health. Yes, we are all
caught up in this madness. And since Baby Aga has great control
over the quality of all our lives, we treat her more like a spoiled
guest than a working member of the crew.*

The coffee maker was nearly as bad. It was not designed to be
on a moving platform. "You were bound to burn yourself every
time you poured the water," Deborah says. And the coffee it made
was terrible. "You had to chew it. But after two months, people
were still coming off watch surprised that the coffee was bad."
Some members of the company gave up coffee for the duration.

It was the steward's responsibility to keep the vessel in order.
One of the few rules on the *Bowdoin* was that people's personal
gear was to be kept in their own bunks or lockers and not in the
common areas. "As good as the mates were, no one wants to say
'make your bunk and pick up your socks,' so that fell to me. I kept
finding myself being the bad guy, hounding people to put their
stuff away," she says, and she didn't like the role and resented the
need of policing.

Things that would be of little or no consequence ashore become monumental problems at sea. Every morning Deborah
found mugs and magazines on the table, foul-weather gear on
the counter, and hats and mittens in the sink, all of which she
had to put somewhere before she could start breakfast. And, as
they came in to eat, people shed their wet clothes onto Deborah's
bunk. She hated finding foul-weather gear there. She was peeved.
No one picked up after themselves, either. She was at a loss how
to communicate to her shipmates how important all this was
to her.

More than one crew member showed Deborah by their
actions that they believed she was not a real crew member. One

student told her, "You're not a mate, I don't have to listen to you." Sometimes she was surprised at the people who attacked her; they were those whom she considered to be her staunchest supporters. "It's the pack mentality," she explains. "If you show any weakness, the pack turns on you. Under stress, genuinely nice, thoughtful people do and say unnecessarily cruel things."

Three weeks into the trip, when the *Bowdoin* came into St. Anthony's, Newfoundland, Deborah was frantic with frustration. Feeling incompetent and helpless, she wondered if she should quit. She says, "I went ashore and pounded the docks till I found a hotel room. When I got back, everyone was hostile. Andy came to me, and I burst into tears." Andy told her to forget dinner. She told him all her worries: about how she wasn't doing her job right, how she couldn't communicate with anyone, how no one would listen to anything she said, no one helped. "I poured my heart out to him. It maybe didn't solve any problems, but I had to say it all. He told me that it was a normal part of the trip, that three weeks in, the steward always loses it. It was reassuring to know I wasn't just some fruitcake, that I shouldn't be sent home because I couldn't do the job. That's what I'd been afraid of. I knew after that that he'd back me up, too."

In spite of her frustrations, though, already Deborah had discovered certain times aboard the *Bowdoin* to be almost magical:

> *What a beautiful time the early morning is. At 0430 the vessel is asleep, all except the mate and three students standing the dawn watch above. I wake in the darkness and warmth of my bunk, under the wool blankets and behind the heavy green curtains. I always burrow deeper in my covers then, though I am listening, waiting for the sounds of boots on the rungs of the ladder in the hatchway. The wait is never long, and in the darkness one of the watch-standers creeps to my bunk and whispers my name.... The 0430 wake-up call is for me alone.*
>
> *I have time to dress in the darkness by the warm stove before climbing the ladder and joining the watch for a cold, gray dawn. That is one of my favorite times, checking the charts to see where*

*we've been in the night and chatting at the helm with some of my
shipmates. After a half hour or so I retreat below to stoke the coal
stove and clean out the ashes. Then I start my baking and get
breakfast on. I wake my galley slave in time to set the table for me,
then I climb the ladder again to ring the old brass bell that
signals meal time.*

The *Bowdoin* moved out into the Labrador Sea, ice-free, but
cold and damp and grey. The temperature had dropped dras-
tically. Deborah wrote, "We have stopped living on deck. The
watch on duty stands above, but the other 12 of us huddle below
by the warm stove and the glow from the lamps." The sea wasn't
always kind, either. From a letter that Deborah wrote:

*These sailors, as befit tradition, do sport an amazing
repertoire of curses and profanity, so I stand out because I very
rarely swear. But last night, just as the first group was seated
'round the galley table and I was pulling the meat from the oven,
we took a death roll and our supper went flying. At that moment,
completely unbidden and surprising to all, a curse that would
make the most salty of sailors proud sprung from my lips. There
was an instant of dead silence before every last one of them burst
into uproarious laughter. They were all so busy clutching their
sides and wiping their tears that none of them grumbled about
having only vegetables for supper. One of the older students
clapped me on the back and said he didn't know I had it in me.
Now, in their eyes, it's official. I'm a true sailor after all.*

Deborah described another aspect of the closeness the crew
experienced aboard:

*You do not know a man until you stand with him, each of you
clad in your underwear, on a pitching ship heading into the far
north. I realized around two this morning, as I was roused from
my bunk to stoke the stove and stood at the task in my underwear,
that under different circumstances it would be an odd thing to be
doing. When Steve joined me on his way to the head—one cannot*

*help but have a tete-a-tete with anyone on their way to the head
when one is standing in that tiny galley—I realized that only in
such a place as this would we stand to chat, we who have known
each other such a short time, by the stove in our skivvies.*

And soon Deborah learned that the same stress that caused
people to do horrible things sometimes made them do uncom-
monly thoughtful things, too. One night when she was really
tired, Jamie was to be galley slave the following day. Without saying anything to Deborah, he told the watch not to wake her, and
he got breakfast himself. She didn't wake up at all until everyone
was eating below her bunk. "He was just as tired as everyone
else—he didn't have to do that," says Deborah. "The caliber of the
gift is so much greater when it costs so much to the giver."

Greenland

"We have so much more than MacMillan had," Elliot noted. "Electronics. Mustang suits. GPS. The exotic wireless that once filled a
whole cabin is now an off-the-shelf item the size of a shoebox. . . .
But we keep the cold and damp, and the dreary half-nights of
these latitudes, the hours of myopic staring into grey mist. And
we keep a feeling that was surely there before, that slight sense of
foreboding, of sailing north into a barren world through a tiny
window of summer."

Each member of the company in 1991 was equipped with a
Mustang suit, a rugged, heavily insulated suit which allows a
deckhand to completely forget about being cold and wet. Elliot
says, "You get out of your bunk in your underwear and just get
right into your Mustang suit, and cold and wet just aren't an issue
any more." He adds, "The Mustang suits are one of Andy's bits of
magic. He has a knack—he's not afraid to ask anyone for exactly
what he wants, and he usually gets it, because they don't know
how to say no." The Mustang Company donated two suits and
made the rest available at cost; several people bought their own,
and others begged for donations from businesses to buy suits

which they would use on this trip and then leave aboard the *Bowdoin*.

Mustang suits are no substitute for survival suits, however— Andy put a Mustang suit to the test in Castine in March, going overboard intentionally. The water temperature was 38 degrees. He was in the water for only six minutes before he had to come out. He didn't think to take his own temperature when he emerged. He wishes he had; in retrospect, he realizes he was already hypothermic. It took him several hours to get warm again. Gumby suits, on the other hand, have kept fishermen alive in frigid waters for two or three days. "You can't work in them, though," Andy explains. "They're strictly survival suits. The Mustang suits are for working—and they'll give you a fighting chance to get someone back aboard if they go over."

At breakfast on July 22, after their first full night of twilight, Greenland showed up on radar, sixty miles off. Only minutes later, a mountain peak was visible over the fog bank ahead. Landfall Greenland! "Now that must be quite a mountain," wrote Andy.

Three days later, at Nuuk (formerly Godthaab) they received a royal welcome from the Home-Rule government, starting with hot showers and a jacuzzi, continuing with a tour of the Royal Greenland Fish Plant, a silver-service feast of Royal Greenland's produce for lunch, followed by a visit to the national museum, and finally the maritime college. The Harbor Master was very helpful, moving another boat so the *Bowdoin* could lay at the passenger berth, and arranging for fuel and water.

Elliot was impressed not only by the red carpet treatment they were given, but by some other local features too. "The mosquitos here bring new meaning to the word," he wrote, commenting as well that doing laundry was the biggest challenge so far; the single coin-operated machine caused the crew frustration to the point of violence.

The next day, the *Bowdoin* headed north to Manitsoq, into head seas. Elliot wrote: "Tonight I brushed my teeth at 11 P.M., in full daylight, in the middle of Davis Strait, aboard a schooner three times my age, in my underwear. It occurs to me that my occupation is not a natural one."

At Manitsoq, again the crew was greeted with extraordinary hospitality, this time arranged by the local director of the Tourist Office, Lena Pedersen. She took the people of the *Bowdoin* to the local museum and to the home of an elderly woman who was teaching native decorative arts, sewing and beading, to all the town's schoolgirls. At night, she was teaching the adult women whose government education had not given them these skills. Deborah, because of her Alaskan Eskimo heritage, was particularly pleased to see the conscious effort being made to incorporate the traditional into modern education. Although the teacher spoke no English, Deborah and the others were able to share their appreciation of the arts being passed on. The woman gave Deborah a tiny, half-completed doll, letting her know that she was to finish it herself. And then she had a special gift for Andy. "Right before we left," Deborah wrote, "she took down a necklace—a man's necklace, a traveler and hunter and brave man's necklace, and placed it around his neck. It was a huge bear claw, strung on a leather thong."

"It nearly brought tears to my eyes," Andy wrote, recognising the importance of such a gift.

As they left the old woman's house, Tom, the photographer, stopped to play with some young children, letting them look at his cameras, and even take a picture with one. "Their laughter followed us down the hill to the *Bowdoin*," wrote Deborah. "We did not need a translator to understand their fun when one of the white strangers stopped to play with them."

The climax for most of the group was "an afternoon jaunt" to the local summer ski area, "just a short trip away by boat," they were told.

"Luckily the story unraveled a little at a time, or I mightn't have gone," Andy says. It started with a twelve-mile journey in the *Bowdoin* through islands and fjords beyond their chart—Lena volunteered her husband Jens as pilot, a fisherman all his life in those waters. "He certainly looked authentic," Elliot wrote, "with a broad white grin and skin like an old leather briefcase. . . . He spoke no English, but was cheerful and quite sure of where we were going. We all hoped that he had not spent his life fishing from a skiff, and walked on needles as we plowed past islands, across a bay, up a fjord, and finally off into the top of a small blind inlet at the foot of a steep valley." There they left the *Bowdoin* at anchor.

The "jaunt" up to the ski area was a hike of nearly seven miles, to a ski resort 10,000 feet above sea level. The "resort" consisted of a portable rope tow, two Snow Cats and a plywood bunkhouse on the ice cap. Some members of the group went snowmobiling; others tried to sleep. Everyone reports that time is irrelevant in constant daylight. At one in the morning, Elliot and Andy were aboard a snowmobile running at 75 miles per hour across the ice cap, following the lead of their guide, the ski center's custodian and would-be Olympic skier. "If you see a crack," he told them as they mounted their machines, almost as an afterthought, "do not try to stop." Go fast, he indicated, and you'll fly over. Stop, and you'll fall in. Unless of course the crack is too wide—then you have to stop. Elliot wrote:

> We stop on a rise that overlooks the icecap proper. Here the black mountains of the coast march inland and disappear into whiteness, as if they are part of an unfinished painting. At this latitude the sun and the moon simply chase each other in a circle around the sky, and right now the sun is barely below the horizon in the north, while a full moon hangs fat and yellow above the mountains, directly opposite. It is perfectly still, and the world has become a deftly folded quilt of purple—gray—black—and the fullest white you can imagine.

The exhausted captain found the bunks in the ski camp to be very comfortable. But he awoke at 0600 hearing a funny noise. "I guess I woke everyone else up when I said, 'Oh *shit*. It's raining.' The magic of last night evaporated. I was fit to be tied. I guessed (correctly) that only about half of us had any foul-weather gear.

Now we had fatigue and hypothermia to confront." The trip back down the mountain was nearly as unpleasant as the trip up. "I was in a frenzy of anxiety," Andy wrote, "fearing that someone would slip and break a leg." He was worried, too, that the schooner would get in trouble while all the professional crew were gallivanting around the ice cap wearing themselves out.

But everyone returned to the schooner safely. The schooner was fine, too.

However, the adventure wasn't quite over. It was low tide, it was still raining, and the wind was blowing hard and directly in their faces. "We were going out through a tricky place for which there was no chart, with a pilot who spoke not one word of English, into a Greenland Gale," wrote Andy. It turned out that Jens knew at least two words of English:

> Jens knew his route—we never saw less than 3 meters under our keel—and soon we were back on the chart, leaping into a mean, steep, 8-foot sea. When we rounded the corner and were briefly beam to it we took a couple of death-rolls, and shipped the first green sea aboard. Jens was very impressed with the boat; he said several times 'good boat, good boat.'

Coming into Sukkertoppen harbor was tricky, too. A big fishing vessel backed off into the channel just as Andy was making his anchoring approach, forcing him to spin the *Bowdoin* around. A tail wind prevented them from rounding up, so they tried to anchor on the fly, and stopped too close to shore. Finally, they went into the dock, finding more shelter there than Andy expected. He wrote: "I fought off exhaustion till dinner time by going up to the Seaman's Club for a shower and laundry."

Deborah and the Inuit

Particularly meaningful for Deborah was her exposure to the Inuit people she met in Greenland. The official Greenlandic language, Inuktitut, is a combination of Inuit and Danish; although it is closely related to Yupik, Deborah could only recognize random words. But it meant a great deal to her to see the careful efforts to keep historic knowledge and skills alive. "I can't tell you how odd and inspiring it is to hear a Native tongue, similar to my own, being spoken by the government officials and in the banks and post offices," Deborah wrote home to a friend. "The Inuit are the middle class here—a far cry from the desperately poor people living in the slums of Fairbanks, as it is with the Natives at home."

The highlight of the trip for Deborah occurred the night the rest of the group trekked to the ski resort. Deborah stayed aboard the *Bowdoin* with Lena, Jens, and an injured crewmember. The two women talked for hours, comparing Inuit and Yupik culture, sharing their lives and experiences, talking about the effects the Danish government had on the Inuit, and the Russians and Americans had on the Alaskan native people.

In Alaska, until the 1960s, the educational policy was to force native children to speak English while they attended compulsory boarding schools away from their own homes, leaving them neither part of the white community nor of their own. In Labrador also, governmental action has destroyed the native lifestyle. But in Greenland, the Danes did not press the local population to dress like Europeans or to become Danish. Although the Inuit were blended into a semi-European economy, their own culture remained important. Traditional hunting and fishing have been respected as a way of life, as has the traditional land base. The Royal Greenland Company must purchase the sea produce caught by the Inuit, although seal and whale meat are not sold internationally; fishing continues as a legitimate way of life for Inuit men. From Deborah's journal:

> *I told her how things are at home, about the poverty and alcoholism that is a lot like the way it is in Labrador. And we discussed the causes, and what might someday bring about change before our culture, if not our people, are entirely destroyed. I was not sure she would understand when I tried to tell her just how bad things were for the people at home, because the situation in*

Greenland is such a far cry from ours. However, she had traveled
and seen the loss and the despair for herself. She did understand,
and I felt like I was talking to an Elder from my own community.
She told me she was proud of me for being proud of my heritage,
and for trying to find ways to live it in the modern world and
protect it. She is very interested in community-building, and
pointed out the things about our people's situation in Greenland
that she dislikes, despite the fact that it is so much better than in
Canada and the U.S., and what she is trying to do about it.

"Don't give up," she told me. "Keep trying to find ways to
help our people. It is how we will survive this century, and the
next, and the next—only if our young people keep trying. The
elders in your village should be proud of you. I am proud of you.
Remember that you are strong, even when it is tough to be a
Native woman in a white world. Always remember that all the
Elders are proud of you."

It is hard to remember, at times, that I am a whole continent
away from home. People like Lena make this feel like home. This
Arctic feels like my Arctic, these People are my People. I did not
know I would sail so far, only to find that I am really at home.

Deborah was impressed by the balance Lena showed between wanting local control of the resources and government,
yet accepting the benefits of contact with the outside. Lena's
political activity was not limited to the local level; she had been
one of three delegates to the recent Inuit Circumpolar Confer-
ence. Tourism has become an important aspect of the Greenlandic economy, in addition to fishing; recently, Greenlandic
glacier ice for cocktails has become a saleable product! One
crewmember took a package of ice home as a gift for his father
to put in his scotch.

Lena told Deborah how the community benefitted from its
contact with MacMillan; she remembered her mother talking of
the *Bowdoin*'s earlier visits. Deborah could see how the Inuit
weren't the naive people described by the MacMillans. They had
been in contact with whalers for a hundred years before Mac
started visiting Greenland, and they had a shrewd awareness of

how to work with the people from away. And their culture stresses making people welcome (no matter if they're making fools of themselves, as no doubt all visitors have done from time to time). If the Inuit were treated by the visitors as appealing little creatures, slightly less than human, they were used to it, and could turn the experience to their own advantage. Deborah, who had felt uncomfortable about the historical relations between the *Bowdoin*'s people and the natives, was reassured after her evening with Lena.

The farewells were emotional. From Deborah's journal:

> *Right before we pulled away from the dock, Andy called down to me. I was busy preparing a meal and didn't want to be interrupted, but I dutifully dried my hands and came up on deck . . . to find Lena, who had come to say good bye.*
>
> *She came carrying a* huge *loaf of raisin sweet bread, which she baked for the crew this morning. For me she had a parka—her own parka, which she removed and insisted I take.*
>
> *I refused at first, saying she was too kind to me, that I couldn't possibly take it. I was really taken aback. But she put the parka in one of my hands and took my other hand in hers.*
>
> *"Take it," she said. "You know it is our way."*

The Arctic

At 1606 hours, July 28, 1991, the *Bowdoin* crossed the Arctic Circle, 66°33′, for the first time in more than 35 years. For Deborah, an Alaskan, the Arctic Circle was an unremarkable part of life, and David Ames had crossed the line during his Navy duty. Together they had planned what Andy calls a "thoroughly humiliating" ritual for the neophytes in recognition of the experience. After a salute with the cannon, the fourteen "Warmbloods" turned to on deck, dressed in only their underwear. Air and water temperature were both right around 40 degrees, accompanied by a good northerly breeze. David read pompously significant words of indoctrination to the assembled company while Deborah painted everyone's noses blue. Then David turned the firehose on the inductees and chased them forward to kiss the *Bowdoin*'s stemhead (subsequently painted blue as well). It didn't take the underwear-clad crew long to go below to dress, although Andy stopped long enough to kiss both Deborah and David, in order to smear their faces with blue food coloring.

The cookstove wasn't working at all this day, so the planned Arctic feast of whale and seal meat, which had been purchased in Manitsoq, was replaced with a less festive meal of sardines, crackers, cheese and peanut butter. "It went down fine," wrote Andy, "though Deb is depressed." The captain broke out a bottle of Greenlandic Aquavit, and everyone drank a toast to the Arctic, the *Bowdoin*, and all her people through the years.

All the while, the barometer was dropping, bottoming out at change of watch in the evening. The northerlies kept building, and by midnight it was really blowing, cold and raining. Because progress wasn't likely, they hove to. "It built to Force 8–9," Andy wrote, "and the seas were 15–20 feet and breaking. The boat took it elegantly. She was practically comfortable, except in the foc'sle where she gave quite an elevator ride. We only rarely got swept by a sea. . . . Just once she punched into one and took a good deal of green water aboard. It was incredible to see her take it with such ease. And the crew held up perfectly."

Late the next morning, when the wind had dropped, backing into the west, they set off again for the 70th parallel, now some ten miles further away than it had been. In fact, they had been blown about a dozen miles back across the Arctic Circle, but of course no note needed taking as they recrossed; they were all old hands now.

Disko Bay's uncountable icebergs included two more wonderful than the rest, according to Andy: "One, a huge irregular cathedral of natural arches, the other a vast white brick twice the height of *Bowdoin* and ten times as long." Tom and Chris took off in the Zodiac to take pictures. Tom took 16 rolls of film circling those two bergs, the rubber boat going one way, the *Bowdoin* the other. "If one of Tom's pictures captures the true colors of the iceberg, no one will believe it," Andy wrote. "They are dynamic sculptures — performance art. They burst, crack, roll, divide right before your eyes." He had a hard time convincing the photography party not to go through the arch in the rubber boat, and as they were returning to the *Bowdoin* a big chunk fell from the arch. (Shades of the 1934 trip when, to Mac's consternation, the Cape Mugford landing party had rowed under just such an arch, which also collapsed.) "It's funny," says Andy, "how everyone always tells you not to get near an iceberg just before they show you a photo of their vessel right next to one."

Elliot describes an encounter in Disko Bay:

> *The vistas of Disko Bay are breathtaking, the scale unimaginable. After dinner we are buzzed by a small powerboat. A woman points a camera at us. Two men wave. The little yellow lapstrake has a Mercury outboard motor, and a freshly killed seal draped over one gunwhale. His blood runs in a red streak, down the topsides and into the bay. After a quick look, they roar off, seemingly to nowhere as their little craft vanishes against the disproportionate landscape.*

At sunset, a half hour before midnight, the *Bowdoin* reached 70° 01'. She rested inside a headland called Akunaq point while Elliot and other members of the crew took the Zodiac ashore to build a cairn to mark their northernmost reach. "The twilight was gentle," Andy wrote, "not vibrant — and remained fully bright enough to write and read on deck until sunrise came at 0130." Steve looked up the point's name in their U.S. Navy dictionary of Eskimo Place Names and Aid to Conversation, which MacMillan had written in 1938. Akunaq, appropriately for the *Bowdoin* in 1991, means "midpoint of one's journey."

The Zodiac's outboard motor, long recalcitrant, now refused to shift into forward gear. The shore party returned to the *Bowdoin* backwards.

Illulisat and Klaushavn

The *Bowdoin*'s next stop was in southern Disko Bay at Illulisat, the former Jakobshavn, where Helga Knudsen Morse spent her childhood. The glacier there creates 70 percent of the icebergs of the North Atlantic, although it takes them two years to float south into traffic lanes. The glacier is five miles wide and a half-mile thick, and it advances 75 feet each day, breaking off enough ice every two days to supply fresh water to all of New York City for a week. A bar at the mouth of the fjord holds the chunks of ice until an abnormally high tide releases it all, as many as a thousand bergs breaking loose in an hour or two, "disgorging enough ice to fill the whole of Disko Bay to an unnavigable confusion of bergs," wrote Andy.

Like each Greenland town they saw, Illulisat was a jumble of pre-fab buildings, none parallel or level. "Roads fit between buildings, not vice versa," wrote Andy. "The real estate between buildings is all rock and gravel, a little mud. Very unattractive, but characteristic of the place. There is no pretense (outdoors anyway) of decoration or adornment. Perhaps their lives are too focused on making a go of it—or at least were, when these habits were formed."

At Illulisat, the canine population considerably outnumbered the 4,200 humans. "A noon whistle sounds here, and is virtually drowned out by the dogs," Andy wrote. The dogs are an economic necessity, used all winter for fishing. They are more reliable than snowmobiles, and are managed in what would be regarded elsewhere as an abusive manner which strengthens them and doesn't cost very much. "They are creatures of work, servile as opposed to tame, and their eyes are hard and cold and bland," wrote Elliot. Nearly every household had a team; dogsleds hung from the balconies of the three-story public housing projects.

The *Bowdoin*'s people were once again greeted as VIPs. They were met at the dock by the Lord Mayor and treated to both showers and a tour of ancient ruins. Elliot was awed, seeing millenia of history before him:

> *Along the crude sand beach at our edge of the fjord are the remains of a Dorset village, two thousand years old. The earthen sills of their houses remain as ridges in the green grass, and the earth here is filled with the bones of their seals, eaten before the Romans came to England.*

> *Along the shore a ways, some Thule graves are concealed*
> *under a jumble of bowling-ball sized stones. In a land of ledge and*
> *permafrost, they are the only practicable medium for burial. In*
> *low wells of stone are skulls, femurs, clavicles ... bleached white*
> *but otherwise immaculate, preserved by the Arctic climate and*
> *undisturbed in their repose for a thousand years.*

The Danish Navy maintains two patrol vessels in Illulisat, which the first mate reported provided "a healthy dose of alcoholic hospitality." Aboard one of the vessels, Elliot met a retired Master who was working on a Greenlandic Coast Pilot for Denmark. He reported that north of 70°, charts are accurate with respect to distances, soundings and ranges, but not with respect to latitude and longitude. Today's sailors, equipped with GPS, have the same experience that MacMillan had in 1921 taking star-sights in Baffin Land, finding themselves theoretically on land while they're quite clearly still afloat.

Andy telephoned back to Maine Maritime Academy. The sound quality was terrible. He learned later that a phone connection is made by radio-link to Nuuk, then bounced off a satellite over South America which relays it by another satellite back to Denmark, and from there the call passes to the United States by transatlantic cable.

Accepting an invitation to join the village of Klaushavn in their 250th anniversary celebration, the *Bowdoin* sailed north again. The majority of Klaushavn's 88 Inuit residents greeted her on the dock waving tiny Greenlandic flags and wearing broad white smiles. There were no Danes in this little village, no roads, no council housing. At first, everyone stood and grinned at everyone else. Finally, someone admitted to speaking a little English, and took the people from the schooner to the town hall, "a small room in a fairly new building," Andy wrote, "which had streamers strung up, and a plate of smoked char, crackers and sodas set out." Everyone enjoyed the hospitality, and returned it with an open house on the schooner. The schoolmaster came aboard, and announced that he had been aboard the *Bowdoin* before, in 1954, when she last was in Greenland. He was four years old at the time.

And the connections with the past continued: the school-master played a tape of a local rock band which included three grandsons of Matthew Henson, the African-American dog-sled driver on Robert Peary's North Pole attempts. "They had a good band," Andy wrote, "very professional, very well-mixed, very good guitar. They sang a children's song, then a song about how he was sad because his plants were all dried up and the flowers withered, because he had been drinking for three days."

The *Bowdoin* blew her whistle as she left Klaushavn, bringing everyone out of their houses to wave goodbye; Andy fired off a cannon salute. The Inuit responded with fireworks. "It was the most complete communication we had with them all day," Andy wrote.

A Long Trip in Distance and Time

The trip was getting to the crew, though. Fatigue, weather, lack of privacy were taking their toll. From Elliot's journal ("Field day" was the weekly stem-to-stern cleanup):

> Southbound from Klaushavn to Faering Nordhavn. Lat 67°49'. Cold and gray, with heavy mist. Barometer steady at 30.00, 4 lowers, force 4 NW'ly. Motored through most of the night and set main in sloppy sea and building breeze at 0700 watch change.
>
> Again the aft cabin is an oasis of dry warmth. At 1445, [the galley slave] is still doing the lunch dishes, and holding up field day:
> Zach: He says he's half done. You should see his expression.
> Andy: He's really milking this one.
> Elliot: Well, I'm not going to tell him to hurry. You tell him.
> Andy: I'm not going to tell him. That would mean going on deck—and I'm freezing right here.
>
> Andy is in his jeans and omnipresent Norwegian sweater. He hugs himself and dives back into his bunk. He is a fixture there, writing letters to Lauren or reading an endless series of thick tomes about people who have gone to the Arctic and met with disaster.

*Up on deck through the hatchway, Josh Smith is in silhouette,
the sardine-can man in his sou'wester and Grundies. He is
hunched on the cast iron dry exhaust pipe, where, with the engine
shut down, only the illusion of warmth exists.*

*The cold is insidious. Your fingers get cold the fastest and
betray you. This morning I told Jamie to man a halyard and he
apologetically showed me that his hands, out of their gloves for
only minutes, were too cold to grip.*

With no darkness, "the body doesn't know when to sleep,"
Elliot says. "Every single day was more incredible than the one
before, and you didn't want to sleep, you might miss something.
Then your body would be feeling strange, and you'd realize you
hadn't slept in 36 hours."

The captain recognized how exhausted everyone was, and at
anchor in a quiet harbor the night after leaving Klaushavn he
left word that there would be no wake-up call. Andy wasn't seen
himself until after ten; some slept until just before Deborah
served a huge brunch at 1130. The rest of the day was spent
recuperating; some went fishing, others walking, some sailing
the dory. Elliot went ashore: "I find some high ground to escape
the bugs along the water, so thick in spots that they fly into your
mouth and get tangled with your chewing gum."

At Sisimiut (Holstenborg), the second largest town in Greenland and just above the Arctic Circle, again the past crept up to
the *Bowdoin*. The town was like the other towns they had seen:
fishplant, concrete block housing project, one department store.
They were received in the same manner as elsewhere: a speech
by the mayor and tours of the Greenlandic Culture school, the
museum, the kayak club, followed by a choir concert. But the
reception provided a surprise—an old woman who remembered
MacMillan. They wondered if she could identify any of the
people pictured in their old *National Geographics*. Looking at a
magazine from 1925, she turned bright red when she saw a
photograph of a beautiful young woman—that was her! She was
21 years old then. Whenever Mac returned, she told them, he
would ask her to dress in her finest clothes for him and he'd take
her picture. Did they want her to dress up, too?

How could they not? Later in the afternoon, she returned in her finest clothes and stood in front of the museum, where she'd stood in 1924 for the first picture, and they took her picture holding the original one, dressed in a newer, but identically-styled costume.

The director of the museum explained to Andy the preservative qualities of the climate, showing him a 200-year-old kayak. "The incredible part is that the wood was 1,000 years old before it was made into the kayak. It all came from Siberian forests, down the glaciers and into the Arctic pack, around the world a few times, out of the pack off the Northeast Greenland coast, down the East Greenland Current, back up with the Irminger Current, and finally ashore on the West Greenland coast to be made into a kayak. Time has different rhythms up here."

New kayaks interested Andy, too. He saw two new authentic sealskin boats, and a large number of fabric ones, but even those were built in traditional manner. "All joints are scarfed (usually hooked scarfs) and tied with string (traditionally caribou sinew), or mortise and tenon with a peg, then tied. Basically the whole frame is tied together with string. This makes for a flexible and very strong boat. The gear on deck for hunting is amazing — they put the megabucks sea kayakers to shame for gadgetry on deck — and all of it is made of bone and hide thongs."

Saying goodbye to the gathered crowd with yet another cannon salute, the *Bowdoin* had barely left the dock when a voice hailed them over Channel 16. "*Bowdoin*, would you like some codfish?" and a small boat came alongside with a bag of cod. Andy gave the fishermen hats and postcards.

Zach wasn't feeling well, so Andy stood his watch from 2300 to 0300. They were running before a building sea and a fresh breeze; Andy wished he didn't have the full main up — "She was a bear to steer." At the change of watch, they brought the main in, and still she zipped along at 5½ knots. But within two hours, Elliot had to start the engine to make Sondrestrom Fjord at 0800 on planned schedule. Andy woke from four hours of stupor to head into Stuart Hotchkiss's fjord.

They motored up the fjord into a strong headwind, admiring the peaks which rose sheer from the water, and looking forward to the run back down the fjord again. Their hope to see caribou and musk oxen wasn't fulfilled, although both were supposed to be plentiful in the area, and a pair of local hunters stopped them, offering them meat from both species. The price was exhorbitant, however, and no sale was made. Eighteen miles up the fjord, when they turned around, so did the wind, and they had to motor back again as well. Andy videotaped landmarks for Stu, though it was hard to imagine that the fjord had changed any since Stu's day.

Back in Nuuk again, a technician finally got the SSB radio at least partially operational. Andy obtained a couple of ice maps that showed the North Labrador coast to be clear, but from Nain south a lot of ice still showed. Andy spoke with the Labrador Coast Guard, which told him there was a shore lead, so he was hopeful that in the two weeks before they would get there, the ice would have freed. But he was relieved that the radio would be able to produce up-to-date ice maps, now that they were headed to Labrador.

Davis Strait Blues

Davis Strait lies between Greenland and Northern Labrador. When the *Bowdoin* crossed westerly in 1991, it was foggy and miserable; everyone aboard had colds and was cranky. Regularly, every day, the stove went out; the sea's tossing would drop green coal onto the live, extinguishing the fire. "Then you'd have to let it cool down, empty it out, and start over," Deborah explains. There were times when she wasn't able to provide enough to eat, let alone comforting, warm food. They ate a lot of emergency rations: tuna, crackers, cheese while it lasted, and the after-cabin's personal supply of sardines was called on for general consumption. When the stove wasn't working, Deborah couldn't even provide hot tea to wash the cold, dry rations down. Stove or no stove, Andy had constantly to remind everyone to drink water to avoid becoming dehydrated.

Nearly everyone grumbled and complained about the food,

particularly first mate Elliot, who didn't like leftovers. He was subjected to harassment from the students who, with great show, kowtowed to him as he entered the galley and pretended to serve him fancier rations than they had themselves. Deborah had a hard time in the galley, as she described to a friend in a letter:

> Would that I could join my fellow travelers above to handle sail through angry seas, but my task is one more humble. The power of the gale is measured for me not by height of seas or force of winds, but by how much coal smoke blown down the chimney I must breathe, how many burns received from boiling water responding to negative gravity when the seas roll the deck to perpendicular, how many gashes from slipping on a sole too wet to grip. This is hardly the stuff of ballad and song. There is no "Hurrah, brave steward!" to be met with for producing the plainest of fare in the face of impossible conditions.
>
> Today, when the seas were at their worst thus far, with efforts that in different conditions would have produced a 7-course gourmet meal for 40 people, I was able to provide a little warmth and a humble pot of beef and rice. This will not be remembered by the others, I am sure, except perhaps with frustration that I did not have more to offer. But what I will remember is watching small comforts register on the weary faces of my fellow adventurers, and Andy's hand on my shoulder as he passed by to climb out of the galley. His words echo with me still. "I can face the seas above, but it's hell down here. If I had to do your job, I'd give up schoonering altogether."

Labrador

Elliot, reading charts of the area they were approaching, wrote that they "have no coloring, no shading, few soundings, and a sparse scattering of printed information that is all bad news.... Forty years later, this is still Mac's coast."

Northern Labrador today feels far more remote than Greenland, and more so even than when the *Bowdoin* regularly traveled up the coast carrying supplies. During the years since the *Bowdoin* had last been there, the Canadian government moved everyone who lived in the far north down to Nain, believing that they couldn't provide services to so remote an area. (Of course, after they were moved, the people then required more services.) Port Burwell, where the *Bowdoin* spent more than a week hanging about in 1934, is now an empty settlement, home only to an unmanned radio relay station. Northern Labrador has little traffic, and still provides most of the navigational challenges of Mac's days.

It was freezing and blowing more than 30 knots as the *Bowdoin* approached Cape Chidley, the northeasternmost point of the North American continent. Elliot describes the cape:

> *Cape Chidley emerged around breakfast from a freezing near-gale, guarded by breaking ledges and rafts of pack ice and looking totally uninviting. The tide rips headed into Hudson Strait from here look like rivers in the ocean, torn into whitewater by gusts that shriek down out of the cliffs. The coast is little more than a jumble of sheer, barren headlands that concentrate the breeze into a roaring maelstrom of Williwaws ... it seems impossible that any harbor could offer a real lee here, in these conditions.*

Andy headed the schooner for Bowdoin Harbour, described by MacMillan as Northern Labrador's finest harbor. Finest or not, the harbor was not inviting. A current of five knots or better runs around Killineck Island; even now there are few soundings on the chart, and the schooner was set sideways on her approach to the harbor. Elliot was in the ice barrel, acting as lookout. As he was coming down the rigging, close to hypothermia, the wind snatched his radio from his pocket. A quick grab saved it, but he felt as if he were sailing around Cape Horn. "We had to strike sail and claw upwind to reach Bowdoin Harbour. To poke your nose into the 100-yard-wide entrance on a day like this one leaves you totally committed, and to lose power would mean going ashore."

Bowdoin Harbour was a disappointment, at least for protection. In the eastern end, "the wind sets down in blasts that blow craters in the water as if they were mortar rounds," Elliot wrote. But no one would have missed the stay there. An anchor watch was left on deck, and at six in the evening, the lookout called to everyone below. Expecting to see the anchor dragging, all hands ran on deck.

To windward of the *Bowdoin*, on the western end of the anchorage, a single polar bear stood, sniffing. He watched for five minutes, and then deliberately, easily, gracefully moved along the rough shore to get downwind. When finally the wind carried their scent to him, he ambled off.

After supper, six Mustang-suited and well-armed men went ashore to check out a cairn the boys built in 1934. (They didn't know that two cairns were built.) Elliot wrote:

> *The cairn sat undisturbed on the hilltop, covered with moss and with a tiny patch of tundra clinging to the rock in its lee. The presence of man represented in so diminutive a fashion against this landscape seemed to heighten the desolation. Far below, the* Bowdoin *swung at anchor, a ghost returned. There were caribou tracks in the soft ground along the shore, and they mingled with those of the bear — the latter deep and oblong prints, larger than my hand.*

They saw no other sign of the bear, a good thing since, as Andy says, it's well known that the only fate worse than being mauled by a polar bear is explaining to the Canadian authorities how you happened to kill one.

The gale still blew fiercely in the morning. A group went ashore to leave a message to any future comers in a detergent bottle in the cairn, having been disappointed to find none there themselves. They reported that it was quiet outside, although the deep and narrow configuration of the valley combined with the wind direction made for vicious winds just within the harbor. The *Bowdoin*'s anchors came up from what may have been the windiest point on the whole coast, and with Elliot once again in the ice barrel, this time "swaddled near to immobility," she headed out to face three or four days of the most difficult and draining navigation Andy had ever experienced. Elliot described it:

> To pilot a vessel on this coast is a meticulous and totally unrelenting task, with tenuous trails of soundings strung out across the white abysses of chartpaper like invisible stepping stones. The fathometer goes tic-tic-tic, your toes remain curled and your muscles tensed for the seemingly inevitable crunch of boat on stone. There is never a break to be afforded by putting yourself in the clear, and few places to get out of this game of blindfolded pinball, even if you had to. Notations make only nominal sense. An illustriously named "island" might be merely an oversized breaking ledge, while a mere starred rock turns out to be a 50-yard whaleback of sullen dry stone.

They anchored each night around ten and were under way again at 4:30 or 5 A.M., the captain or mate glued to the radar and depth sounder. The GPS wasn't useful for navigating; "there's no use in knowing where you are if you don't know what's around you," says Andy, but he adds it was good to be able to note locations of things they found.

They followed the single track of soundings on their chart as closely as they could, "but every once in awhile there would be a rude surprise as the fathometer shot up from 30 fathoms to 10, or in one case, five," Andy wrote. He set a routine of running the engine at 1,250 rpm when the depth was more than 20 fathoms. Under 20, he cut back to 1,000; below 10, he matched the depth in fathoms to rpms in hundreds—at 7 fathoms he ran the engine at 700 rpm. "Below five was idle, anything below four is stop or back full. The real problem is when you find it so shallow you don't know which way to turn." The first day Andy kept a mate in the ice barrel all day, but between the glare and the rough seas, it didn't help much.

Andy asked Deborah to delay lunch for an hour that first day on the Labrador coast because no one could leave their stations to eat. Deborah, not one to belt out a song in public as a general rule, felt compelled to sing "The Wreck of the Bay Rupert":

Well, they got no charts for the Labrador,
All you hear is "Stay away,"
For it's rocks and ice, dark as hell at night
From Jack Lane's Way to Bromfield Bay.
They've got wooden ships, steamer ships;
They've got frozen men below.
They've got mountains right beneath your keel,
So, for God's sake, don't you go.

"Oh, shut up!" said Andy, to whom the mountains beneath their keel were all too real.

Eclipse Harbour was populated only by caribou; a cache of outboard motors and a pile of geological samples on the beach gave evidence of former human presence. The *Bowdoin* spent a night at anchor there, just one of many over the years. Her crew went ashore to do all the things their predecessors had done in past decades: climb cliffs and push boulders off and roast marshmallows at a fire on the beach. The radio picked up the first local weather reports in weeks. Although the forecast was not looking very pleasant, in the morning, the *Bowdoin* was under way. Elliot wrote:

The morning is grey and blustery. Winds from the West and a rising glass would indicate that the system is to the North and East of us. We go out under power, with the fore and jumbo set, but as we turn the corner at the entrance the puffs screaming out of the mountains build to force 8 and 9, and we strike them. Added to a knockdown is the very real danger under sail of being unable to stop when, racing along before the wind, your depth sounder suddenly shoots skyward. As it is, with it blowing 50 dead offshore and a narrow chain of soundings between the cliffs and an area offshore simply marked, "Numerous uncharted rocks and shoals," we are reduced to the point where few things can be

allowed to go wrong. The mountains, right at the water's edge,
resemble huge, pointed piles of coal....
In two days, we will be on a real chart, if we can get to it.

On August 14 at 1600 hours, the *Bowdoin* reached Saglak
Fjord which offered the first sight of present-day human activity
since leaving Greenland—a navigational beacon and radome
tower. Six hours later, they anchored at Hebron, before the old
mission settlement buildings. The village was abandoned, the
buildings crumbling. Elliot went ashore:

> *Hebron is a place of quiet and simple ghosts. The rambling*
> *old mission hall—rooms—stairways—the* Bowdoin, *a ghost*
> *herself, seen through a wavy old windowpane. Thirty-four years*
> *ago, she carried bags of mail and supplies here, and people came*
> *down to meet her.*
>
> *In the attic is an old mangle, the rusted gears still work-*
> *able ... stapled to a wall an old provisions invoice for canned*
> *food ... cigarettes ... marmalade.*
>
> *There are the bones of an old woodstove. On a desk is a pile*
> *of welfare forms for the sight-handicapped, dated 1961. I read*
> *their legalese gobbledegook and wonder how it must have sounded*
> *to the Inut, thirty years ago before their lives vanished....*
>
> *There is a tiny graveyard on the hillside above the buildings.*
> *On the way up, the path crosses little streams on silvery skeletons*
> *of old boards. One brook is cut so deep into the gravel below the*
> *swale that the water is invisible, and it lives only as a steady*
> *bubbling sound, heard through a crack in the earth.*
>
> *Piles of rusted steel cans. Barrel hoops. I look at the hundred-*
> *year-old gravestones—clean white marble from far away, and I*
> *wonder at these people, at the force that brought them here and*
> *whatever strength it was that allowed them to stay ... until it was*
> *decided to give the land back to the caribou.*

Deborah said that from the hill over Hebron she looked
down at the *Bowdoin* and was almost afraid to look away, for fear
that the schooner would disappear.

Andy meant to get ashore at Hebron, but couldn't pull himself out of bed after the three days of intense piloting.

Heading Home

A good sail in a fresh northwesterly, with an almost warm sun, took the *Bowdoin* to Cutthroat Harbour, today the northernmost settlement on the coast. It was a summer fishing camp to a few Inuit families who lived in five buildings and had a radio antenna and three boats—a beat-up Novi and two outboards.

The next night the barometer again was dropping: "We have by this point become almost blasé about watching the changes in weather and are simply responding to them ... the transitions are so abrupt and erratic that it is useless to do much else," Elliot wrote.

At the Port Manvers run, Elliot picked an alder twig and brought it aboard the *Bowdoin*. "It smells of home, and although it is hard to imagine feeling sentimental about this cockroach of the tree family, I tape it into my diary."

The Maine Maritime gang were not the only people to have felt distant in this locale. From Elliot's journal: "The pervasive loneliness of the land is manifest in the culture of its people. A tall cairn on a ride at the run's entrance is actually an Innukshuk—a structure meant to mimic the silhouette of a human and thus relieve the solitude."

Students took over navigation, starting the Junior Watch Officer program as they saw increasingly more indications of civilization. Finally, Nain. From Elliot's journal:

> At the foot of the hill, Nain is the last word in grim arctic welfare towns. The web of dusty streets wind between rickety houses ... pell-mell children with dark, empty eyes and runny noses. Piles of junk. Skidoos conspicuous in their shiny sophistication. The idle fish plant and the high school are cold, new buildings of pressure-treated lumber and rough-look brick, helplessly alien structures that cannot possibly have been spawned

from local money. Puppies root through trash. Kids throw stones.

At the Aluatsik Lodge the hollowcore room doors clear their sills by a good three inches at the bottom. In the dining room the crew of the Bowdoin *keeps watch at the formica tables.*

Laundry. Phone calls. Tom and Steve at the Cribbage Board, waiting to fly home. The dauntless Valerie races about and tends to our every need — Double Lamb's Rums — french fries — showers. She is the owner's daughter, 20, heavy and pale, a ball of pent-up energy. Her brother Marcel is 16, lean and darkskinned, quietly friendly. Another brother was murdered in a knife fight here, just a few months ago.

There is no beer. No mixers. No fresh fruit. All are presently being unloaded from the M/V Northern Cruiser, *tied up at the wharf while a single crane lifts pallets onto a single stakebody truck. Valerie's father owns more trucks, but is short of trustworthy drivers.*

At the top of the hill over town I am standing next to another cairn of stones, waist-high and slightly lopsided. It was built last year by the crew of the Schooner Bowdoin, *at her farthest North since 1958. I add a stone, pick up a small one that has fallen to one side and put it in my pocket.*

At Nain, Steve and Tom left the *Bowdoin*. It was an emotional farewell, Deborah reports. Full fuel tanks, fresh vegetables and potato chips all came from Nain, where six New England canoeists came aboard for a visit to tell of their own adventures.

In Makkovik, some of the crew visited with Rupert MacNeil, who had been in a wheelchair a year before. Now, Rupert was up and around and working on a skiff, "the roughest skiff I'd ever seen," Elliot wrote. "He told us it was the first boat he'd built since 1960. He is 72 now, and it will probably not outlast him." MacNeil told tales of his harbor from days when more happened there and showed a photograph of West Turnavik with a brigantine, two schooners, a dozen smaller vessels, and many houses no longer to be seen. He told how, in 1938, he found an abandoned float plane, an upside-down Canadian flag, and the frozen bodies of two timber cruisers. He had only seen a single airplane before that one: Charles Lindbergh's.

Webeck Island seemed to Andy like a good harbor to make in the dark, because it had an easy entrance. "I should have been concerned. The bloomin' place was full of ice ... I was on the foredeck with the spotlight, Chris was in the ice barrel, Elliot was at the wheel. We bumped a few pretty good, but no damage. ... We dropped the hook off of Steve Tooktoshina's camp ... and then watched the ice pans come down on us ... they would fetch up on the chain, then rotate and slide down the side." One big one had to be shaken loose.

Hurricane Bob, which had recently devastated parts of the New England coast, sent its leftovers toward the *Bowdoin* as she progressed down the Labrador coast. Everyone on board was ready to get home. The mosquitos arrived in swarms at Gready where the whale processing plant was now just a jumble of rusty machinery, yet another ghostly site of former endeavors.

The wind increased to a full gale. Elliot described it: "The run inside to the Punchbowl is tight, tricky, and filled with bergs that become phantom islands on the radar. We do it on a screaming broad reach—9.5, 10, 10.2 knots. White knuckles. In the midst of the maelstrom Andy gets out the camera and starts shooting video. The diminutive Gil is in danger of being spun upside-down at the wheel. Finally, there's room to round up and get the main down."

Andy reported that the sail-striking went very smoothly, and they motored into Punchbowl. "That entrance is so narrow you have to take a deep breath to get through, and exhale on the other side." Anchoring was a job too, in the howling wind, but on the second try, with both anchors out, the *Bowdoin* finally stayed put.

Not a single fish had been caught there that summer, and the Punchbowl, the little unmarked harbor that had been so busy last year, was closing down. Where a hundred families had been, mostly Newfoundlanders, there were now perhaps twenty people. At least, Elliot noted, they "are from a place they can go back to. To the Labrador native at the end of a broken season there is nothing. ..."

The *Bowdoin* took on 200 gallons of diesel fuel, and Andy called back to MMA, asking that a new lid for the Aga be shipped to Baddeck, as it had melted down its own the night before.

On the schooner everyone had gotten touchy. Elliot reported another crew member getting on his nerves, and later wrote: "For the first time I can see down into the fatigue at the bottom of my energy."

Near Battle Harbour, under a pile of lumber, lies the telegraph board from which Peary's announcement of his successful Pole expedition was sent out in 1909. In this village, like the others on the Labrador, time has passed on, leaving unused fish-barrels, old dories, unused manila, caulking mallets and a 1933 ledger, all remnants of another age. "The place is history. . . not preserved, but intact," Elliot wrote. "On the hill above the wharf is a cottage built and occupied by Sir Wilfred Grenfell." This was the site of Labrador's first white settlement, first hospital, first church. Sixty summer residents now come to fish or work on restoring the church—there is some awareness of the history here, but no year-round residents. From Elliot's journal:

> *A few of the older men on the dock remember the boat when she was new, when she used to stay here for a few days of last-minute outfitting on her way north and there'd be dancing ashore, with the young men of the* Bowdoin *and the girls from the island, and the crews of the hundred or so boats that were always at the dock in those days, waiting to unload fish.*
>
> *The full moon rises over Grenfell's white clapboard cottage, and the green hill where the old radio mast is dwarfed by new Loran towers. . . .*
>
> *Just visible over the boulders of South tickle is the loom of a lighthouse. Ashore on the mainland, for the first time I can see lights burning.*

The *Bowdoin* faced more gales as she passed through the Straits of Belle Isle. The land had changed, now "a bland expanse, a continuous hill that rolls to the sea in a wave the color of camouflage," Elliot wrote. They spent a night in Red Bay, with yet another silent fish plant and the remants of a long-gone whaling industry. There are trucks, though, "REAL trucks, from someplace else. With license plates."

They were waiting for the gale to blow out, which Elliot wrote might not happen until next July:

> We imagine that the gale has veered to the West somewhat, grow restless and short on time to wait. . . . The town needs us to clear the wharf for an incoming coastal freighter. We grit our teeth and push out into it. . . .
>
> It is every bit as much fun as we had imagined. Day 2 of what will turn out to be a three-day gale, blowing directly up the nine-mile bottleneck of the Straits of Belle Isle. The seas are steep, breaking, 10–15 feet high and as we slam into it they begin to break across the deck. Soon the foc'sle is a swamp — an aqueous roller coaster. The reefed main stays up for about 20 minutes before we strike it in a cacophony of slamming spars and hoarse wet shouts.
>
> We hang on. . . . There is a singularity to each moment in heavy weather . . . a sort of sameness that makes time stand still, as the normal indeces of passing minutes are eclipsed by the cold wet roar and the need to hang on. Ears keened against the gale hear the main engine's roar and urge it on piston by piston. Shoulders are hunched in anticipation of some THING going wrong and demanding action and decisiveness in an environment where doing nothing requires effort.
>
> At sunset, the sky is clear. It howls. The waves are roiled, translucent — the color of jade.
>
> The barometer has been rising like a shot since its 1000 nadir of 29.3, a point that marked the bottom of a 48-hour descent of nearly an inch.
>
> Wave aboard. Duck. Water down my neck. With a Sou'wester over the high collar of my Mustang suit, I can pull my head in and close the opening like a turtle, but only if I can master the impossible skill of guessing which waves have my name written on them. Chris calls the foc'sle "Skylab" on days like this. It is grey

*and dank down there. The air has a close damp texture when you
breathe it in, and numerous small deck leaks deal out misery far
out of proportion to their volume.*

*Lunch is chewy grey beef and watery rice. Not for the faint of
heart. Dinner is minestrone soup from cans. I am fortified with
my private stock of crackers, and of Bonine.*

*By morning all that's left are a bright sunny day and the
human toll of bad weather: stupid minds, fingers dopey with
residual Bonine, wet bedding, and bodies cramped from sleeping
wedged-in. Jumped up nerves from too much caffeine. Salt is caked
behind my ears like beach sand.*

Deborah Gets It Together

One day during the last leg of the trip, Deborah found dirty
mugs in the sink once too often, and Elliot reported, "This morning Deborah threw all the extra coffee cups over the side in the
latest and most evocative chapter of her personal war." Elliot said
the captain put the episode into perspective: "Andy draws on his
store of bemusement and knowledge of far greater problems
elsewhere. We learned this morning of a coup in Russia, a hurricane at home, and, closer by, a marine gear mistakenly drained
of all oil . . . hopefully with no harm done."

But during the course of the voyage, Deborah had learned
a great deal. "I felt I should miraculously make our nonoperational stove work right (which couldn't happen). As a result, I
took people's complaints about the cold, damp quarters and the
lack of hot food personally. I got defensive, and spent three-quarters of the trip working against people instead of with them.
I wavered between being one of the guys and a bad guy."

Deborah feels very fortunate for having had Andy as captain. Although he had whims which, due to his rank, she had to
accommodate, he was also very supportive in his quiet way; with
a different captain, her job might have been intolerable.

One of Andy's whims was that he had to have a weekly

shower. Salt water for on-deck showers was heated on the stove when it was working and when it fit in with the cooking schedule. "One time, Andy ran out of water," Deborah describes, "and there he was in his undershorts, dripping all over the galley, trying to warm up some more water." Andy also demanded butter, not margerine, Grey Poupon mustard, not French's, and he insisted upon a particular creamer for his coffee. He wouldn't use canned milk. "We ran out of the creamer, but I filled the thing up with powdered milk, and he never knew the difference." But Deborah says Andy was good to cook for. "You could set a plate of mud in front of him, and he'd say, 'This is damn good mud.' He had a sense of how hard everyone's job was."

She eventually realized that her bunk was the easiest place for everyone to toss their hats and mittens, but that no one meant any harm by doing so. In fact, in the extreme head-seas Hurricane Bob sent their way in the Straits of Belle Isle, those men whose quarters were in the foc's'le couldn't sleep; their bunks were wet, and it was a constant elevator ride. During the day, Deborah's bunk attracted multiple nappers. This, too, was all right. She understood that personal space wasn't necessarily a matter of physical boundaries. She developed the habit of getting up early to sit quietly on deck for a half hour before starting breakfast, just for the solitude.

"If I were to do it again—which I never would, not as steward," she says, "I would do a much better job." She would love to go to sea again, but on deck. "As steward, you're not part of the on-deck cameraderie, you're not part of the system." But in any case, she knows better now what needs to be set up ahead of time, and how to handle things as they come along. She understands how groups work together far better than she did when she started. And she cherishes some friendships she never would have made on land: "Dave, he's Mr. Harley, he's an ex-Navy guy, tattoos all over. On the surface, we're so different, we never would have run in the same circles at home, but he's one of the sweetest people I've ever known. On the boat it doesn't matter what your lives are like off the boat, you need each other, you're like family. How sad it would have been never to have known Dave."

The Return of Stuart Hotchkiss

Nearing Cape Breton, the *Bowdoin*'s crew got their first taste of summer-like weather. From Cape Horn to the face of God he experienced in Greenland and Labrador, Elliot was now back where he started. Everyone was silent as they tied up at the pier. Soon, they were eating fresh food and doing laundry, and David was painting the *Bowdoin*'s stemhead blue, in honor of the Arctic crossing.

One crewmember disembarked, and the *Bowdoin*'s World War II skipper, Stuart Hotchkiss, now 78 years old, joined the schooner. "Stuart Hotchkiss is short and stocky," Elliot wrote. "He has a mane of white hair and a twinkle in his eye, and looks as if he could still bend a steel bar if he needed to."

Deborah was unhappy with the personnel change at Baddeck. "We felt we'd been to hell and back, and it was very much 'Us' and 'Them;' I wasn't feeling welcoming at all." Stu came below while she was preparing dinner; she felt disgruntled and intruded upon. Without looking at Stu, Deborah made an impersonal apology about dinner being on the fly. "I'm just so happy to be here, you could feed me anything at all," Stu said. With that, he won her over completely and immediately. "Ten minutes later I was in love with him," she says. "He just exudes warmth. He fit right in and became one of 'Us.' He didn't understand the crew jokes, but he understood the context that crew jokes emerge in."

Mealtimes, which Deborah had been very careful to keep on schedule throughout the trip, became a little slack with Stu aboard. People gathered around him at breakfast, lunch and supper, listening to him tell of the differences on the *Bowdoin* between 1991 and how he remembered her in 1942. "Let me tell you about the time when. . ." a lot of stories began, and no one was in a hurry to sleep or get back on deck. Sometimes he would punctuate a tale with the words "but that's another story," and no one would let him go without telling that story, too. And Deborah says that Stu is like Andy—"He eats what's given him and calls it damn good."

Home

The good weather held, and the winds increased. Fifty miles east of Halifax, Elliot wrote:

> *The breeze has built to a near-gale behind us and we are screaming along at 10.5, 10.7, 11 knots, as if the boat is ready to be home. . . . Carried the full mainsail well into the white-knuckles zone, and finally replaced it with the trysail at 1900. We are still averaging 8 knots. Stu has been at the wheel steering for most of the day, grinning like a fool.*
>
> *At 2130 Andy and I lean with tired elbows on a chart that, for the first time, contains home at its periphery. We poke at it with dividers in the weak light, where the trail of two months and 5,000 miles wanders into New England waters. We mutter half-formed ideas in half-coherent voices . . . discuss the logistics of ordering pizza in Bar Harbor, until our conversation seems too surreal and we start to laugh, a bit raggedly.*
>
> *On deck it has flattened out, the high moved in and the barograph steady.*

Off Cape Sable they passed their furthest south point of the voyage, 42° 50′N, 1,691 miles from Disko. They stopped to fish for cod on Brown's Bank, and enjoyed chowder for supper that night. Elliot wrote:

> *At sunset the sky was the color of pumpkin. Stu stood at the rail with a fishing rod, perhaps only slightly short of complete rapture. If his legs were still young he would be uncontrollable. All the same he is the proverbial child at Christmas. This man with five Navy commands and the world behind him has returned to delight us all.*

No fog this year for the entry into Mount Desert. Deborah wrote:

> *Today the* Bowdoin *sailed into Bar Harbor. Back amidst the chatter of schooner calling schooner on the radio — chatter where for so long there has been silence. Back amidst the summer schooner fleet — strangers to us, we who have seen no summer. Back amidst the noise of a crowded harbor. Dogs barking. Children shouting. Cars that we can hear even from the boat. The Augusta Navy is out in force, and a woman is speaking, over-loud, from the rented catamaran next to us: "Harry . . . Harry, are you* sure *you know where we're supposed to park this thing?"*

In silence, Andy and Deborah went ashore to get pizza for everyone. "I see no joy in Andy's face at being back in 'civiliza-tion'" Deborah wrote. "I thought I would be glad to be back. But there is no joy for him to see in my face either. Only bewilder-ment. Was the world this noisy before?

"'Oh, look,' one of us said, 'Look at all these people with their Big Hair.' But suddenly it seemed hollow — I felt an overwhelm-ing dread. What do we have in common with these people any more? And then I felt we were losing something."

The next morning, on the way back to Castine, everyone turned out for a final field day to polish the schooner for her return home. When all their laundry was hung out to dry, a squall hit. "Not so bad it wouldn't have been fun to sail through," Andy says, "only we were in the middle of field day. And there was a bunch of schooners around, sails up and having a great time, and here we are, the bold sailors returning from the Arctic with our tails between our legs, motoring along with just the foresail up. I was hoping someone would give me a call on the radio so I could make excuses, but no one did."

At Mount Desert, Elliot ended his journal:

> *There is a feeling of something finished, already drifting into the past.*

*Earl and David disagree on where to hang our set of caribou
antlers. I scoop up a* Newsweek *and then hesitate—do I care?*

*Last night rites—shots of Aquavit with a taste like rye bread
and JP-4—readings from journals, from Rockwell Kent. To
quantify our experience is impossible from such a short vantage,
but the effort is made, the words are said.*

— Welcome back, Stu.

— Here's to us.

— Here's to the boat.

— Here's to EIGHTY North. . . .

*The dipper hangs in the sky, and a cold front whispers on
the wind.*

Epilogue: Deborah

I have come to the realization that we live among ghosts. I would say that we live with Mac's ghost, since he was and is such a part of the *Bowdoin*. But living with his ghost is not so true as living with his memory. The *Bowdoin* remembers him, if we cannot, and his name is on all our lips like he was an old friend to us all. We refer to his days aboard like they were our own fond memories, and we refer to Mac as though he were still the heart of the crew, as if he will be down with all of us tonight eating supper in the fo'c'sle.

But with Mac's memory there are certainly ghosts, shadows of others who sail north with us still. When I wake in the night to the sound of our sails snapping and luffing in the gusty Arctic breeze, I cannot tell by sight or sound if I am on the voyage of 1991 or the voyage of sixty years past. When I stand at the bow and look out over gray mists and rocky coastline, over slate-gray seas to a landscape that has not changed visibly in a hundred human lifetimes, I realize that there is nothing anchoring us in time. All of us have remarked to each other that we go below and expect to see the shipmates of a half century ago, to find that we have somehow slipped back, become a part of that time when men made their way north by guess and by God. The *Bowdoin*'s memories are so palpable that we can almost touch them, be a part of them, remember them for ourselves.

I sit now listening to the usual order of the evening: the nightly round of cribbage being played. Tonight, John is 36 points ahead. Last night, Tom was in the lead by over 20. The numbers mean nothing and yet they do. They separate night from night, for John being ahead by 36 points sets this day apart from yesterday, apart from all the yesterdays that the *Bowdoin* has seen. In these far north waters, where we sail past icebergs, ever changing yet never changing, ghosts like this time-voyager on which we sail, the round of points in a cribbage game are somehow more tangible things, anchoring us in this mutable shadow called time.

Deborah Harrison, letter home,
July 30, 1991

Afterword

*I*n 1994, the *Bowdoin* returned to Greenland, captained by Elliot Rappaport. Among ten trainees, only one was a student from Maine Maritime Academy; a quarter of the complement was over the age of 50. One other repeater from the 1991 trip sailed, photographer Tom Stewart.

Nearly everyone on the trip reports terrible weather. "Mostly," says Elliot, "the weather was just cold and wet and dreary." But there was one full day of Force 10 winds. Sid Clemens, a long-time blue-water sailor herself and *Bowdoin* trainee in '94, says she was amazed at how seaworthy the schooner was, and then corrects herself. "No, not amazed — she was built for that. Even in the full gale, when you couldn't open your eyes on deck, she rode beautifully. She's perfect for what she's doing."

The highlight of the trip for many, including Elliot, was Furthest North, Umanak Fjord, 71° 25′. Elliot says this region with its many glaciers is the most spectacular place he's ever been. "The drama of the scenery jumps by another exponent from Disko Bay." With the *Bowdoin* tied to an iceberg at midnight, sun above the horizon, Elliot describes seeing the Karrats Isfjord: "A solid pile of bergs the size of soccer stadiums, lit the color of peach. . . . It is a moment when people try to talk and then go silent, that seems to demand testimony and mute awe simultaneously."

The *Bowdoin* was 85 miles north of her extreme of the '91 trip, fulfilling Elliot's dream of expanding his range with the schooner.

Of next summer, however, Captain Rappaport says with a laugh but some seriousness as well, "My goal is to not go out of sight of Vinalhaven." As always, the official mission in '94 was sail training and education at sea; on shorter trips during the next few years, more MMA students will be able to schedule and afford the experience, and more younger students will be encouraged to participate as well.

But the northern missions are an essential part of the *Bowdoin*'s life. Andy Chase says so, Elliot says so, everyone who knows and loves the schooner says so. Miriam said so, in her day. It was the thought of the schooner going north again that kept John Nugent going, all those miserable months of the rebuild. "There's a difference," says Elliot, "between a schooner that goes to the Arctic and one that has been to the Arctic."

Appendix

Below is steward Deborah Harrison's provisioning list for the *Bowdoin*'s 1991 trip to the Arctic.

Budget: $7/person/day = $122 per day for 66 days = $7,392, not including housekeeping supplies. Of this, approximately $6,000 was spent before embarkation.

Delivered to the dock the day before departure:

> 250 lbs. white flour
> 175 lbs. whole wheat flour
> 100 lbs. white sugar
> 30 lbs. brown sugar
> 6 lbs. powdered sugar
> 90 dozen eggs
> 25 lbs. powdered milk
> 5 cases evaporated milk (240 cans)
> 2 cases canned corn (12, #10 cans)
> 1 case mushrooms
> 5 cases crushed tomatoes
> 5 cases whole tomatoes
> 5 cases diced tomatoes
> 1 case mayonnaise
> 1 case ketchup
> 2 cases Dijon mustard
> 1 case vegetable oil
> 1 case brownie mix
> 20 lbs. dried beans

25 lbs. dried peas
25 lbs. canned tuna
7 cases crackers (28 boxes)
30 lbs. peanut butter
10 cases fruit juice (120 cans)
30 lbs. rice
75 lbs. onions
30 lbs. carrots
200 lbs. potatoes
60 lbs. margerine (for cooking only)
30 lbs. butter
45 lbs. cheddar and swiss cheese
10 lbs. parmesan cheese
1 case cream cheese (10 large boxes)
40 lbs. apples
24 lbs. oranges
60 lbs. grapefruit
20 lbs. sour cream
2, 35 lb. hams
2, 15 lb. turkeys
210 lbs. roasting beef
80 lbs. stew beef
80 lbs. ground beef
120 lbs. boneless chicken breasts
30 lbs. sausage
20 lbs. bacon
25 lbs. cornish game hens
40 lbs. hot dogs
30 lbs. frozen blueberries
2 cases canned peaches
1 case pears
30 lbs. oatmeal
50 lbs. chocolate chips
2 cases canned clams
2 cases fruit jelly
15 lbs. honey
5 cases coffee

1 case tea
20 boxes hot chocolate
10 cases Hershey bars
12 lbs. M&M's

Emergency food included one case each of the following:
chowder, tomato soup, vegetable beef soup, minestrone.

Additional provisions, which Deborah had not ordered ahead, purchased
in Ellsworth, Maine, just before departure:

fresh greens
fresh fruit
milk
condiments and spices
international coffees, Moxie as special treats
peanuts
pretzels
cocoa
vinegar
horseradish
10 lbs. of garlic (Deborah used it all)
syrup
olive oil
30 lbs. macaroni
more honey
cans of pumpkin
four boxes of grits (to indulge the captain's whim — only
    one other crew member ate grits)
Cream of Wheat
Bisquick
Crisco

Items for special occasions:
balloons, streamers, candles, poster board, finger paints,
food coloring, sprinkles for cakes and cookies

Virginia Thorndike

*H*ome port for author Virginia Thorndike is Lincolnville, Maine. Ms. Thorndike grew up near Boston and graduated from Boston University, majoring in history. Her love of sailing reaches back to childhood summers spent on Maine's Islesboro Island in Penobscot Bay. Sailing is in her blood—her great-grandfather was three times the America's Cup defender, and her grandfather, a designer of sailing yachts, was also an America's Cup contender. Her grandfather, Frank C. Paine, also designed the *Gertrude L. Thebaud*, which was the most successful American racing-fishing schooner to compete against the Canadian *Bluenose*, and which plays a part in the *The Arctic Schooner Bowdoin: A Biography*.

When not on the water, Ms. Thorndike is tending to her animals. A former dressage and trail competitor, she keeps several pleasure horses, three dogs and four cats. While living in New Hampshire in the 1980s, Ms. Thorndike and her husband raised cows and were proud to have the highest producing herd per cow in the state for three consecutive years. Today, she is a town selectman and active in local planning.

Ms. Thorndike has previously written *Windjammer Watching*, a guide to the large sailing vessels on the coast of Maine, and is currently working on her next book which she says will be "a celebration of lobster boats."